Professional Tips and Workarounds for QuickBooks Online

Improve your QuickBooks Online and bookkeeping skills using advanced techniques and best practices

Ashley Beetson

BIRMINGHAM—MUMBAI

Professional Tips and Workarounds for QuickBooks Online

Group Product Manager: Rohit Rajkumar

Senior Editor: Mark D'Souza

Content Development Editor: Aamir Ahmed

Technical Editor: Simran Udasi

Copy Editor: Safis Editing

Project Coordinator: Rashika BA

Proofreader: Safis Editing

Indexer: Sejal Dsilva

Production Designer: Alishon Mendonca

First published: November 2021

Production reference: 1221021

Published by Packt Publishing Ltd.

Livery Place

35 Livery Street

Birmingham

B3 2PB, UK.

ISBN 978-1-80181-037-1

www.packt.com

For my wife, Sarah, who fully supports me in everything that I do, and our children, Hannah and Owen. Not forgetting mum and dad – thank you.

– Ash Beetson

Contributors

About the author

Ashley Beetson has worked in various bookkeeping and accounting roles over a career spanning 30 years. This has included working in law firms, manufacturing, and an accounting practice, as well as operating his own bookkeeping business for 10 years. In 2014, Ash was invited to join the UK Trainer Writer Network, assisting Intuit in creating training materials for QuickBooks ProAdvisors. In 2021, Ash was included in the Top 100 list of ProAdvisors as compiled by *The Insightful Accountant*.

In 2019, Ash co-created nettTracker, a third-party software application that integrates with QuickBooks Online. It is designed specifically with accountants in mind to simplify fixed-asset processes, and there are plans to add further features that will help accountants and bookkeepers.

When he's not working, you'll probably find a bass guitar in Ash's hands as he's a regularly gigging musician, playing at different venues 3-4 times a month.

Thank you to my wife, Sarah, as my first proofreader, and to all the team at Packt for the help and guidance while writing my first book. Also, to everybody I have worked with over the last 30 years, I thank you. It's through all the knowledge gained working with different people and businesses that this book is possible. I hope my past learnings will be useful to others, saving people time and some head-scratching.

About the reviewer

Aaron Patrick is a Chartered Accountant and Head of Accounts at a state-of-the-art accounting practice called Boffix, which uses cloud technology to make sure that clients have the information they need at their fingertips.

He is also a UK Intuit QuickBooks Certified Trainer, delivering Core and Advanced QuickBooks training to accountants and users alike. Finally, he has a dedicated YouTube channel called *Aaron Patrick the QuickBooks Chap*, which delivers training and support one video at a time!

Table of Contents

Section 2 – Adapting QuickBooks Online to Suit Different Business Types

3

QuickBooks Online for Manufacturing Businesses

4

Recording Income for Retail Businesses

5

Handling Client Money

6

The Secret to Success with Projects in QuickBooks Online

7

Handling Foreign Currencies in QuickBooks Online

Section 3 – Reviewing and Reporting Data in QuickBooks Online

8

Best Practices When Reviewing Financial Records

9

Enhancing the Consistency of Your Financial Statements

10

Reconciling the Balance Sheet

11

Closing the Year-End, the Audit Log, and More

Other Books You May Enjoy

Index

Preface

QuickBooks Online is a fully cloud-based accounting software solution for small-to medium-sized businesses. It has also become popular with bookkeeping and accountancy firms that provide bureau bookkeeping services.

At the time of writing, QuickBooks Online has close to 5 million users worldwide with different levels of subscription available. This book will concentrate on using the Plus subscription, which is the most popular.

Accountants and bookkeepers with a QuickBooks Online Accountant subscription will benefit from being able to access different QuickBooks client files from one area. In addition, there are some Accountant-only tools that are not available to standard users. No Accountant tools are used in the book, so the features used should be available to all with a Plus subscription.

The purpose of this book is to provide you with additional tips and workarounds that reflect real-world scenarios. Although there is some flow between the chapters, they can be read in any order.

Who this book is for

This book is aimed at anybody that would like to get the most out of their QuickBooks Online subscription.

For a business owner using QuickBooks reading this book, not every chapter will be relevant. If you are a bookkeeper or accountant, the book should become a great reference tool. As and when you need to help different business types that are getting started with QuickBooks Online, simply jump to the appropriate chapter.

When businesses grow, they may need to implement different apps. This book looks at how QuickBooks Online can be adapted to suit most business models by only using the tools that are available in QuickBooks Online. This is perfect when getting started and working to a budget.

The book does not cover the very basics and general use of the software. The book is designed for readers already familiar with QuickBooks Online. If you need assistance with the basics, please check out other titles from Packt, and the free webinar tutorials provided by Intuit that help when getting started.

What this book covers

Chapter 1, *Creating and Reviewing Opening Balances in QuickBooks Online*, looks at how, when it's not possible to automatically convert data to QuickBooks Online, manual adjustments may be required to ensure the balance sheet is reporting the correct figures. This chapter explains the entries required.

Chapter 2, *Useful Tips and Tricks Every QuickBooks User Should Know*, with QuickBooks ready to use, provides some guidance to help keep things simple, together with some quick tips that can generally save time.

Chapter 3, *QuickBooks Online for Manufacturing Business*, is the first specialist chapter, which details specific settings and workflows for businesses that manufacture products. This includes the handling of the bill of materials and adjustments for stock.

Chapter 4, *Recording Income for Retail Businesses*, looks at different methods of recording income when invoices are not raised. This includes options to update price lists and revalue stock.

Chapter 5, *Handling Client Money*, provides a detailed suggestion on how QuickBooks can be used for lawyers, investment brokers, and property agents, who often handle money on behalf of others – client money.

Chapter 6, *The Secret to Success with Projects in QuickBooks Online*, provides one of the most detailed guides you will find to using the Projects feature in QuickBooks.

Chapter 7, *Handling Foreign Currencies in QuickBooks Online*, explains, as multicurrency can sometimes be a little confusing, exactly how the feature works, and what to look out for when things are not always straightforward.

Chapter 8, *Best Practices When Reviewing Financial Records*, is not simply about using tools in QuickBooks. It also includes guidance on generally accepted accounting principles and concepts and how they can be applied when reviewing data in QuickBooks Online.

Chapter 9, *Enhancing the Consistency of Your Financial Statements*, following on from *Chapter 8*, *Best Practices When Reviewing Financial Records*, looks at how adjustments can be made to ensure the profit and loss is reporting the correct values.

Chapter 10, Reconciling the Balance Sheet, includes tips that will make the process of getting ready to prepare annual financial statements for a business from year to year, including checking the balance sheet thoroughly, easier.

Chapter 11, Closing the Year-End, the Audit Log, and More, looks at how, with the accounts of the business complete, the year should be closed. This chapter includes some basic steps to take, and how to investigate any balances changed, that should not have.

To get the most out of this book

Only refer to the chapters that you really need – those that are relevant to you. *Chapter 1, Creating and Reviewing Opening Balances in QuickBooks Online*, and *Chapter 2, Useful Tips and Tricks Every QuickBooks User Should Know*, provide tips on setting up and using QuickBooks regularly and are relevant to everybody. *Chapter 8, Best Practices When Reviewing Financial Records*, through to *Chapter 11, Closing the Year-End, the Audit Log, and More*, are also relevant to all as they are concerned with reviewing information in QuickBooks.

Chapter 3, QuickBooks Online for Manufacturing Business, to *Chapter 7, Handling Foreign Currencies in QuickBooks Online*, are aimed at niche business types or those that require specific features, such as using Projects or Multicurrency. For example, a marketing agency may find Projects useful, but *Chapter 3, QuickBooks Online for Manufacturing Business*, to *Chapter 5, Handling Client Money*, may not be of much interest.

Download the color images

We also provide a PDF file that has color images of the screenshots and diagrams used in this book. You can download it here: `https://static.packt-cdn.com/downloads/9781801810371_ColorImages.pdf`.

Conventions used

There are a number of text conventions used throughout this book.

`Code in text`: Indicates code words in text, database table names, folder names, filenames, file extensions, pathnames, dummy URLs, user input, and Twitter handles. Here is an example: "The supplier's name used in this example was `Contra adjustments`."

Bold: Indicates a new term, an important word, or words that you see onscreen. For instance, words in menus or dialog boxes appear in **bold**. Here is an example: "The **Sales** tab of **Account and settings** contains the option to use **Progress Invoicing**."

> **Tips or important notes**
> Appear like this.

Get in touch

Feedback from our readers is always welcome.

General feedback: If you have questions about any aspect of this book, email us at customercare@packtpub.com and mention the book title in the subject of your message.

Errata: Although we have taken every care to ensure the accuracy of our content, mistakes do happen. If you have found a mistake in this book, we would be grateful if you would report this to us. Please visit www.packtpub.com/support/errata and fill in the form.

Piracy: If you come across any illegal copies of our works in any form on the internet, we would be grateful if you would provide us with the location address or website name. Please contact us at copyright@packt.com with a link to the material.

If you are interested in becoming an author: If there is a topic that you have expertise in and you are interested in either writing or contributing to a book, please visit authors.packtpub.com.

Share Your Thoughts

Once you've read *Professional Tips and Workarounds for QuickBooks Online*, we'd love to hear your thoughts! Scan the QR code below to go straight to the Amazon review page for this book and share your feedback.

https://packt.link/r/1-801-81037-0

Your review is important to us and the tech community and will help us make sure we're delivering excellent quality content.

Section 1 – General Tips and Shortcuts

It's important that a QuickBooks Online company file is set up correctly, reflecting the financial position of an organization at the point that QuickBooks Online was put into use.

Once the initial Opening Balances are in place, review the general setup of the QuickBooks company, ensuring that it contains just the right amount of account categories. Too few, and it can be a struggle to code transactions; too many, and reporting can become a little messy.

As QuickBooks is used each day, there are a few little tips that can generally save time no matter what type of business you have. So, just for starters, we'll advise you of some of those.

This section comprises the following chapters:

- *Chapter 1, Creating and Reviewing Opening Balances in QuickBooks Online*
- *Chapter 2, Useful Tips and Tricks Every QuickBooks User Should Know*

1

Creating and Reviewing Opening Balances in QuickBooks Online

As described in the preface of this book, QuickBooks Online is a cloud-hosted accounting software solution for small to medium-sized businesses. Accountants and bookkeepers can assist their clients by being able to access all the information they need at any time.

Opening balances reflect the financial position of a business at the point when QuickBooks Online is brought into use. Where a business has only just been set up and they choose to use QuickBooks from the very beginning, there will not be any opening balances to speak of except for cash or equipment introduced by the business owners.

Where a business has been operating for some time and has perhaps used spreadsheets or other accounting software in the past, there will be a financial history that results in values that will affect the balance sheet in different ways.

It is very important, especially when moving from one method of accounting to another, to ensure there is continuity. Without a correcting starting position, future profits could be over or understated, and the values filed in various tax returns could be incorrect.

In this chapter, we will cover the following topics:

- Should opening balances be in place before using QuickBooks?
- Opening balances – Customers
- Opening balances – Suppliers
- Opening balances – Bank
- Opening balances – VAT/GST/Sales Tax
- Other opening balances

Should opening balances be in place before using QuickBooks?

Before we explore opening balances, we need to know whether it is necessary for our opening balances to be in order when we make the switch from our old method of keeping books to QuickBooks.

The simple answer to this question is no. As soon as you have a subscription in place and set QuickBooks Online up with the required settings, you are likely to want to start creating customer invoices before you do much else.

However, it is best to get some opening balances in place as soon as possible. As customers start to pay for products and services supplied before QuickBooks is in use, it is important to have a record of any of those unpaid amounts in place. This will also be the case when it is time to pay suppliers for amounts owed against historic bills.

We can build our opening balances in stages – it is not necessary to do it all at once. In some instances, it is not possible to deal with all the opening balances because all the information required is not readily available. Therefore, we can put into place the values that are easy to deal with, such as the amounts owed by customers and to suppliers.

What dates are used for opening balances?

Before we answer this question, it is important consider the date you start using QuickBooks Online. You can of course start using QuickBooks at any time, but it can generally make life easier to do so when a clear "line in the sand" has been drawn.

The following are good starting points for a new QuickBooks Online file:

- Any time for a new business (no historical transactions to worry about)
- Start of new financial year/tax year
- Start of new VAT/GST/Sales tax period

Using these starting positions can make life a little easier when preparing financial statements and tax returns. Otherwise, data may need to be merged from two systems, which can increase time consumption and the cost of work required.

Once you select the start date, ensure the financial year date is set correctly in QuickBooks. To do this, select the gear icon found in the top right of the main screen menus and choose **Account and settings** from the **YOUR COMPANY** list.

Figure 1.1 – Selecting the financial period start date

From within the **Advanced** tab, we select the first month of the financial year. In this example, the year-end is `March 31`, so the first month is set as April. This company is going to use QuickBooks from `April 1, 2021`.

Now that we have selected our start date, we will visit some examples of opening balances.

Opening balances – Customers

At any given point, it is highly likely that a business is owed money from customers for goods and services already provided in a previous period; this needs to be considered when a business decides to change its bookkeeping system.

There are various methods to create the opening balances for amounts owed from customers, but we will stick with the one that is advised by most professionals.

A business should have a list of the invoices sent to customers and of those that remain unpaid at the date they start using QuickBooks. Taking that list, we will already have the following:

- Customer name
- Invoice date
- Invoice number
- Net charge
- VAT/GST/sales Tax
- Invoice total

From the preceding list of items, we have pretty much all the information we need to create our opening customer balances in QuickBooks. That will be done by creating invoices in QuickBooks that reflect those that are unpaid. In addition to the items listed, we will need to add either **terms** or a **due date**, and we will need to use **product/service item** information. But how do we decide on which product/service code to use?

Which Product/Service Item to use

Product/Service items dictate how the values entered on invoices are presented in different reports.

You can use one of the default items, but it is advisable to create a specific service item for invoices that are created that form part of your opening balances. This makes them easier to identify and will also assist with the reconciliation process when checking that opening balances have been completed.

The following figure shows how the Product/Service code should be created.

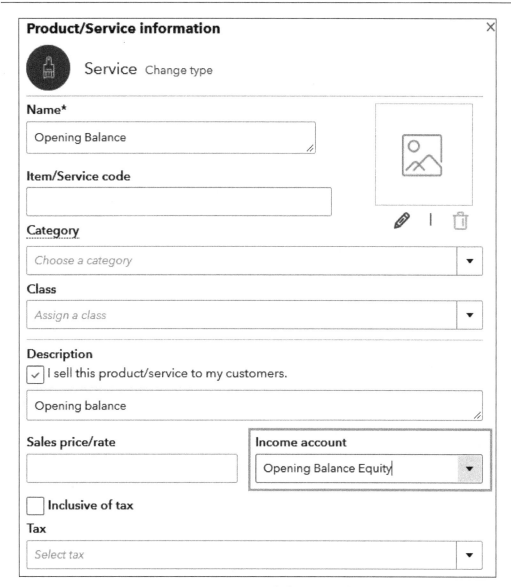

Figure 1.2 – Item/Service code for opening balance

Notice the **Income account** value selected here is **Opening Balance Equity**. This account name may vary in different regions and could be **Retained profit balance forward account**. The important thing to consider here is that this account forms part of our *Double-Entry* when dealing with our opening balances.

You can create and use your own balance sheet account. If you do, ensure it is an **Equity account**, with a detail type of **Accumulated adjustments**.

When we create our opening balances for customers using invoices, the following accounts will be affected:

- **Debit**: Debtors/Accounts receivable (total amount of unpaid invoice)
- **Credit**: Opening balance equity
- **Credit**: VAT/GST/sales tax if applicable

> **Important Note**
>
> VAT only needs to be split on the invoice for the opening balances for *Cash Accounting* purposes. For *Standard VAT accounting*, the invoices can be entered gross using **No VAT**. Any further adjustments for VAT on Customer/Supplier balances could be made using **Journal entry**. (This is explained in the *Opening Balances – VAT* section.)

If VAT (or the sales tax appropriate for your region) is submitted on a **cash basis** or for any other reason the invoice was not reported on the previous return, the invoice should be recorded exclusive of tax. Below is an example of a single opening balance customer invoice:

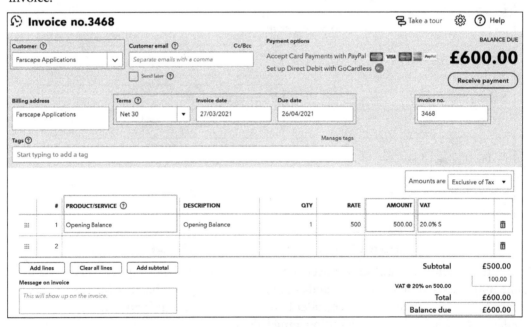

Figure 1.3 – Customer invoice screen

The preceding image reflects one of the invoices owed from a customer named `Farscape Applications` as of `March 31, 2021`. The invoice date used is per the original invoice sent that is unpaid.

This invoice is for a company filing VAT/GST on a cash basis, so the sales tax has not been filed. For standard VAT accounting where the tax had already been filed, the amount would be £600 inclusive using NO VAT/NO TAX, which can vary depending on the region you are working in.

If this customer owes £1,800 for 3 months, three separate invoices should be created. Separate invoices should be created because this will help ensure that future payments are allocated correctly. Also, if payment reminders are required, or statements are sent to customers, it will be easier for customers to agree on the values displayed.

To complete the creation of our opening customer balances, separate invoices should be created for each unpaid invoice for all customers. If you have a lot of unpaid customer balances, you can save a lot of time by importing the data using a `.csv` file.

Depending on your region, you may not have the ability within QuickBooks alone to import invoices. The **Import Data** option in the UK version appears as follows.

Figure 1.4 – Import Data options (UK)

If you do have a large amount of unpaid customer invoices and the import feature is not available, it may be worth temporarily subscribing to an app such as SaasAnt Transactions Importer – details can be found at `www.apps.com`.

After all the customer invoices have been created (by manual input or data import), we must run some reports to check whether our unpaid customer balances are correct:

- Accounts receivable aging summary report
- Accounts receivable aging detail report
- Trial balance

All reports can found within the reports center, which can be accessed from the left-hand navigation pane. You will also be able to search for reports from this area. The first two reports listed above should be run and checked as per the last period. In this chapter, we considered that our company will start using QuickBooks from `April 1, 2021`, so the reports should be run and checked as of `March 31, 2021`. The summary will provide the totals owed by each customer and the detailed report will list all unpaid invoices.

The trial balance report will display a summary of accounts used so far, up to the date we run the report, which in this scenario is `March 31, 2021`:

QuickBooks Tips		
Trial Balance		
As of March 31, 2021		
	DEBIT	CREDIT
Debtors	3,600.00	
VAT Control		600.00
Opening Balance Equity		3,000.00
TOTAL	£3,600.00	£3,600.00

Figure 1.5 – Trial balance report after customer opening balances are updated

- **Debtors**: The total owed by customers that will agree to the accounts receivable reports
- **VAT Control**: The value of sales taxes not yet filed (GST/sales tax)
- **Opening Balance Equity**: The account linked to the product/service used for opening balances

Opening customer balances – Summary

- Create invoices for all unpaid values that reflect historical invoices sent.
- Use the original dates and invoice numbers.

- Enter values gross if taxes filed; enter net + tax if the amounts have not previously been included on VAT/GST returns.

- Save time importing when there are large volumes to deal with.

With customer balances now complete, it is time to look at opening balances for suppliers.

Opening balances – Suppliers

Dealing with opening balances for suppliers is similar to the method used for our customer balances. This time, we will be creating supplier bills for the amounts due. Again, there are different methods for creating opening balances, but we will stick with one preferred by professional advisors.

Creating supplier bills that reflect exactly what was owed before QuickBooks was put into use means that there will be values that match direct debits that appear on bank feeds, and there will be bills that we can agree to supplier statements:

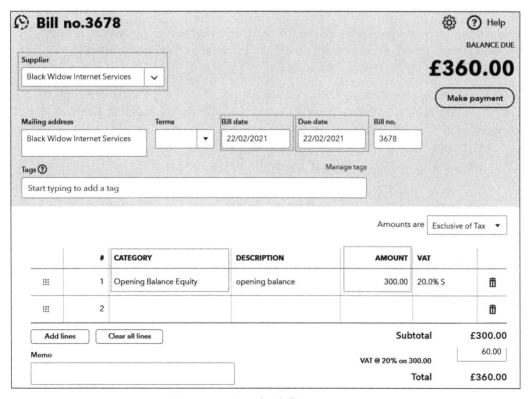

Figure 1.6 – Supplier bill input screen

The fields within the red boxes are mandatory when adding the supplier bill. Note the same **chart of account code** linked to the service item for customer invoices, that is **Opening Balance Equity**, is being used. All opening balance adjustments should affect the same account.

Just as in the case with customer balances, the VAT/GST will need to be accounted for if the amounts have not been included on previously filed returns. If the bill had already been included within a filed VAT return, it would have been entered as £360 NO VAT.

After all supplier bills have been entered (and if necessary, any supplier credits), the following reports should be checked to the date before the QuickBooks start date. For example, if starting from April 1, 2021, all the reports will be run to the date March 31, 2021:

- Accounts payable aging summary

- Accounts payable aging detail

- Trial balance

The first two reports should be compared to the details held within our old accounting records. It's important that the amount that QuickBooks reports as being owed to suppliers at our chosen start date is as expected.

The trial balance report will now include creditors that will agree to the totals on the accounts payable report. In the example shown in the following figure, **VAT Control** has been reduced to reflect the purchase tax claimed on supplier bills:

QuickBooks Tips

Trial Balance

As of March 31, 2021

	DEBIT	CREDIT
Debtors	3,600.00	
Creditors		840.00
VAT Control		460.00
Opening Balance Equity		2,300.00
TOTAL	**£3,600.00**	**£3,600.00**

Figure 1.7 – Trial Balance report after supplier balances updated

With opening balances in place for customers and suppliers, it is now time to look at ensuring the opening balances for any bank accounts are correct.

Opening balances – Bank

When dealing with the opening bank balance, the following must be taken into consideration:

- The balance per the bank statement at the start of the day when QuickBooks is put into use – in this example, the closing cleared balance on March 31 was £5,000.

- Payments made (checks) or deposits received that were originally recorded before the date QuickBooks was put into use, but have not yet cleared the banking system.

- Whether a live bank feed is in place for the bank account.

Dealing with the last point, in some instances, when a bank account is connected to QuickBooks Online, an *opening balance* is automatically created. Sometimes this opening balance will be OK; however, sometimes it will be incorrect and will need to be deleted.

There are a couple of ways to check to see whether an opening balance has been automatically created. If no bank reconciliations have been performed against a bank account, there will be a beginning balance within the reconciliation screen as shown here, where the beginning balance will normally be 0.00:

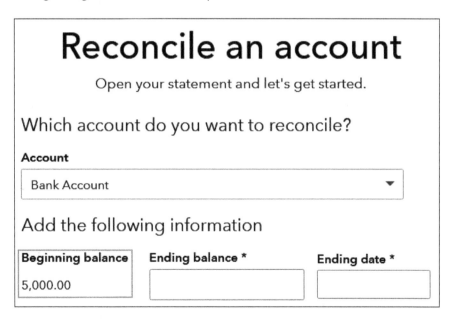

Figure 1.8 – Bank reconciliation

The other way to check whether an opening balance has been created by connecting a bank feed is to run the trial balance report for *all dates* and then click on the value associated with **Opening Balance Equity** or **Retained profit balance forward**.

This will display a list of all entries made to this account. Where an automatic opening balance has been created, it should be clearly visible in the list as shown in the following figure.

			QuickBooks Tips								
			Transaction Report								
			All Dates								
DATE	TRANSACTION TYPE	NO.	ADJ	NAME	MEMO/DESCRIPTION	ACCOUNT		SPLIT	AMOUNT	BALANCE
▾ Opening Balance Equity										
15/01/2021	Invoice	3470	No	Farscape Applications	Opening Balance	Opening Balance Equity		Debtors	500.00	500.00
15/01/2021	Invoice	3471	No	Ash Beetson Bookkeeping	Opening Balance	Opening Balance Equity		Debtors	250.00	750.00
15/02/2021	Invoice	3469	No	Farscape Applications	Opening Balance	Opening Balance Equity		Debtors	500.00	1,250.00
22/02/2021	Bill	3678	No	Black Widow Internet Services	opening balance	Opening Balance Equity		Creditors	-300.00	950.00
22/02/2021	Bill		No	Stationery and Supplies Co.	opening balance	Opening Balance Equity		Creditors	-400.00	550.00
15/03/2021	Invoice	3473	No	nettTracker	Opening Balance	Opening Balance Equity		Debtors	1,000.00	1,550.00
15/03/2021	Invoice	3472	No	Ash Beetson Bookkeeping	Opening Balance	Opening Balance Equity		Debtors	250.00	1,800.00
27/03/2021	Invoice	3468	No	Farscape Applications	Opening Balance	Opening Balance Equity		Debtors	500.00	2,300.00
31/03/2021	Deposit		No			Opening Balance Equity		Bank Account	5,000.00	7,300.00
Total for Opening Balance Equity									**£7,300.00**	
TOTAL									**£7,300.00**	

Figure 1.9 – Opening Balance Equity transaction report

What if no opening balance is created?

If there is no chart of account category in place, one will need to be created. If a bank account has been set up, then choose to edit it. Simply enter the cleared balance as per the bank statement date the day before QuickBooks was put into place:

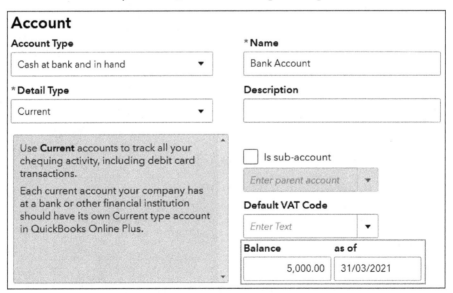

Figure 1.10 – Editing the chart of accounts code with the opening balance

The *double-entry* to the value to be entered in **Balance** will affect the **Opening Balance Equity** account. If the bank account is overdrawn, be sure to enter a negative value.

> **Tip**
> Using the balance within the chart of account code to account for the cleared balance will automatically mark the account as reconciled at the specified date.

What about uncleared checks and deposits?

Where any checks were written out before QuickBooks was put into place and there were funds received that had not cleared the bank prior to setting up QuickBooks, entries are required so that they can match future transactions as they appear on the bank feed.

To do this, a journal entry is required. Checks that have not yet cleared the bank will need to credit the bank, and deposits will require debits. This information should be obtainable from the last bank reconciliation from the accounting system in use prior to QuickBooks.

In the example shown in the next figure, the following entries had not cleared the bank as of March 31, 2021:

- Check 000345 dated February 16, 2021, for £300

- Deposit 000222 dated March 31, 2021, for £250

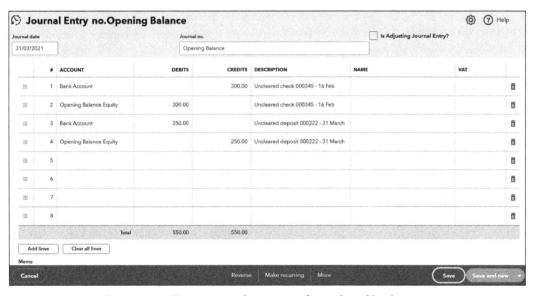

Figure 1.11 – Using a journal to account for uncleared bank entries

The *double-entry* is always made to the **Opening Balance Equity** account.

With all the entries made that reflect the opening bank balance, again run the trial balance to the day before QuickBooks was brought into use, that is `March 31, 2021`.

QuickBooks Tips
Trial Balance
As of March 31, 2021

	DEBIT	CREDIT
Bank Account	4,950.00	
Debtors	3,600.00	
Creditors		840.00
VAT Control		460.00
Opening Balance Equity		7,250.00
TOTAL	£8,550.00	£8,550.00

Figure 1.12 – Trial Balance report after opening bank balances

The bank balance here of £4,950 reflects the following values:

- Balance of £5,000 as per the bank statement as of `March 31`.
- Less the uncleared check for £300.
- Add the uncleared deposit of £250.

To summarize, £5,000 - £300 + £250 = £4,950.

With the bank added, we can now add a credit card balance owed for £750 as follows:

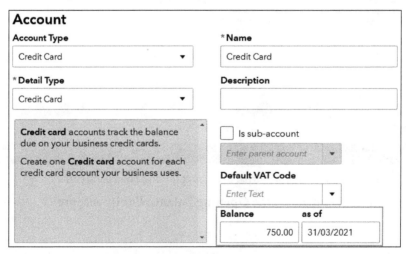

Figure 1.13 – Opening balance for credit card

Opening balances – VAT/GST/sales tax

If the business using QuickBooks is not VAT registered or similar, then you will not have to enter any opening balances for VAT. However, for a business that files VAT returns, we must consider the following:

- Is the date we start using QuickBooks in line with a new VAT period?

- Is there an overlap? For example, 2 months from the old system and 1 month from the QuickBooks start date will be used to file the next quarter.

- Is there any unpaid VAT from previously filed returns?

- Is VAT filed on a cash basis (dates of payments) or standard accrual basis using the dates of invoices and bills?

In the example within this book, the opening balances have been created for a business that files VAT on a cash basis. The unpaid customer and supplier balances have been entered net plus VAT, and that has resulted in the balance appearing in **VAT control**.

If all VAT has been paid, and there is no overlap at all, there would be nothing further to do. However, this is going to be unlikely.

Let's look first at VAT already filed but not yet paid. The example here is for a UK company but the principle will work the same in other regions – there will just be different terminology and tax rates.

If the VAT was filed, or about to be filed to March 31, but QuickBooks was only put into use on April 1, there will not be any information held in the software for the quarter January–March to enable us to create a return. However, we can fix that.

First, check whether the VAT settings reflect the start of the VAT period not filed/paid. So, here we have January selected even though we started using QuickBooks in April.

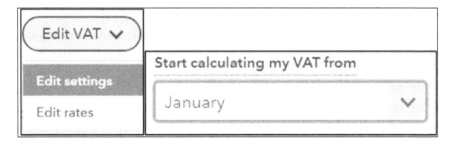

Figure 1.14 – VAT settings

What we will need to do next is take information from the VAT return that has already been filed, or information from our old accounting system, so that we have the following:

- Summary of sales with a specific tax rate applied and amount of tax
- Summary of purchases with a specific tax rate applied and amount of tax

With the preceding information to hand, we will create a journal dated to the last quarter, and this should be entered as shown here.

Journal date								Is Adjusting Journal Entry?
31/03/2021			Journal no. opening balance					
	#	ACCOUNT	DEBITS	CREDITS	DESCRIPTION	NAME	VAT	
⠿	1	Opening Balance Equity		40,000.00	Value of net sales - 20% VAT		20.0% S (Sales)	
⠿	2	Opening Balance Equity		5,000.00	Value of net sales - Zero 0% VAT		0.0% Z (Sales)	
⠿	3	Opening Balance Equity	10,000.00		Value of net purchases - 20% VAT		20.0% S (Purchases)	
⠿	4	Opening Balance Equity	1,000.00		Value of net purchases - Zero 0% VAT		0.0% Z (Purchases)	
⠿	5	Opening Balance Equity	40,000.00		Opening balances for VAT return			
⠿	6							
⠿	7							
⠿	8							
		Subtotal	51,000.00	45,000.00				
		VAT @ 20% (Sales)		8,000.00				
		VAT @ 0% (Sales)		0.00				
		VAT @ 20% (Purchases)	2,000.00					
		VAT @ 0% (Purchases)	0.00					
		Total	53,000.00	53,000.00				

Figure 1.15 – Journal entry required for VAT balances

Every journal line must be posted to the same account **Opening Balance Equity**. All values that need to appear on the return must have a VAT rate applied and this will add a VAT value at the bottom of the journal.

The balancing line on this journal is entered into the same chart of account code but does not have a VAT rate applied.

The result of creating the preceding journal will affect our VAT return, as shown in the following figure.

> **Tip**
> When creating journals like this, it is possible to attach documents (option available at the bottom left of the journal screen). It is a good idea to attach your spreadsheet workings in case you need to refer to them later.

VAT Return		VAT
HM Revenue & Customs (VAT)		
QuickBooks Tips (VAT registration # 123456789)		Cash basis
01/01/2021 - 31/03/2021		Submission date: 04/06/2021

VAT due on sales and other outputs.	Box 1	£8,000.00	Adjust
VAT due on acquisitions from other EC Member States.	Box 2	£0.00	Adjust
Total output tax due.	Box 3	£8,000.00	
VAT reclaimed on purchases.	Box 4	£2,000.00	Adjust
Net VAT to pay (or reclaim).	Box 5	£6,000.00	
Net value of sales.	Box 6	£45,000.00	Adjust
Net value of purchases.	Box 7	£11,000.00	Adjust
Net value of supplies to other EC Member States.	Box 8	£0.00	Adjust
Net value of acquisitions from other EC Member States.	Box 9	£0.00	Adjust

Figure 1.16 – VAT return summary after the opening balances are updated

We can see that entering a summary of data from a previous period into the journal will populate the VAT return exactly as required. If the VAT return has already been filed with the authorities, it can be manually *marked as filed*, where the payment can be recorded later.

If you have not filed the VAT return yet for the last quarter, we will now be able to submit the return digitally (if available in your region).

If the business had more than one VAT period unpaid, journals can be created for every period and the VAT returns recreated this way. You must work on the oldest period first, because it would not be possible to create a return for an earlier period once a return has been filed for a later period.

If there was an overlap between the VAT period and the date the business started to use QuickBooks, then a journal could be created that reflects sales and purchases for 2 months from the old system, and sales and purchases from QuickBooks would be used for the third month of the quarter.

As with all other opening balances, we should check our trial balance to see what the effect of making entries has made.

QuickBooks Tips 🖉		
Trial Balance		
As of March 31, 2021		
	DEBIT	**CREDIT**
Bank Account	4,950.00	
Debtors	3,600.00	
Creditors		840.00
Credit Card		750.00
VAT Control		6,460.00
Opening Balance Equity		500.00
TOTAL	£8,550.00	£8,550.00

Figure 1.17 – Trial Balance report after adjustments made for VAT

Creating the journal for the VAT has increased liability in the VAT control account and reduced the **Opening Balance Equity** account further. When all opening balances have been entered, the **Opening Balance Equity** account should finally balance to zero.

Let's move on to look at more common opening balances that may be required.

Inventory (stock)

Product/Service items for inventory can be imported – see *Figure 1.4*. Stock that is imported will be valued by multiplying the quantity on the import sheet by the purchase cost price set against an item.

This creates an opening stock adjustment, which is similar to a journal entry. One side of the entry will *debit* the **Stock Asset** account, and the other side of the entry will *credit* **Opening Balance Equity**.

Opening Balances – Other

So far, we have looked at opening balances where information should be readily available to business owners: the cash in the bank, what our customers owe, what is owed to suppliers, and the current VAT/GST/sales tax position. However, other values that appear on the balance sheet may require further investigation.

In some instances, the accountant may not have finalized the accounts for the previous financial year, so the opening balances cannot be completed until there is a balance sheet that all figures can be agreed to.

The following sections contain details of the different types of opening balances. They can all be set up in the same way; this will be explained toward the end of this chapter.

Other business taxes

This is the balance of tax, insurance, and pension contributions that has been deducted from employees, and the corporation tax payable by the company.

Fixed assets (Plant and Machinery)

The value of all assets held by the company. This usually includes the original cost and provision for depreciation already made. This information is found on the fixed asset register (This is often held by the accountant).

Loans and Hire Purchase Agreements

The current balance owed on any loans that the company has in place. This will include the original loan value, less payments to date, and accrued interest.

Shareholdings

This is the value of shares in place. This information will be found on the last set of completed accounts.

Director's loans

The balance funds owed to the director, or, in some cases, funds owed from a director if the director's loan is *overdrawn*.

Provisions for prepayments and accruals

These values are often calculated by the accountant and relate to income and expenditure that will be adjusted in other periods: for example, an annual subscription paid, 6 months of which will cover a different financial year.

The opening balances for these categories can be created as follows.

When creating/editing a chart of account code and adding a balance as at a specified date, this method can save time as you are creating the opening balance at the same time as creating/editing the chart of account code.

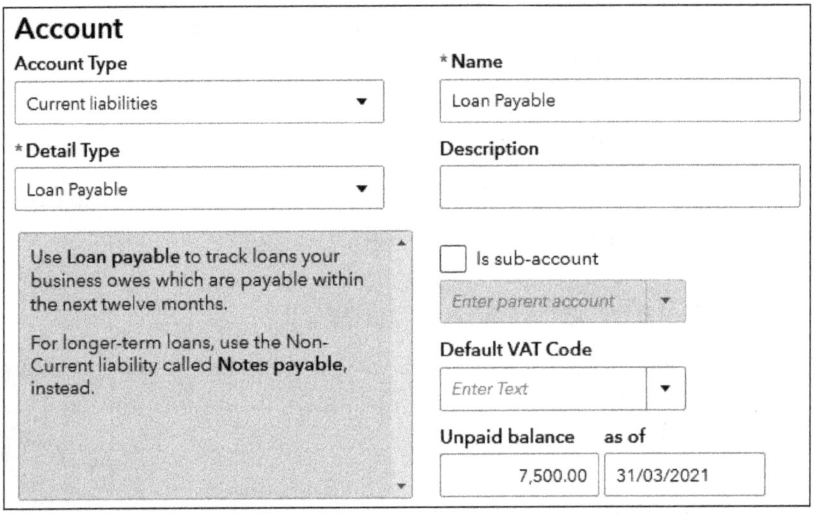

Figure 1.18 – Editing the chart of account category with the opening balance

If you have all the necessary chart of account codes in place, it will be quicker to use a journal entry to create the opening balances. All liabilities (monies owed to others) need to be entered as credits and all assets are entered as debits.

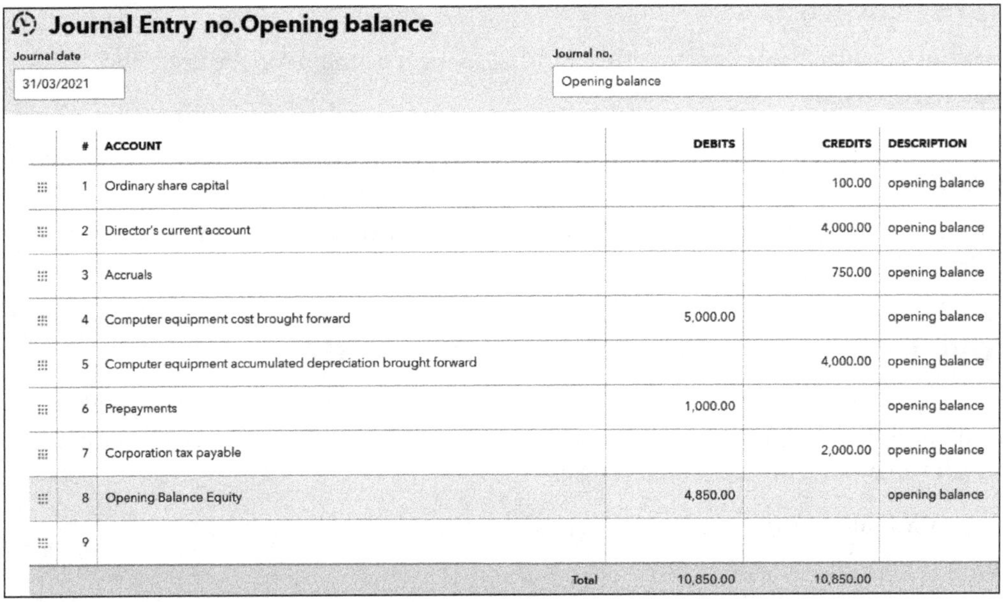

Figure 1.19 – Using a journal to edit further opening balances

The final balancing line will be entered into **Opening Balance Equity**.

After creating this journal entry, the trial balance report appears as follows:

QuickBooks Tips 🖉		
Trial Balance		
As of March 31, 2021		
	DEBIT	**CREDIT**
Bank Account	4,950.00	
Debtors	3,600.00	
Prepayments	1,000.00	
Computer equipment accumulated depreciation broug…		4,000.00
Computer equipment cost brought forward	5,000.00	
Creditors		840.00
Credit Card		750.00
Accruals		750.00
Corporation tax payable		2,000.00
Director's current account		4,000.00
VAT Control		6,460.00
Opening Balance Equity	4,350.00	
Ordinary share capital		100.00
TOTAL	£18,900.00	£18,900.00

Figure 1.20 – Checking the Trial Balance report

After making all the entries to this company so far, the balance within **Opening Balance Equity** is £4,350, but it should balance to zero once complete, so what could be missing?

If the business has been trading for over a year, there should be a balance in the **Retained Earnings** account, which is a result of the cumulative profit/loss of the business in previous years. Errors could also have been made along the way, which is why this account contains a balance.

Using the example that has been worked on in this chapter, it has been found that the Computer Equipment cost is £50,000 (not £5,000) and depreciation is £40,000 (not £4,000). The value of retained earnings from prior years should be £4,650 in credit.

As with all of the entries made in QuickBooks, edits are easily made. There are many different ways to locate an entry. One of the simplest is to run the Trial Balance report for the desired period and click the balance against the account where the balances appear to be incorrect. That will list all of the transactions made to the account in the selected period. Click on the transaction that is incorrect, make the required edits, and save.

After correcting the journal for the value of assets, the opening balance equity now contains the value that should appear in retained earnings, so a simple journal will fix that.

⏱ Journal Entry no.opening balance

Journal date	Journal no.
31/03/2021	opening balance

	#	ACCOUNT	DEBITS	CREDITS	DESCRIPTION
⠿	1	Retained Earnings		4,650.00	Opening balance
⠿	2	Opening Balance Equity	4,650.00		Opening balance

Figure 1.21 – Final journal adjustment to correct balances

After making our final adjustment, the Trial Balance report should be checked to ensure that all opening balances are correct to the last closed period. In this example, that's March 31, as we are starting using QuickBooks from April 1.

QuickBooks Tips
Trial Balance
As of March 31, 2021

	DEBIT	CREDIT
Bank Account	4,950.00	
Debtors	3,600.00	
Prepayments	1,000.00	
Computer equipment accumulated depreciation broug...		40,000.00
Computer equipment cost brought forward	50,000.00	
Creditors		840.00
Credit Card		750.00
Accruals		750.00
Corporation tax payable		2,000.00
Director's current account		4,000.00
VAT Control		6,460.00
Opening Balance Equity		0.00
Ordinary share capital		100.00
Retained Earnings		4,650.00
TOTAL	£59,550.00	£59,550.00

Figure 1.22 – Trial Balance report after the opening balances are completed

The opening balances are now complete. Once the opening balances have been fully agreed, it is a particularly good idea to close the books with a password, using the options within the **Advanced** tab of **Account and settings**.

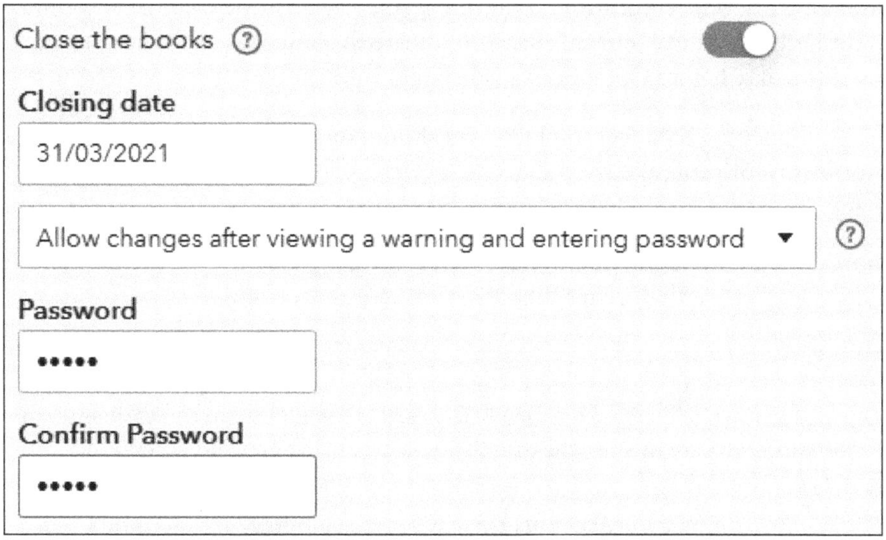

Figure 1.23 – Set books as closed with a password

Summary

This chapter has explained in detail how opening balances can be created when a company shifts to QuickBooks at any given point.

Here is a very brief recap:

- **Customer Balances**: Create invoices/credit notes that mirror those that were unpaid in your old system prior to the switch to QuickBooks. Use a product/service for opening balances linked to the **Opening Balance Equity** account. If *Cash Accounting* for VAT, invoices should be entered net + VAT; otherwise, enter the invoices to reflect the total gross amounts due, ignoring VAT.

- **Supplier Balances**: Create supplier bills/credits that mirror those that were unpaid in your old system prior to the switch to QuickBooks. The bills should be coded to the **Opening Balance Equity** account category, and if reporting VAT on a cash basis, values should be entered net + VAT.

- **Bank Accounts**: Edit the chart of account code and enter a balance as at the last closed period (the day before QuickBooks was brought into use). Uncleared payments and deposits can be listed within a journal.

- **VAT/GST/Sales Tax**: Entering customer invoices and supplier bills net + VAT will populate values within the VAT control account. Journals can be used to recreate VAT returns for prior periods and adjust the VAT control account.

- **Other Balance Sheet Accounts**: Edit the balance against the chart of account code at a desired date or use journal entries to create the balances to the last closed period (the day before QuickBooks is brought into use).

With all of your opening balances in place, you should be all set. The following chapter includes some tips for general day-to-day use, as well as some additional settings you should check.

Furthermore, if you have made a complete mess setting up, it's possible to scrap all the data and start over, so we shall cover that too.

> **Tip**
>
> During each step of creating opening balances, it is a good idea to run various reports and compare them to the data that was held using previous accounting systems.
>
> For example, running the **Accounts payable ageing summary** and **Accounts receivable ageing summary** reports is always a good place to start to ensure the opening balances for customers and suppliers are correct at the date QuickBooks Online was first put into use.

2

Useful Tips and Tricks Every QuickBooks User Should Know

Some chapters within this book are for specific business types that can help users tailor QuickBooks Online to meet their specific requirements. This chapter, as well as the chapters toward the end of this book that refer to reviewing and reporting, apply to all types of organizations – large and small.

It is important that QuickBooks is made as easy to use as possible for everybody that needs to access and use it. Within this chapter, you will learn how to put various methods into practice that will do exactly that.

In this chapter, we will cover the following topics:

- Purging a QuickBooks company
- Using the KISS principle
- General tips for regular use

To start with, we are going to take a look at what we might need to do if things have gone wrong in the very early stages of getting QuickBooks set up.

Purging a QuickBooks company

Purging a company that's been set up in QuickBooks gives you the option to *start over*. Purging a company will remove all the data that is currently in place.

If mistakes have been made when setting up a company in QuickBooks, too much time can be wasted trying to correct them all. In such a scenario, starting from scratch can be the easiest option. Purging a company allows us to do so without having to sign up for a new subscription.

There are some limitations to using this option and they will vary, depending on the region you are working in. In some countries, it is not possible to purge a company if it has been in use for more than 30 days, while in others, you may have up to 90 days to purge a company. However, if you find that you are unable to purge a company, there are other options:

- Contact the Intuit QuickBooks care team; they may be able to purge the company for you.
- Cancel the current subscription and start another.

> **Note**
> Purging will remove all data and disable settings such as Multicurrency. If sales tax still appears to be in place, try refreshing the browser or logging out from and back into QuickBooks. You should find that the VAT/GST settings will also have been removed.

Using the Purge Company option

You will not find the option to purge a company within any of the menus and settings. The reason for this is to protect users from purging a company in error; this reason is also why there is a limited time in which you will be able to purge a company without having to contact Intuit.

Any area you are accessing in QuickBooks will always be displayed in the address bar of your browser. As shown in the following screenshot, when viewing the **Dashboard** in QuickBooks, the word **homepage** appears at the end of the web address:

Figure 2.1 – Web address for the Dashboard

To access the function that will allow you to purge a QuickBooks Online company, click on the web address within the browser, remove the **homepage** text, and replace it with purgecompany, as shown in the following screenshot:

Figure 2.2 – Web address required to access the Purge Company function

Once the text has been entered into the address, press *Enter* on your keyboard. You will be presented with the information that's displayed in the following screenshot:

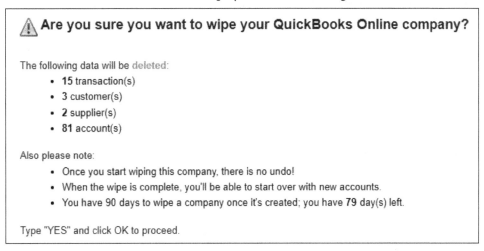

Figure 2.3 – Warning before purging a QuickBooks Online company

This warning is advising you of what will happen once you have confirmed this action. It states the number of transactions, customers, suppliers, and chart of account codes that will be removed. If you are sure that the data needs to be wiped, confirm this by typing YES into the box at the bottom right of the screen:

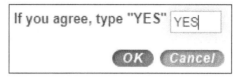

Figure 2.4 – Confirming the option to purge the company

After confirming that you wish to proceed with purging a QuickBooks company file, there are two further options to select before the data is wiped:

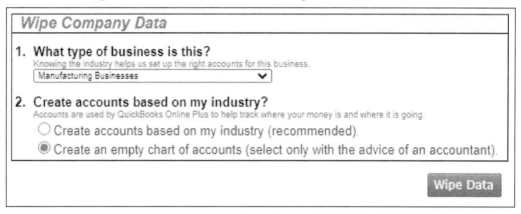

Figure 2.5 – Final options before purging a company file is complete

You can select a company type that matches your business (or close to) from the dropdown options for option 1.

For option 2, you can choose for QuickBooks to recreate a set of chart of account codes based on your company type, or you can have an empty chart of accounts be created. Choosing the latter means that you can start creating the categories exactly as you would like, without having to remove any chart of account codes that you are never likely to use.

If you are not sure what to do, seek assistance from a professional advisor.

Even after selecting the option to create an empty set of chart of account codes, you will find that there could be a dozen or so in place. You will be able to make some of these inactive; this will be covered later in this chapter.

The following screenshot shows the bare minimum chart of account codes for a UK QuickBooks file after the data has been wiped:

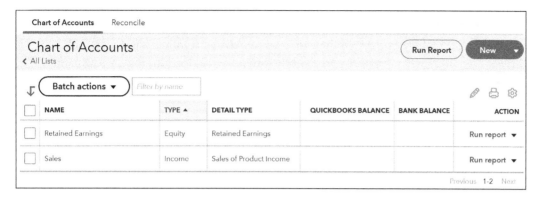

Figure 2.6 – Chart of Accounts once data has been wiped

Now that you have learned how to purge a company (if needed), let's look at how the KISS principle can be applied when setting up QuickBooks Online.

Using the KISS principle

The **KISS** acronym means *keep it simple, stupid.* When it comes to setting up systems and procedures for businesses, both large and small, it is better to avoid complexity wherever possible.

When setting up a QuickBooks file, it is important to ask yourself the following:

- Who is accessing the QuickBooks file regularly?
- What are the regular reporting requirements of the business?
- What are the statutory reporting requirements of the business?

Why are these considerations so important?

When we know who is going to access QuickBooks the most (for bookkeeping) and we fully understand the reporting requirements of the business, we will be able to follow our KISS principle.

It is important that QuickBooks has been set up so that the following is true:

- It is easy to use – especially if the business owner will be doing the bookkeeping.
- Reports are easy to understand – for the business owner and the accountant.
- Statutory requirements have been met (sales tax and employee tax, for example).

How can you make QuickBooks easier to use?

It does not matter where you are in the world – QuickBooks Online is going to look and feel the same. There will always be some subtle differences in terminology, with *vendors/suppliers* being one example and different tax options being another. It is not possible to change the layout or menu titles, but we can edit and change the names of items within *Lists*.

The following would fall within this category:

- Chart of Account Codes
- Products/Services
- Customers (including sub-customers and projects)
- Suppliers/Vendors
- Classes/Locations and Tags (Optional if in use)

When transactions are coded in QuickBooks, a chart of account code is always in use. Even when a customer invoice is created using a Product/Service, a chart of account category is connected to the Product/Service code – this ensures the values on invoices appear on reports as desired.

When reviewing the setup of the QuickBooks file to ensure it meets the needs of the business and follows the KISS principle, the chart of account codes is the best place to start.

Chart of account codes

The chart of accounts is a list of codes that are used to carry out our bookkeeping. When reviewing the setup, we need to consider the following:

- How many codes are required?
- How should they be named?
- Do we need sub-accounts?
- Do we need to use account numbers?

Let's start by looking at the first query on this list.

How many chart of account codes should I use?

We are trying to keep things as simple as we can, so the answer to this is as few as possible. A good reference can be to start looking at the last set of accounts that have been prepared for the business by the accountant, if available. This is likely to reflect the absolute minimum number of categories that the business will need.

Do not forget that there are a lot of different reports that can be run from QuickBooks. Even though materials could be purchased from different suppliers, it is not necessary to have a different chart of account category for each as we can produce an **Expenses by Supplier** report.

The same applies to our income categories. It is possible that one income category, called *Sales*, will be sufficient as there are reports such as **Income by Customer Summary** and **Income by Product/Service Summary** that will produce the necessary breakdown required for sales reporting.

Occasionally, more chart of account codes will be required than what is used by the accountant for tax purposes. This will help give more clarity to the business owner and the chart of account codes could be named differently too. A good example is **Insurance Expenses**. For tax purposes, the accountant may always have everything under one heading, but the business may incur different types of insurance costs and may want to display them separately.

Now, let's look at how we can modify the chart of accounts so that it can be tailored to suit the needs of the business.

Tailoring the chart of accounts

You can access the chart of accounts from a couple of areas in QuickBooks – even more if you are logged in as an accountant. We will not be using *Accountant-only* tools, so all these features will be available to everybody. We will use the *gear* icon, which is located at the top right of the screen. **Chart of Accounts** can be found under **YOUR COMPANY**.

With our **Chart of Accounts** list on the screen, we can do some instant tidying. The QuickBooks file could be brand new, recently purged, or perhaps been in use for several years. Whichever the scenario, it is likely that accounts that we do not require are in place. **Batch actions** comes into play here. On the far left of every account code is a small tick box. As shown in the following screenshot, use your mouse to tick all the account codes that are surplus to requirements, use the **Batch actions** tool, and select the **Make inactive** option:

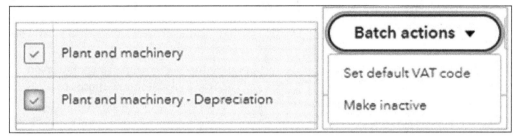

Figure 2.7 – Using Batch actions within our Chart of Accounts

As you can see, you can also apply default VAT codes (or GST sales tax in other regions) against the chart of account codes using **Batch actions**.

> **Note**
>
> If the batch option to make a chart of account category is not available in your region, a single account can be made inactive using the delete/**Make inactive** option, which can be found in the drop-down action menu on the far right of each chart of accounts code.

Remember that making a chart of account code inactive simply hides the code from your list – it is not permanently deleted. When the **Include inactive** option is selected from the cog list within the chart of accounts and the word deleted is entered in the search bar, all the accounts that were previously made inactive will appear on the list. These accounts can be made active again:

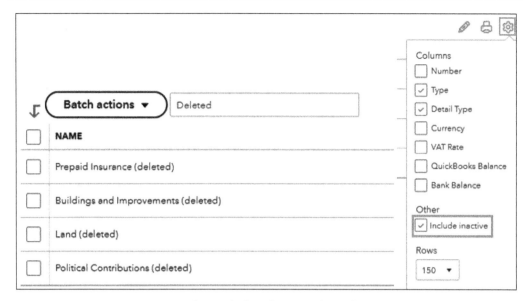

Figure 2.8 – Displaying the list of inactive chart of account codes

After removing any chart of account codes that are not required, we should carefully review what is left. QuickBooks may have created a set of chart of accounts, but in some instances, you may just like to change the names a little.

Within the *drop-down menu* on the far right of each chart of account code, you will find the option to *edit* an account. However, if you have several names to edit, using the *batch edit pencil* will save a lot of time.

The batch edit pencil option can be found at the top right of the chart of accounts list:

Figure 2.9 – The batch edit pencil

Selecting the batch edit pencil opens the chart of accounts in a table view where names can be edited quickly and easily. Simply click inside the text fields, edit the name as desired, and save it:

Donations	Expenses
Entertainment	Expenses
Equipment Rental	Expenses
Heat and light	Expenses

Figure 2.10 – Using batch edit against the chart of account names

After making the required edits, the same account categories will appear as per the following screenshot. The business owner/bookkeeper will now be using the account names they could have used in a previous bookkeeping system:

Charitable donations	Expenses
Client entertainment	Expenses
Equipment hire	Expenses
Electricity	Expenses

Figure 2.11 – Chart of accounts once edits have been made

Using more than one chart of account code for similar types

Be mindful that the chart of accounts needs to be as straightforward as possible; creating lots of chart of account codes should be avoided if possible. However, there are instances when more than one account for a similar type is required. The most common are bank accounts.

In a statutory financial report for a company, there is likely to be one value that reflects *cash in the bank and in hand,* but this could be a value that consists of a current account, savings account, and petty cash. These accounts must be kept separate in QuickBooks so that each bank account can be reconciled correctly.

It is often the case that accounts that affect the profit and loss (income, cost of sales, expenses, other income, and other expenses) can end up with more categories than are required.

For example, would four accounts for insurance, three accounts for telephone, and six accounts for motoring expenses be necessary, or would one of each suffice? This can be the difference between a profit and loss report that runs over three pages and is difficult to read, or a report that fits on one page that is much clearer and easier to understand.

If you do need multiple accounts for similar types, it is highly advisable to group them using **sub-accounts**.

Using sub-accounts

Using sub-accounts means that if you create different accounts for similar expense types, you can group them easily on your reports. Taking motoring expenses as an example, this could be made up of fuel, repairs, and lease payments.

We are going to use four chart of account categories for motor expenses. Motoring expenses will be the parent, while the other three will be sub-accounts of that.

The following is an example of the chart of account category for fuel that is part of the group of accounts for motor expenses. To ensure that the account is grouped correctly, it must be set up using the same **Account Type**. A tick must be placed against the **sub-account** where the parent account that is to appear at the top of the group is selected:

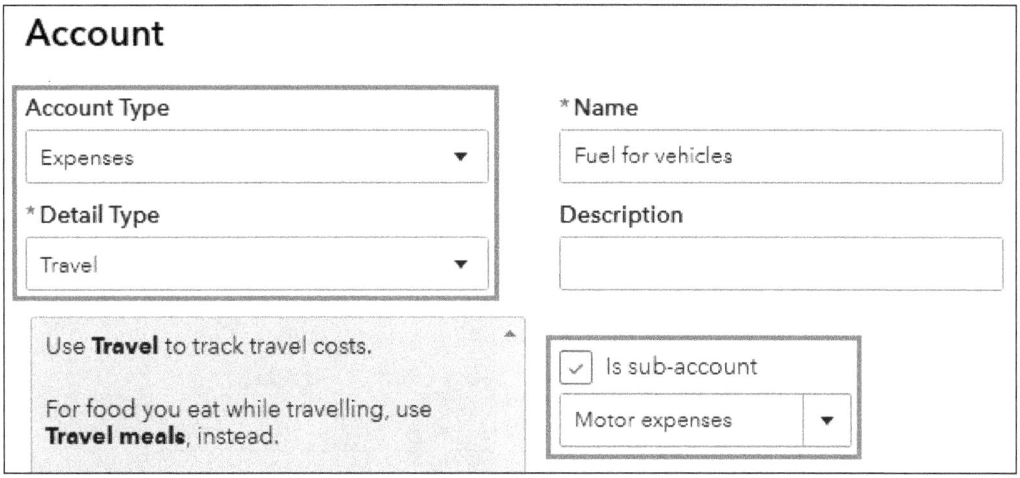

Figure 2.12 – Creating a sub-account

With three sub-accounts created below motor expenses, they would appear in the chart of accounts as shown in the following screenshot. A sub-account will always appear indented below the parent of the category:

☐	Motor expenses	Expenses	Travel
☐	Fuel for vehicles	Expenses	Travel
☐	Leasing payments	Expenses	Travel
☐	Vehicle repairs	Expenses	Travel

Figure 2.13 – Sub-accounts listed below the parent in the chart of accounts

Using sub-accounts helps ensure that categories appear within your profit and loss/balance sheet reports as desired. Using the motoring expenses example, the costs will appear in the profit and loss section, as shown here:

Motor expenses	
Fuel for vehicles	350.00
Leasing payments	625.00
Vehicle repairs	180.00
Total Motor expenses	**1,155.00**

Figure 2.14 – Sub-accounts displayed on the profit and loss report

If you wish to produce a report that displays the total for the group without the detailed breakdown, toward the top of the report screen, you can **Collapse** a report so that only the totals of a group are displayed.

Figure 2.15 – Collapsing a report

The option to **Collapse** will change to **Expand** once it's selected. Clicking on this option again will display the breakdown that was shown previously:

	TOTAL
▾ Income	
Sales	3,000.00
Total Income	**£3,000.00**
GROSS PROFIT	£3,000.00
▾ Expenses	
Accountancy fees	100.00
Heat and light	300.00
Motor expenses	1,155.00
Shopify charges	200.00
Subscriptions	250.00
Total Expenses	**£2,005.00**
NET OPERATING INCOME	**£995.00**
NET INCOME	**£995.00**

Figure 2.16 – The profit and loss in a collapsed view

Using account numbers with the chart of account codes

Using account numbers within your chart of accounts is a matter of personal preference. It is not mandatory, so if you prefer to refer to a category by name alone, it is probably best to leave the feature switched off. However, there are a few benefits of using it. These are when the following are true:

- Account numbers were used previously, and everybody is familiar with them.
- You wish to change the order in which categories appear on reports.
- Accountants may wish to set up the same account numbers in QuickBooks that are used in the tax preparation software.

To enable the use of account numbers, access the **Advanced** tab within **Account and Settings**. From here, you can enable the use of account numbers and choose if account numbers should be visible on reports:

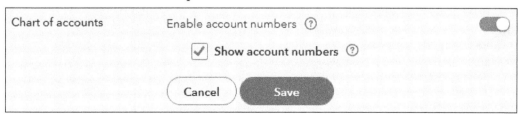

Figure 2.17 – Enabling account numbers

With this feature enabled, you can edit the chart of account numbers using the batch option, as described earlier in this chapter. QuickBooks does not come with its own set of numbers; you can apply your own.

When reports are produced in QuickBooks, the default is to sort them in alphabetical order within each section of a report. As shown in *Figure 2.16*, the categories within **Expenses** are sorted alphabetically, starting with `Accountancy Fees`.

The following screenshot shows the same report but with account numbers in use. This time, the report is sorted in account number order:

QuickBooks Tips	
Profit and Loss	
1 May - 18 June, 2021	

	TOTAL
▾ Income	
1000 Sales	3,000.00
Total Income	**£3,000.00**
GROSS PROFIT	**£3,000.00**
▾ Expenses	
3995 Subscriptions	250.00
3996 Heat and light	300.00
3997 Shopify charges	200.00
3999 Motor expenses	1,155.00
4001 Accountancy fees	100.00
Total Expenses	**£2,005.00**
NET OPERATING INCOME	**£995.00**
NET INCOME	**£995.00**

Figure 2.18 – Profit and loss report with account numbers in use

Products and services

When reviewing the products and services that are in place, we are applying the same logic that we used when looking at the chart of accounts. A sole proprietor using QuickBooks online, who only provides consultancy services, may only require one service item called *Consultancy*. All the sales invoices that are raised could be coded to this single item.

However, if the business owner provides different services and would like to check which one is generating the most income, then it makes sense to create the different product/service codes. This means that reports such as **Sales by Product/Service Summary** will separate the values for the different services provided.

Generally, a business will only require a lot of different Product/Service items if they are buying and selling goods and need to monitor stock levels. We will look at how stock is handled in *Chapter 3, QuickBooks Online for Manufacturing Businesses*.

Customers

All businesses need to have customers, but again, we can consider how many are created in QuickBooks. When goods or services are provided with credit terms, a customer must be created so that a business can track who owes them money.

However, where payment is received at the point of sale, a different customer does not have to be created each time. We shall cover these scenarios in *Chapter 4, Recording Income for Retail Businesses*.

Suppliers

Like customers, when we receive a supplier bill, it is coded to a supplier account so that we can keep track of how much we owe to other businesses. When purchases are made and paid for immediately, it is not necessary to create a supplier every single time.

If a new supplier was created for all the different gas stations that were used when paying for fuel, or different grocery stores or fast-food outlets that were used, the number of suppliers in the supplier list can become exceptionally long.

The only time you might want to create a supplier, even if you have paid for the goods on receipt, is if you wish to report on this supplier later using **Expenses by Supplier Summary**. For small one-off purchases, it can be advisable to create a supplier called `Sundry Suppliers` so that they can easily be found within supplier reports, as well as the profit and loss reports.

Classes, locations, and tags

Unlike other list items, the use of classes, locations, and tags is optional. In *Chapter 9, Enhancing the Consistency of Your Financial Statements*, and *Chapter 10, Reconciling the Balance Sheet*, we will look at how these features can be applied when reviewing and reporting against the data held within QuickBooks Online.

So far, we have looked at areas we should consider when setting up QuickBooks Online in terms of our opening balances, as well as the number of different categories we need to use. Throughout the following chapters, we will look at different business types and how QuickBooks Online can be set up to suit the needs of the business.

As well as covering different business models, we will be looking at best practices with regard to reviewing and reporting financial data. This applies to all business types.

For now, let's look at some quick tips that can be followed when you're using QuickBooks daily.

General tips for daily use

QuickBooks Online offers various features that can help simplify bookkeeping, and some of these are hidden. Let's take a look at a few quick tips that can be used daily when using QuickBooks:

- Merging accounts
- Date shortcuts
- The calculator function
- The advanced search
- Duplicating the tab of your browser
- Other shortcuts

Merging accounts

Occasionally, two different list names may be created and both contain records. However, where two currently exist, there should only be one. Where the list name is used, this refers to any of the following:

- Customers
- Suppliers
- Chart of account categories
- Products/services
- Classes and locations

Let's say that, within our supplier list, two suppliers have been created with slightly different names, the first being *Intuit* and the other being *Intuit QuickBooks*.

This sort of duplication is common and can lead to entries being made against both suppliers at different times in the year, leading to confusion – checking supplier statements is a good example of this. We can correct this easily by merging.

How are accounts merged?

You will not find the option to merge within any menus. The following screenshot shows the two suppliers in our supplier list:

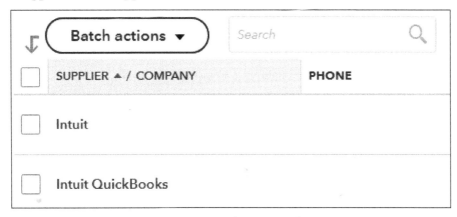

Figure 2.19 – Duplicating suppliers

First, click on the name of the account that is using the incorrect name. In this example, we wish to keep the account with the full name and remove Intuit from the list. Any records that are made to that account should be merged with the supplier we are keeping.

To do this, click on the name of the account to be removed and click **Edit**. The **Display name as** field should be edited so that it contains the supplier name we wish to use moving forward:

Title	First name	Middle name	Last name	Suffix

Company

Intuit

*Display name as

Intuit QuickBooks

Figure 2.20 – Display name, as edited with the correct name

After editing the account's name, the following message will appear on the screen:

Please Confirm

That name is already being used. Would you like to merge the two?

No   Yes

Figure 2.21 – Confirming the merge of accounts

After confirming that the account is to be merged with another of the same name, the account being edited becomes inactive. All the transactions that were previously found against two separate named accounts will now only show in one.

The merge feature works in the same way when editing customers, chart of account categories, products and services, classes, and locations.

Date shortcuts

When data is being entered manually in QuickBooks Online, time can be saved if you are familiar with some simple data shortcuts. Entering letters in a date field (in lowercase) will create the following dates based on the date already being shown:

- *t*: **T**oday's date
- *w*: The first day of the **w**eek
- *k*: The last day of the wee**k**
- *m*: The first day of the **m**onth
- *h*: The last day of the mont**h**
- *y*: The first day of the calendar **y**ear
- *r*: The last day of the calenda**r** year

> **Tip**
> To remember these shortcuts, think of the words *today*, *week*, *month*, and *year*, and the letters found at the beginning and end of each word.

As well as using these letters, pressing the plus (+) key will add a day to the date displayed. Pressing the negative/minus button (-) will reduce the date by a day.

Let's say that the current month is June and that the year is 2021. If only the day of the month is entered – for example, 14 – the date will autocorrect to June 14, 2021.

Keeping the same year in mind, let's we need to make an entry for May 14, 2021. Here, the only value that's required in the date box is 1405.

If an entry was required for May 14, 2020, the digits 140520 are all that is required.

The use of slashes or dashes is not required when entering a date, and using the preceding shortcuts saves time versus entering full dates or scrolling through dates manually.

The calculator function

The calculator function allows us to check calculations within a value field in QuickBooks, without the need to go hunting for a calculator. Imagine that the annual insurance cost for a business was £1,475 and that the accountant needs to prepay for 2 months of this value. This value could be calculated while creating a journal.

As shown in the following screenshot, we would need to enter the value, divide it by 12 months, and then multiply it by 2. These are simple formulas, and unlike Excel, there is no requirement to use the equals sign (=) at the beginning. If you wish, you can use brackets within the formula.

The result of this calculation gives us a value of £245.83:

Figure 2.22 – Using the calculator function in the value field

- + Addition
- - Subtraction
- / Division
- * Multiply

The advanced search function

The magnifying glass icon displayed toward the top right of the dashboard menu is a basic search and recent transactions tool. Clicking this icon will provide some search tips and display the last 10 transactions that have been created. If you need to investigate this further, the **Advanced Search** option (as shown in the following screenshot) can be extremely useful:

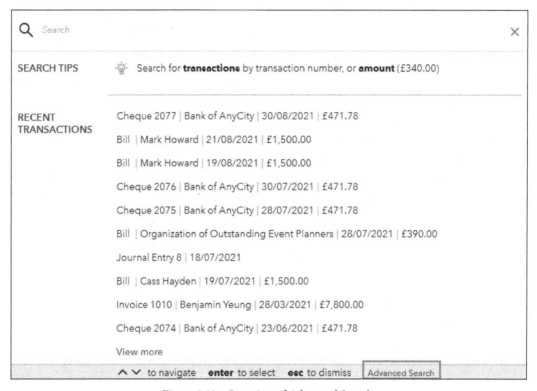

Figure 2.23 – Location of Advanced Search

Using **Advanced Search** allows you to create a filtered search. After selecting the type of transaction or value you are looking for, click the **Filter** option (do not click search).

This allows you to search for different things within a single search by building the filter. As shown in the following screenshot, there is a search for **Bills** against the Intuit QuickBooks supplier, where the value is greater than £10 but less than £30:

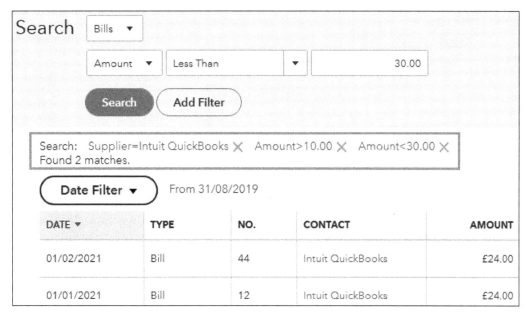

Figure 2.24 – How a filtered search appears

If the preceding search still produces a lot of records, the list can be reduced further by applying a date filter.

Duplicating a tab in the browser

It is only possible to have one QuickBooks company file open at the same time when using one internet browser. However, you can have multiple tabs open for a single company at the same time.

For example, this can be useful if, during a bank reconciliation, you would like to check a customer account. Instead of having to close the bank reconciliation completely, it could remain open in one tab; then, customers could be viewed on the other.

Accountants have a **New window function** within **Accountant Tools**, but all users can apply the following without any special QuickBooks features.

With the browser open, point your mouse to the browser tab that's open for QuickBooks and right-click. Select **Duplicate** from the menu that appears, as shown in the following screenshot:

Figure 2.25 – Duplicating a tab in the browser

You can have multiple tabs open for different areas of QuickBooks Online at the same time, which is even more useful if you are working with multiple displays:

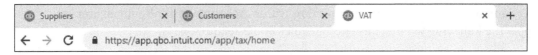

Figure 2.26 – Multiple tabs open

Other shortcuts

There is a selection of other shortcuts available that can be accessed by pressing the *ctrl/control* and *alt/option* keys at the same time with one other key. To view this list of shortcuts, press *ctrl/control* and *alt/option* keys together with the *?* key; the following will appear on the screen:

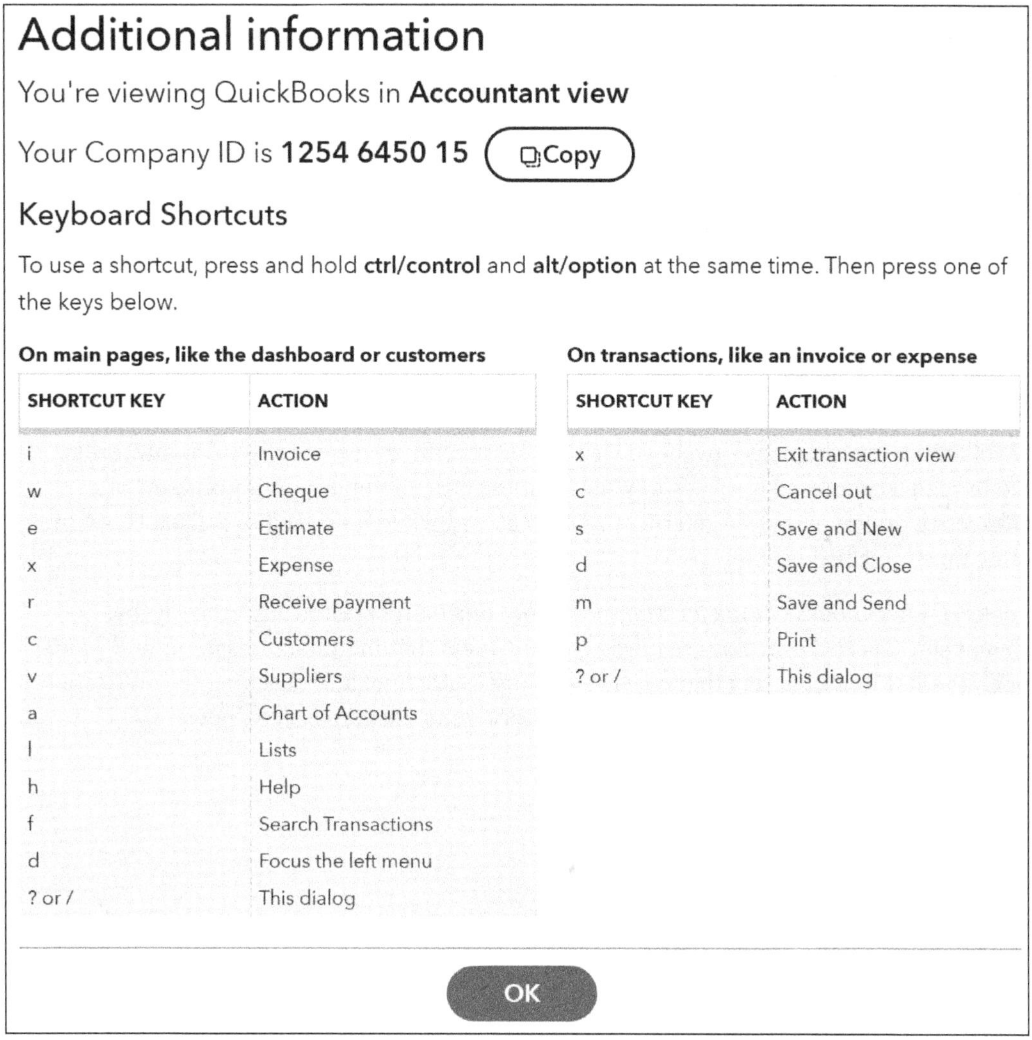

Additional information

You're viewing QuickBooks in **Accountant view**

Your Company ID is **1254 6450 15**   (🗐Copy)

Keyboard Shortcuts

To use a shortcut, press and hold **ctrl/control** and **alt/option** at the same time. Then press one of the keys below.

On main pages, like the dashboard or customers

SHORTCUT KEY	ACTION
i	Invoice
w	Cheque
e	Estimate
x	Expense
r	Receive payment
c	Customers
v	Suppliers
a	Chart of Accounts
l	Lists
h	Help
f	Search Transactions
d	Focus the left menu
? or /	This dialog

On transactions, like an invoice or expense

SHORTCUT KEY	ACTION
x	Exit transaction view
c	Cancel out
s	Save and New
d	Save and Close
m	Save and Send
p	Print
? or /	This dialog

(OK)

Figure 2.27 – List of shortcuts

As well as being presented with a list of shortcuts, the QuickBooks Online Company ID will be displayed. You will need this information if you raise a support query with Intuit.

Summary

This chapter covered how a QuickBooks company can be purged, should we wish to completely wipe our data and start from fresh, without the need to cancel a subscription and sign up for another.

When using the KISS principle, it is a best practice to avoid complexity whenever we can, and this starts in QuickBooks by looking at the number of chart of account categories the business requires, followed by the use of products and services, customers, and more.

Using date shortcuts and the calculator function, merging accounts, and duplicating the browser when using QuickBooks can save us time when using QuickBooks on a day-to-day basis.

The following five chapters have been written for specific business types. You may only need to read a chapter that relates to your business type. If you are an accountant or bookkeeper, you may wish to refer to a section as and when you need to assist a client in setting up a QuickBooks file.

Chapter 3, QuickBooks Online for Manufacturing Businesses specifically looks at the different settings and processes required by a business that manufactures items and holds stock. The last four chapters that cover reviewing, reporting, and checking the audit trail are relevant for all business types, so skip the upcoming chapters as you need to.

Section 2 – Adapting QuickBooks Online to Suit Different Business Types

QuickBooks Online is designed to be used for small- to medium-sized businesses and there can be many different types of businesses that may want to use QuickBooks. It's important to understand that not every business will be set up in the same way, and not every user will have the same requirements.

There can be some limitations when using QuickBooks Online, and it can be necessary to use additional third-party applications that increase some of the functionality required. However, with a thorough understanding of how the software works, it is possible to mold QuickBooks Online to meet the needs of almost any business type.

This section comprises the following chapters:

- *Chapter 3, QuickBooks Online for Manufacturing Businesses*
- *Chapter 4, Recording Income for Retail Businesses*
- *Chapter 5, Handling Client Money*
- *Chapter 6, The Secret to Success with Projects in QuickBooks Online*
- *Chapter 7, Handling Foreign Currencies in QuickBooks Online*

Depending on the type of organization using QuickBooks, not every chapter is going to be relevant.

3
QuickBooks Online for Manufacturing Businesses

A large manufacturing company is likely to require a full **Enterprise Resource Planning (ERP)** system. Often the cost of this software can run into tens of thousands of dollars a year.

For a small company or a start-up, a full ERP system is not required, and possibly not affordable. QuickBooks Online can be adapted to meet the needs of most industry types.

When setting up QuickBooks Online, there will always be some similarities between different business types. However, the accounting requirements for some businesses can be specific.

Within this chapter, you will learn how to work through the entire end-to-end accounting process of a manufacturing company, starting from the initial customer order through to the point where goods have been manufactured ready for the sales invoice to be raised.

There are some specific accounting entries required within manufacturing, and it is important to understand why. There may be a considerable impact on the Profit and Loss reports if QuickBooks is not set up correctly.

In this chapter, we will cover the following topics:

- Chart of account categories used for manufacturing businesses
- Accounting entries required through the manufacturing process
- Products and services – Raw materials
- Bill of Materials (BOM)
- Workflow of a manufacturing company

If accounting within a manufacturing company is new to you, the whole process may feel a little daunting. However, with the correct settings in place, QuickBooks can produce all of the necessary accounting entries.

In the *Workflow of a manufacturing company* section, there is an end-to-end process containing seven steps. Once you have the correct settings in place, you may find it beneficial to work through the steps within your own QuickBooks file.

At the end of the *Workflow of a manufacturing company* section, there is also a simplified option that you could use if you felt the entire process was not required.

Chart of Accounts for manufacturing

Like most businesses, a manufacturing company will have sales, purchases, and general overheads. This business type will also have the following considerations:

- Raw materials
- Stock assemblies
- Work-in-progress
- Finished goods/closing stock

In addition to the common account categories used by all business types, such as insurance, bank charges, and accountancy fees, the following chart of account categories could be used within manufacturing.

Additional chart of account categories for Profit and Loss:

Account Name	Type	Detailed Type
Raw materials	Cost of sales	Supplies and materials – COS
Direct labor*	Cost of sales	Cost of labor – COS
Opening work-in-progress**	Cost of sales	Supplies and materials – COS
Closing work-in-progress **	Cost of sales	Supplies and materials – COS

> **Important Note**
>
> *Traditionally, employee costs fall within your expenses (overheads) – part of payroll costs. Where an employee is paid to manufacture an item that will be sold to customers, the employee time is a cost that is directly associated with sales. Therefore, these costs should fall within the *Cost of sales*.
>
> **Adjustments for *work-in-progress* will be required to account for materials taken from stock used for manufacture but that are still in the process of being used to build the finished item.

Additional chart of account categories for the Balance Sheet:

Account Name	Type	Detailed Type
Stock (Raw materials)	Current assets	Stock
Stock (Finished goods)	Current assets	Stock
Work-in-progress	Current assets	Stock

As well as having the relevant chart of account categories in place, a manufacturing company will need to handle inventory. Where quantities are being monitored, relevant product/service items will need to be created.

Products and services – Raw materials

Raw materials are essentially the different items required to build a finished product. A furniture company that builds desks could require wood, metal, nuts, bolts, and screws. These items will be required in order to manufacture the finished product.

A company may not manufacture fully from scratch, but simply purchase the component parts and assemblies only. The accounting entries are pretty much the same for either business model, or often it is a combination of the two.

Raw materials need to be created as stock items. As shown in the following screenshot, three chart of account categories are associated with a stock item. These are **Stock asset account**, **Income account**, and **Expense account**.

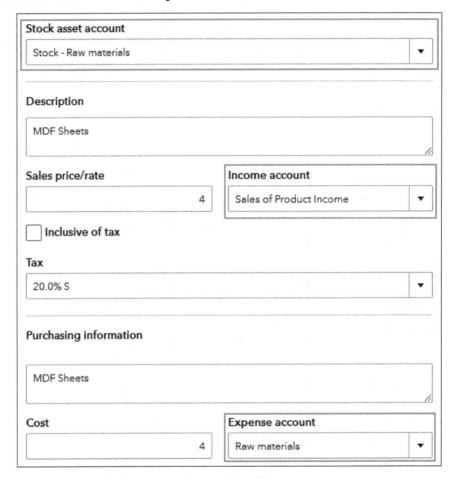

Figure 3.1 – Inventory/stock item accounts

The **Stock asset account** is affected when the goods are purchased. For example, the balance sheet entries could be debit stock and credit creditors.

If a customer invoice is created using an inventory item, all three accounts are affected. These are how the double entries would be created (ignoring sales tax):

Debit Entries	Credit Entries
Debtors/Accounts Receivable	**Income account**
Expense account	**Stock asset account**

> **Note**
>
> Raw materials are not usually sold to customers. Adjustments for raw materials are explained later in this chapter.

Within manufacturing, various items (raw materials) are required to produce the finished product. In the next section, we can learn how to use the tools in QuickBooks Online to group those required items.

Bill of Materials (BOM)

A **BOM** is simply a list of items required to build a finished product. QuickBooks Online itself does not contain all the tools required for BOMs and assemblies. There are some third-party apps that can help, but we will look at using the tools in QuickBooks Online alone to work through this.

When product/service categories are created, there is an option to use a bundle. A bundle can be used to help create a BOM. Multiple items can be associated with a bundle – all the materials required to build a desk, for example.

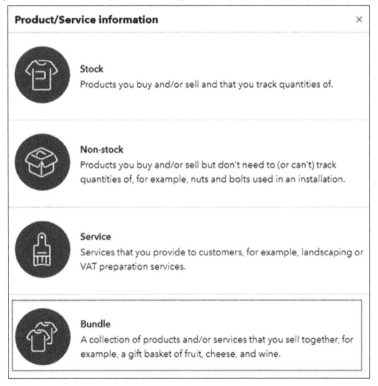

Figure 3.2 – Bundle option when creating a new product/service

When creating the Bundle, we select the quantities for each of the raw materials required to build the finished product.

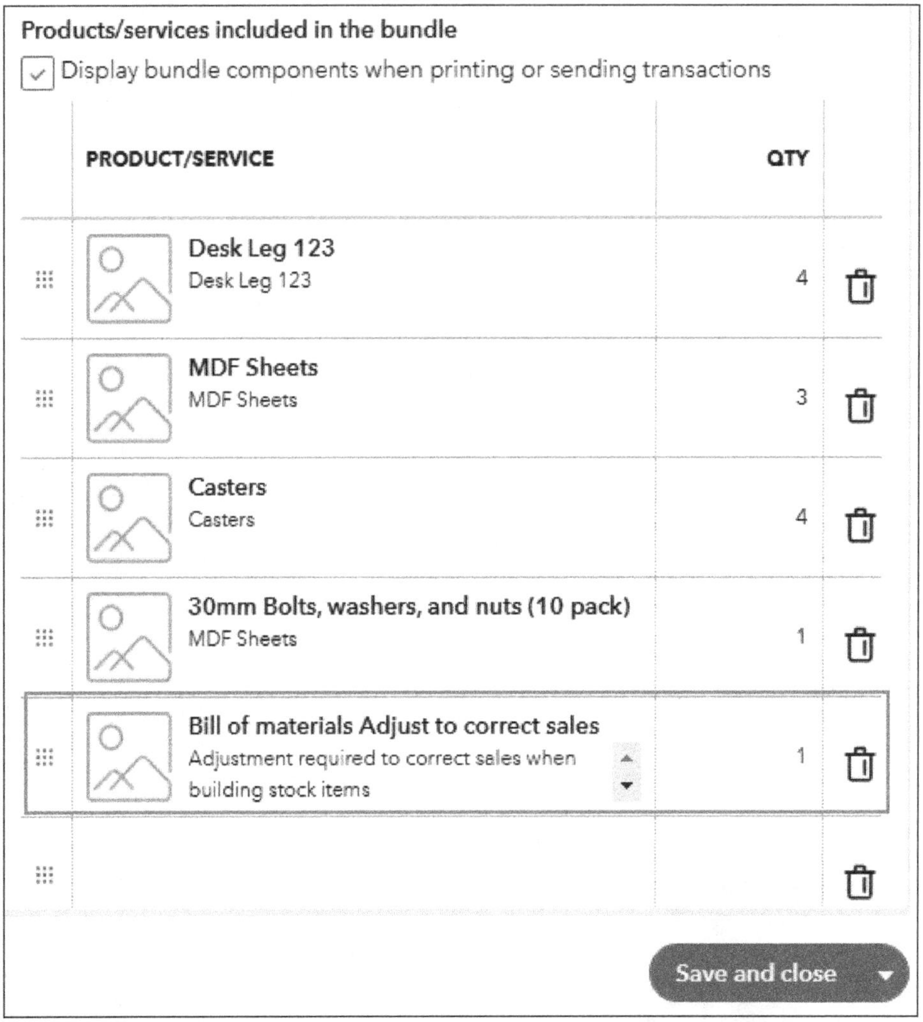

Figure 3.3 – Items listed within a bundle

In addition to the raw materials required to build the product, an additional product/ service item needs to be created to correct sales values that could be generated in error. This will be explained later in this chapter when we use this bundle as part of the workflow.

The last item on the list as highlighted in *Figure 3.3*, **Bill of materials Adjust to correct sales**, should be set up as shown in *Figure 3.4*. This is a non-inventory item where the **Income account** uses the category **Sales of Product Income**.

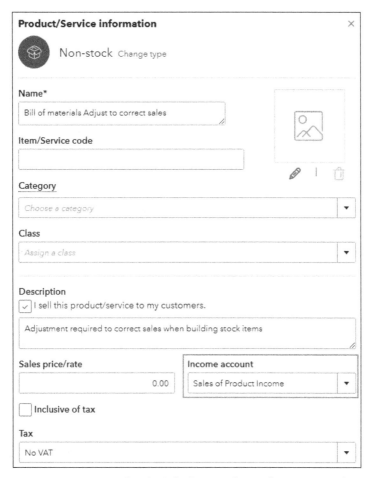

Figure 3.4 – Item used in the Bill of Materials Bundle to correct sales

Within a manufacturing company, different processes are often required. From the point at which materials are purchased to when goods are finally sold to a customer, let's look at how we can create those processes in QuickBooks Online.

Workflow of a manufacturing company

When it comes to producing goods for resale, there will usually be a process that is followed from start to finish. The order may vary slightly depending on whether products are produced at the request of a customer or whether there are materials or finished goods already in stock. Here is an example workflow:

1. A purchase order is raised for raw materials from the supplier/vendor.

2. Goods are delivered with a bill from the supplier.

3. A sales order is received from a customer.

4. A BOM is created to produce finished goods from raw materials.

5. Work-in-progress calculations are required.

6. Products are manufactured and stock is adjusted.

7. Goods are dispatched to a customer, and the customer invoice is generated.

> **Note**
>
> Work-in-progress reflects the value of products that are still being manufactured but are not part of the finished stock values on the balance sheet.

Let's work through the entire process above using the tools that are available in QuickBooks Online.

Purchase order for raw materials (Step 1 of 7)

Before we start, a *Plus*-level subscription will be required to use this feature.

Within the **Expenses** section of **Account and Settings** in QuickBooks Online, you will find the option to enable **Purchase orders**, as shown here:

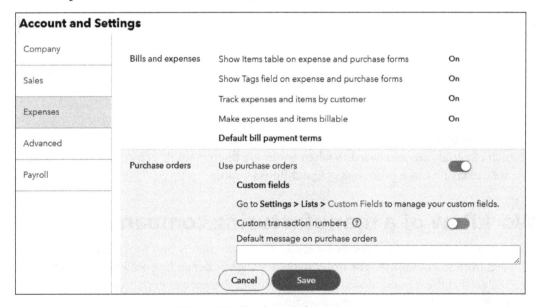

Figure 3.5 – Purchase Order settings

Once the feature has been enabled, there are multiple areas from which the purchase order can be raised. These are as follows:

- From the **New** button, choose the option below **Suppliers**.

- From the *action menus* available within the **Supplier** center.

- Using the **Reorder** option within the action menu in **Products and Services**.

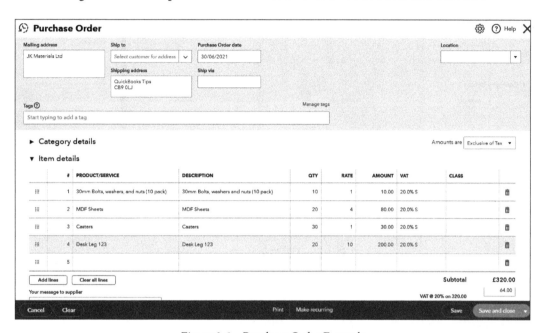

Figure 3.6 – Purchase Order Example

The purchase order looks very much like a supplier bill, but it is a *non-posting* entry. This simply means that the accounts are not affected in any way.

Stock quantities will not be adjusted to reflect the stock on order. However, if you run an **Inventory/Stocktake Worksheet** report (the report name may vary in different regions), the number of stock items on hand and the quantity on order will be displayed.

Goods delivered and supplier bill created (step 2 of 7)

When the goods have been delivered and the supplier bill received, the original purchase order can be used to automatically create the supplier bill in QuickBooks.

Using the option to create a supplier bill, the purchase order will appear on the right-hand side of the screen. Choose the **Add to Bill** option to add the purchase order to the bill.

Figure 3.7 – Creating a Bill from a Purchase Order

> **Note**
> After adding the purchase order to the supplier bill, it is possible to adjust the quantities. If the supplier had only part-delivered some items, the purchase order will remain open with the number of items not yet delivered.

Sales order from a customer (Step 3 of 7)

At present, there is no full sales order process within QuickBooks Online; however, we can use an estimate. First, we need to create a template entitled `Sales Order`.

From within the gear icon (top right of the main menu), the **Custom form styles** field can be found under the **Your Company** options.

From within **Custom form styles**, a **New Style** of **Estimate** needs to be created.

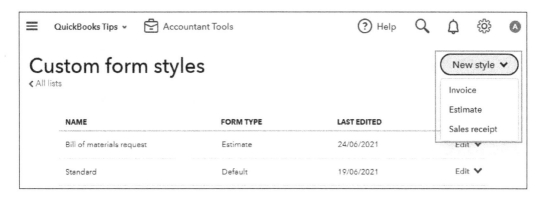

Figure 3.8 – Creating a new custom form style

The template will be edited to meet the requirements of the business, but to ensure that `Sales Order` appears on the document when printed or emailed, the **Form name** must be edited within the **Content** section.

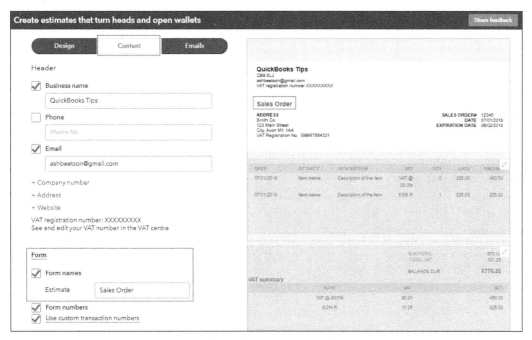

Figure 3.9 – Editing the Form Name of an estimate

Once completed, the template can be set as the default option for **Estimates**.

NAME	FORM TYPE	LAST EDITED	ACTION
Sales Order Template	Estimate	30/06/2021	Edit ∨
Bill of materials request	Estimate	24/06/2021	Preview PDF
			Rename
Standard	Default	19/06/2021	Delete
			Make default

Figure 3.10 – Setting an estimate as a default for sales orders

Now that there is a suitable template in place, a sales order can be raised on QuickBooks Online using the **Estimate** feature.

> **Tip**
> Consider using **Custom fields**. They can be created from the gear icon and are found under the **Lists | All lists** section. Custom fields can be used with purchase orders, estimates, and invoices. For example, a custom field could be created for the customer purchase order reference.

The current maximum number of custom fields that can be used for customers is three with the Plus subscription. QuickBooks Online Advanced allows you to create more custom fields. You can name the fields as you wish to meet the requirements of the business. You can choose whether they are for internal use only, or whether they are visible when printed or sent by email.

Custom fields

‹ All Lists   Give feedback   Add field

Include inactive ⬤

CUSTOM FIELD NAME	SALES RECEIPT	INVOICE	ESTIMATE	CREDIT NOTE	REFUND RECEIPT	PURCHASE ORDER	ACTIONS
Customer Purchase Order No.	✓	✓	✓	✓	✓	✓ ⊝	Edit ∨
Sales Rep	✓	✓	✓	✓	✓	✓	Edit ∨
Credit Checked by	✓	✓	✓	✓	✓		Edit ∨

Figure 3.11 – List of Custom fields

Before creating the sales order (using **Estimates**), the finished stock item should be created in QuickBooks. There will be no quantity on hand, but you will be able to work out the total cost of raw materials from all the items required in a bundle used for the BOM.

After considering labor costs, you will agree on a standard sales price. In this example, the following accounts are being used for the inventory item for the desk.

Account Type	Chart of Account Code
Stock asset account	**Stock – Finished goods**
Income account	**Sales of Product Income**
Expense account	**Raw materials**

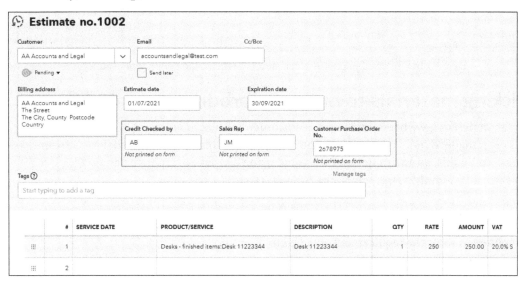

Figure 3.12 – Finished Stock Item in the list of Products and Services

Now that we have most of our settings and items in place, we can create the customer sales order using the **Estimate** feature.

Notice that as per the estimate in *Figure 3.13*, custom fields are being used for **Credit Checked by**, **Sales Rep**, and **Customer Purchase Order No.**:

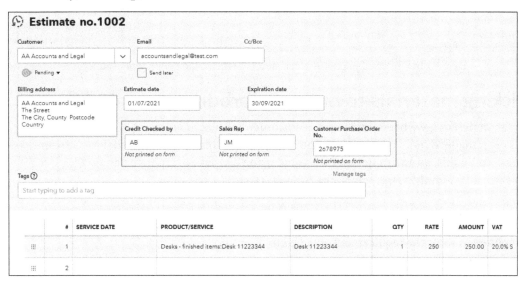

Figure 3.13 – Estimate used to create a Customer Sales Order

If there are no finished goods in stock, an internal purchase order can be raised to request that the product needs to be built. In this example, a supplier has been created with the name **Production Use Only**.

The purchase order is created for the finished item. The purchase order can also make use of custom fields so that they can be cross-referenced with customer purchase orders.

As mentioned previously, the cost that appears on this purchase order will reflect the total cost of raw materials required.

Figure 3.14 – Internal purchase order raised to request the building of products

Picking materials to build the product (step 4 of 7)

So far, materials have been purchased, a customer has placed an order, and a request has been made to build the product. The next step is to remove the raw materials from stock. To do this, an **Estimate** can be created using a separate template named Bill of Materials – in the same way as the Sales Order.

In the example shown in *Figure 3.15*, a customer named Bill of Materials (for internal use only) is being used. As you can see, the estimate can be adapted and simplified to meet the requirements needed to fit the purpose.

It is important to note that the item on this estimate is the bundle that reflects the BOM as discussed earlier in this chapter.

QuickBooks Tips
CB9 0LJ
ashbeetson@gmail.com

Bill of Materials (pick from stock)

ADDRESS
Bill of Materials (for internal use only)

BILL OF MATERIALS 1003
(PICK FROM STOCK)
NO.
DATE 01/07/2021

CUSTOMER PURCHASE ORDER NO.
2678975

DESCRIPTION	QTY	RATE
Bill of materials list to build desk 11223344	1	57.00
Desk Leg 123	4	10.00
MDF Sheets	3	4.00
Casters	4	1.00
MDF Sheets	1	1.00
Adjustment required to correct sales when building stock items	1	0.00
TOTAL		**£57.00**

Figure 3.15 – Using an Estimate to produce a picking list of items

Estimates, like Purchase Orders, are non-posting entries that will not affect our accounts at all. Just creating this entry will not reduce the stock levels of raw materials.

Once the items have been picked and removed from stock and moved to the factory floor, the Estimate should be converted to an invoice.

There are two important things to note here as the estimate and invoice are purely being used for internal purposes only:

1. The invoice total will need to be adjusted to zero using the final line entry.
2. VAT/Sales tax must be ignored – using the **No VAT** code, for example.

The following screenshot shows how part of the invoice screen should appear when converting the estimate to an invoice. A value of negative £57 was entered against the final line to balance the invoice to £0.00.

PRODUCT/SERVICE ⑦	DESCRIPTION	DUE	QTY	RATE
Bill of materials - Desk	Bill of materials list to build desk 11223344 Your customer will see all items in this bundle	0.00 of 57.00	0	57
Desk Leg 123	Desk Leg 123	40.00 of 40.00	4	10
MDF Sheets	MDF Sheets	12.00 of 12.00	3	4
Casters	Casters	4.00 of 4.00	4	1
30mm Bolts, washers, and r	MDF Sheets	1.00 of 1.00	1	1
Bill of materials Adjust to cc	Adjustment required to correct sales when building stock items	-57.00 of 0.00	0	0

Figure 3.16 – Items on invoice converted from the estimate

At the bottom of most transaction entry screens is a **More** option. To check that our accounting entries are correct, we can view the **Transaction journal**.

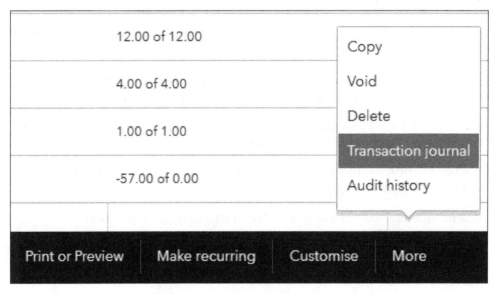

Figure 3.17 – Location of Transaction journal within More

Using the example that has been worked through, we can see in *Figure 3.18* that the debtor balance has not been affected and that the overall total posted to sales will be nil.

ACCOUNT	DEBIT	CREDIT
Debtors	£0.00	
Stock - Raw materials		£40.00
Sales of Product Income		£40.00
Cost of sales	£40.00	
Stock - Raw materials		£12.00
Sales of Product Income		£12.00
Raw materials	£12.00	
Stock - Raw materials		£4.00
Raw materials	£4.00	
Sales of Product Income		£4.00
Sales of Product Income		£1.00
Raw materials	£1.00	
Stock - Raw materials		£1.00
Sales of Product Income	£57.00	
	£114.00	£114.00
	£114.00	£114.00

Figure 3.18 – Entries made when raw materials are taken from stock

Accounting for work-in-progress (step 5 of 7)

Taking into account the entries made so far, and perhaps some labor, QuickBooks would report a loss. No goods have been dispatched or sales invoices raised. As you can see in *Figure 3.19*, the **Profit and Loss** window displays the value of **Raw materials** taken from stock as well as the wages paid.

QuickBooks Tips	
Profit and Loss	
July 2021	
	TOTAL
▾ Income	
Sales of Product Income	0.00
Total Income	£0.00
▾ Cost of Sales	
Direct labor	100.00
Raw materials	57.00
Total Cost of Sales	£157.00
GROSS PROFIT	£ -157.00
Expenses	
Total Expenses	
NET OPERATING INCOME	£ -157.00
NET INCOME	£ -157.00

Figure 3.19 – Profit and Loss with no sales recorded

This doesn't reflect the true cost for the period, so we can make an adjustment for work-in-progress. A business is likely to adopt its own method for calculating work-in-progress.

One method could be to run a report of open purchase orders raised against the supplier `**Production Use Only**` and use a percentage of labor costs for the period.

QuickBooks Tips					
Open Purchase Order List by Supplier					
All Dates					
DATE	NO.	MEMO/DESCRIPTION	SHIP VIA	AMOUNT	OPEN BALANCE
▾ **Proudction Use Only**					
01/07/2021	1002			57.00	57.00
Total for **Proudction Use Only**				£57.00	£57.00
TOTAL				£57.00	£57.00

Figure 3.20 – Open Purchase Order List by Supplier

In this example, we will calculate the work-in-progress to be the value of materials currently in use, and 50% of the direct labor spend for the period. This will reduce the loss by £107. To do this, a journal entry will be required, as shown in *Figure 3.21*:

Journal date				Journal no.	
31/07/2021				adjust	

	#	ACCOUNT	DEBITS	CREDITS	DESCRIPTION
⋮⋮	1	Work-in-progress	107.00		Valuation of work-in-progress
⋮⋮	2	Closing work-in-progress		107.00	Valuation of work-in-progress

Figure 3.21 – Journal to adjust work-in-progress

Line 1 of the journal created will debit our balance sheet for **Work-in-progress**. Line 2 will credit the cost of sales within our **Profit and Loss** sheet. This entry will need to be reversed in the following month.

After a journal has been saved, a **Reverse** option will be available at the bottom of the screen:

Figure 3.22 – The Reverse Function

Reversing will duplicate the journal, and will be dated the first day of the following month by default. Debit and credit entries are swapped around, but before saving, the debit entry needs to be adjusted to **Opening work-in-progress**.

Journal date				Journal no.	
01/08/2021				adjustR	

	#	ACCOUNT	DEBITS	CREDITS	DESCRIPTION
⋮⋮	1	Work-in-progress		107.00	Valuation of work-in-progress
⋮⋮	2	Opening work-in-progress	107.00		Valuation of work-in-progress

Figure 3.23 – Journal entry reversed the following month

After creating the journals, **Profit and Loss** will now reflect the cost over two months.
Notice how the use of account numbers can assist to sort the **Profit and Loss** report into
the desired order.

Profit and Loss July - August, 2021			
	JUL 2021	**AUG 2021**	**TOTAL**
▾ Income			
1001 Sales of Product Income	0.00		£0.00
Total Income	£0.00	£0.00	£0.00
▾ Cost of Sales			
900 Opening work-in-progress		107.00	£107.00
901 Raw materials	57.00		£57.00
902 Direct labor	100.00		£100.00
903 Closing work-in-progress	(107.00)		£(107.00)
Total Cost of Sales	£50.00	£107.00	£157.00
GROSS PROFIT	£(50.00)	£(107.00)	£(157.00)
Expenses			
Total Expenses			£0.00
NET OPERATING INCOME	£(50.00)	£(107.00)	£(157.00)
NET INCOME	£(50.00)	£(107.00)	£(157.00)

Figure 3.24 – Profit and Loss after adjustments made for work-in-progress

Updating stock with finished goods (Step 6 of 7)

Earlier in this chapter, when the sales order was created (using an estimate), an internal
purchase order was raised to request the build of a stock item. To update stock with the
finished goods, the purchase order will be converted to a bill.

In the same way that the BOM estimate was converted to an internal invoice, the purchase
order will be converted to a bill that totals zero. This is purely an internal entry to update
stock.

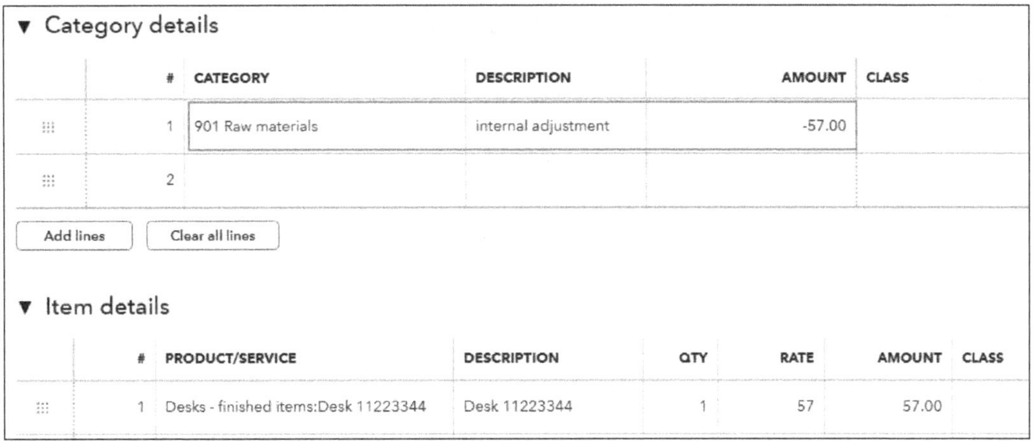

▼ Category details

	#	CATEGORY	DESCRIPTION	AMOUNT	CLASS
⋮⋮	1	901 Raw materials	internal adjustment	-57.00	
⋮⋮	2				

[Add lines]   [Clear all lines]

▼ Item details

	#	PRODUCT/SERVICE	DESCRIPTION	QTY	RATE	AMOUNT	CLASS
⋮⋮	1	Desks - finished items:Desk 11223344	Desk 11223344	1	57	57.00	

Figure 3.25 – Supplier Bill Adjusted from Internal Purchase Order

After converting the internal purchase order into a bill, the **Item details** area will be populated with the quantity and cost value of the stock item created. Within the category section of the bill, a negative value will be entered against raw materials.

Figure 3.26 shows the double entries created from this internal bill:

ACCOUNT	DEBIT	CREDIT
Creditors	£0.00	
Stock - Finished goods	£57.00	
901 Raw materials		£57.00
	£57.00	£57.00

Figure 3.26 – Double entries made after creating an internal zero value bill

Goods delivered and an invoice raised for the customer (Step 7 of 7)

Now that the finished goods have been booked into stock, we can now look back at the original sales order. The original customer order was created using an estimate and this can now be converted to an invoice for the customer.

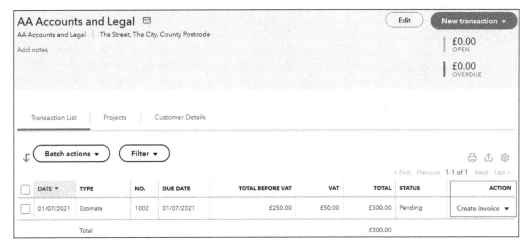

Figure 3.27 – Creating an invoice from the pending Estimate

The invoice raised will reflect the rate set against the finished goods item for sales, in this example, £250 excluding VAT.

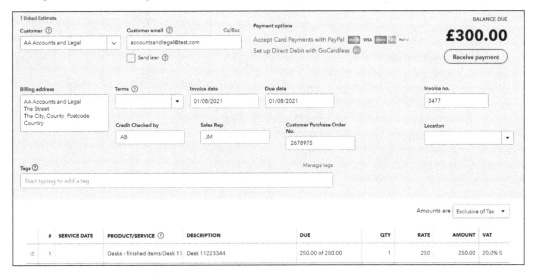

Figure 3.28 – Sales invoice converted from an Estimate

As we have done previously, check the **Transaction journal** available from within the **More** options at the bottom of a saved invoice.

This will show all the double entries created from this transaction.

ACCOUNT	DEBIT	CREDIT
Debtors	£300.00	
901 Raw materials	£57.00	
Stock - Finished goods		£57.00
1001 Sales of Product Income		£250.00
VAT Control		£50.00
	£357.00	£357.00
	£357.00	£357.00

Figure 3.29 – Double entries arising from the creation of a customer invoice

Now that the process has been covered from end to end, after running the **Profit and Loss** report again for the two months, a different picture is painted.

Profit and Loss July - August, 2021			
	JUL 2021	AUG 2021	TOTAL
▼ Income			
1001 Sales of Product Income	0.00	250.00	£250.00
Total Income	£0.00	£250.00	£250.00
▼ Cost of Sales			
900 Opening work-in-progress		107.00	£107.00
901 Raw materials	57.00	0.00	£57.00
902 Direct labor	100.00	100.00	£200.00
903 Closing work-in-progress	(107.00)	(100.00)	£ (207.00)
Total Cost of Sales	£50.00	£107.00	£157.00
GROSS PROFIT	£ (50.00)	£143.00	£93.00
Expenses			
Total Expenses			£0.00
NET OPERATING INCOME	£ (50.00)	£143.00	£93.00
NET INCOME	£ (50.00)	£143.00	£93.00

Figure 3.30 – Profit and Loss report reflecting the full end-to-end process

We can see that by making work-in-progress adjustments to account for the cost of labor or materials for unfinished products, a more realistic profit or lost report is produced.

The value of work-in-progress at the end of July for £107 was adjusted to the balance sheet. At the beginning of August, this was adjusted back as a cost within the profit and loss to match the sales recorded within the same month.

So far, we have worked through an end-to-end process that follows the accounting entries required for materials purchased and stock sold. But there are other things that need to be considered.

Simplified Option

Some businesses may not require the full end-to-end process as detailed within the section *Workflow of a manufacturing company*. If that is the case some of the steps could be removed.

Raw materials could be consumed as and when they are required, but without recording all movements. A single stock adjustment could be made when finished goods have been created.

Bear in mind that this option would mean that inventory records in QuickBooks would not always reflect quantities of raw materials on the shelves. It would also be difficult to calculate the value of work-in-progress.

In the example shown in *Figure 3.31*, a stock adjustment can be used to reduce the quantity of raw materials and increase the quantity of finished goods:

Stock Quantity Adjustment no.7

Adjustment date

23/07/2021

Stock adjustment account

Raw Materials

	#	PRODUCT	DESCRIPTION	QTY ON HAND	NEW QTY	CHANGE IN QTY
⠿	1	MDF Sheets	MDF Sheets	20	16	-4
⠿	2	Nuts, Bolts and Washer (10 pk)	Nuts, Bolts and Washer (10 pk)	100	99	-1
⠿	3	Aluminum Legs - 4 pack	Aluminum Legs - 4 pack	20	19	-1
⠿	4	Desk - Finished Goods	Desk - Finished Goods	0	1	1

Figure 3.31 – Single Stock Adjustment for Finished Goods

The example shown in *Figure 3.31* shows individual items being adjusted, but multiple items could be adjusted using a single **Bundle**.

The net effect of this entry within the Profit and Loss report would be nil. This would simply move the value of the stock on the balance sheet from raw materials to finished goods. Profits would be fully calculated when the finished goods were sold.

	22 JUL, 2021	23 JUL, 2021
Stock - Finished Goods	0.00	100.00
Stock - Raw Materials	2,215.00	2,115.00

Figure 3.32 – Balance Sheet movements following stock adjustment

Now that you have learned how a simplified option works, in the next section, let's look at some other considerations a company should make when working with stock.

Other Considerations

As well as the process of purchasing materials, manufacturing products, and selling them, other elements that a manufacturing company may need to consider can include the following:

- Theft of stock
- Donating stock (charities or promotions)
- Damaged stock
- Scrapping obsolete stock
- Revaluation of stock

The revaluation of stock items and updating price lists are covered in the next chapter of this book, which looks at retail-based businesses in more detail. The first four listed previously can all be dealt with in the same way as they all involve adjusting stock quantities.

Stocktakes and adjusting stock quantities

Periodically, a business that sells stock will do a stocktake. This simply means counting all the stock items held. The frequency with which this is done is likely to depend on the size of the business, the number of items held, and the manpower required to carry out the task.

To assist with this process, the **Stocktake/Inventory Worksheet** report can be run from the **Reports** Center. The report contains current quantities on hand and quantities on order. The idea is to print the report and write down the counted amounts within the **Physical Count** column and then make adjustments in QuickBooks when necessary.

Whether it is established that items have been given away as part of a promotion or goods have been found as damaged, the way the stock is adjusted will be the same, the only difference being the chart of account category used to make the adjustment.

From within the **Products and Services** list, when one or more items have been selected, the **Batch actions** option becomes visible.

Figure 3.33 – Batch actions in Products and Services

Within **Batch actions,** you will find the **Adjust quantity option**. The products selected will appear on the screen, where values in either the **NEW QTY** or **CHANGE IN QTY** columns can be adjusted.

The screen as shown in *Figure 3.34* will also allow you to decide which account is to be used to record the stock adjustment:

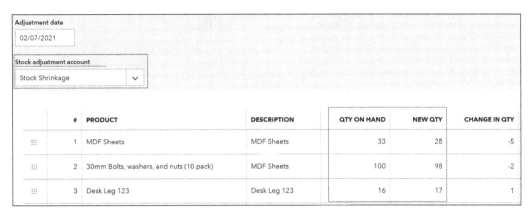

Figure 3.34 – Adjusting stock

In the example in *Figure 3.34*, the **Stock Shrinkage** account is being used, but this could be changed to **Advertising & Marketing** if stock has been given away at a trade event, for example.

Stock is recorded in QuickBooks Online on a **FIFO (First In, First Out)** basis. Adjustments will be made in QuickBooks to reflect historical transactions. One side of the entry will affect the stock value in the balance sheet. The other will affect the stock adjustment account chosen.

Summary

As we have seen throughout this chapter, QuickBooks Online can be adapted to meet the needs of a manufacturing business. For small businesses and start-ups working within a tight budget, this is good news.

Understanding all the options that can be used is important if you are a business owner or a bookkeeper/accounting professional setting up QuickBooks.

By way of a brief recap, we have covered the following topics:

- Raised purchase orders and received bills for raw materials
- Created a customer sales order by adapting an estimate
- Used a purchase order to request an item be manufactured
- Used an estimate to create a BOM request to pick stock
- Created an internal invoice to remove raw materials from stock
- Checked reports and created a journal to account for work-in-progress

- Converted the internal purchase order to a bill for the finished stock item
- Created an invoice for the finished goods from the original sales order
- Made an adjustment for inventory/stock after completing a stocktake

The next chapter will look at how a retail business can make use of QuickBooks Online, which will include an element of how an inventory is updated.

4
Recording Income for Retail Businesses

The main thing that differentiates retail from other business models is when payment is received. This is usually at the point of sale – when goods or services have been provided. 30-day payment terms, for example, are not used.

In this chapter, you will learn how to optimize the settings and features within QuickBooks Online to help save time on a lot of unnecessary data entry.

When setting up QuickBooks Online for a retail business, there are a few things to consider that can specifically relate to a retail-based business model:

- Inventory (stock) requirements
- The sales environment (shop/online/market)
- How sales are recorded
- Accepted payment methods
- The systems that may currently be in place

Understanding the different methods of recording income is important. Choices that are made will impact the amount of time required, not only to set up QuickBooks but also the time it will take to create bookkeeping entries. How sales data will ultimately be reported is also a factor to be considered when choosing how income is recorded.

There is an increasing number of third-party apps becoming available to help in this area. By visiting the QuickBooks apps store (`www.apps.com`) and searching for `Retail` or `E-Commerce`, you will find a few that you may want to consider choosing from.

OneSaas was recently purchased by Intuit, so it will be of no surprise to find an increasing number of features appearing within the Banking area of QuickBooks at some point.

We will not be using any apps in this chapter – only the tools in QuickBooks alone. Apps are great and can help us save a heap of time. However, it's a good idea to understand the bookkeeping entries required first. This means that when the volume of transactions increases, you know the areas of bookkeeping where time savings are required.

Let's start by taking a look at the first item on our list, which is inventory.

Using Inventory

Using inventory can sometimes require careful consideration. The main purpose of using inventory is for increased reporting capabilities and checking if items for resale are in stock.

A small sole trader retailer with a hotdog stand might purchase hotdogs, sauces, and drinks. There could be little benefit to coding these purchases in the **Products & Services** inventory. Instead, they can simply code purchases directly to a **Cost of Sales** chart of account category.

Using the small sole trader with a hotdog stand as an example, there is likely to be a quick turnaround from the time items are purchased and when they are sold. A larger franchise with an outlet in a shopping mall is likely to require the use of an inventory as larger quantities of stock are purchased.

Consider the purchase of one-off items for resale. Creating lots of inventory items within the **Products & Services** inventory that are only purchased and sold once could result in an exceedingly long list.

The main benefit of creating an inventory item is the reporting functionality you can gain. This will only work if the sale is recorded appropriately. If a Product/Service item was created for hotdogs, sales of the same item must be recorded using the same item details. Failure to do so will result in overstated stock values on the Balance Sheet, and overstated profits on the Profit and Loss report.

The difference between coding a purchase to a Product/Service item compared to a Chart of Account category is shown in the following screenshot. Quantities and rates are used with items:

▼ Category details

	#	CATEGORY	DESCRIPTION	AMOUNT (GBP)
⠿	1	Cost of sales	Purchase of 500 Hot Dogs	100.00
⠿	2			

[Add lines] [Clear all lines]

▼ Item details

	#	PRODUCT/SERVICE	DESCRIPTION	QTY	RATE	AMOUNT (GBP)
⠿	1	Hot Dogs	Hot Dogs	500	0.20	100.00
⠿	2					

Figure 4.1 – Category and product/service on a supplier bill

For simple straightforward accounting, you only need to use the **Category details** area. If you're monitoring stock fully, the purchase needs to be coded within the **Item details** area. If the inventory feature is in use, items may require price updates and revaluations. The *Considerations for inventory* section explains how inventory can be revalued and how sales prices can be updated in bulk.

Now that we've considered if tracking inventory is required, we need to think about how the sales are going to be recorded and how payments will be accepted.

The Sales Environment and the different methods of Payment accepted

These two considerations have been placed together because the environment in which a business sells is often going to determine the various payment options in use.

A simple example is that an online retailer is not likely to be receiving any payments in cash. Likewise, a business running a hotdog stand will not receive many payments through PayPal. However, with more mobile payment options such as **Apple Pay** and the increasing use of QR codes, it makes this much more of a possibility than it was a couple of years ago.

After establishing how a business is going to be paid for the sales they have made, we need to decide how the income should be recorded in QuickBooks. In retail, payment is received at the point of sale, so we do not need to raise an invoice.

Ignoring journal entries for the time being, there are two other options we should use to record income when invoices are not raised. These are *sales receipts* and *bank deposits*, but which option should we use?

Sales receipts versus Bank deposits

When it comes to using either a sales receipt or a bank deposit, it boils down to the reporting requirements of a business. Both options will update our Profit and Loss reports and sales taxes, and both can affect the Sales by Customer reports in QuickBooks.

The only difference is that the sales receipt makes use of Product and Service items. If you need to track stock quantities or easily produce gross margin reports and report against the different types of goods or services sold, then you should use the **Sales receipt** option.

It is also worth noting that the use of products and services with sales receipts means that you can use a minimal number of charts of account categories. This is because multiple products can all be directed to use the same profit and loss account for sales – `Sales of Product Income`, for example.

Let's look at some examples of sales receipts and bank deposits so that you fully understand the difference between these two options.

Bank Deposits

We can record income that's been received in a chart of account category of our choice when using the bank feeds within QuickBooks Online:

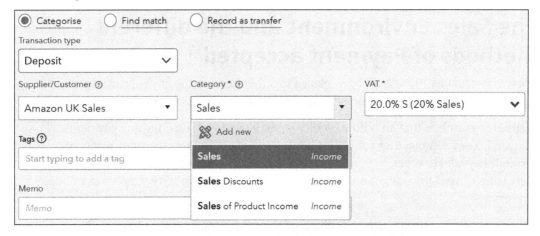

Figure 4.2 – Recording sales as a bank deposit from bank feeds

As per the image in *Figure 4.2*, the customer's name can be selected, as well as the chart of account category and VAT rate. The value of VAT (sales tax) cannot be specified or seen on this screen. This value is always recorded inclusive of tax. If the total received was £1,800, it will automatically be recorded as £1,500 + £300 VAT.

As well as entering bank deposits using bank feeds, they can be entered using the **New** button in QuickBooks Online, where the **Bank deposit** feature can be found below the list of **Other** options.

The exact same entry, when entered manually or viewed after being entered from bank feeds, is shown within *Figure 4.3*

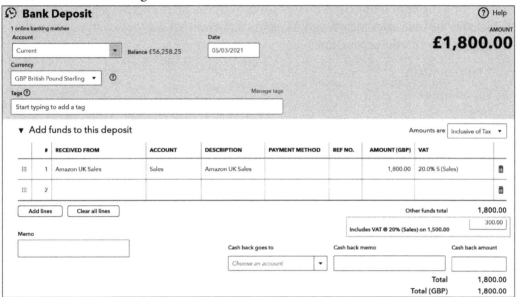

Figure 4.3 – Bank Deposit entry screen

The VAT value is visible within the **Bank Deposit** entry screen and can be edited if necessary.

Sticking with using a bank deposit, the amount that's received in the bank might not be a true reflection of the total sales. The amount could be the result of total sales minus commission or bank charges.

Using the same example, let's see how we can account for a sales total of £1,900 including VAT, minus commission charges of £100 exempt from VAT.

Splitting bank deposits

If we need to account for sales and commission charges within the same bookkeeping entry, we will need to split the transaction into multiple lines.

When we categorize from the bank feed, there is an option to **Split** the transaction:

Figure 4.4 – Split option for recording entries from bank feeds

After selecting the **Split** option, it is now possible to record all the details that are required. This includes the total sales including VAT on the first line and the total charges deducted as a negative value on the second line:

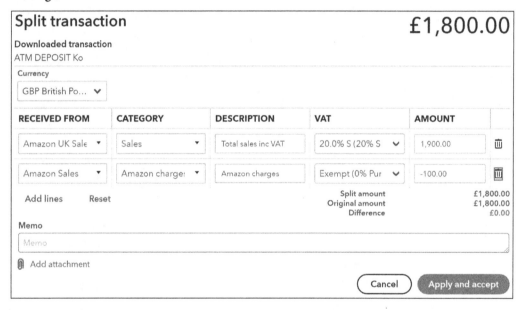

Figure 4.5 – Using the Split option

> **Tip**
> If income is being recorded after you've downloaded and viewed various reports – for example, sales reports from Amazon – those reports can be attached to this transaction.

If we view the same transaction again from the manual **Bank Deposit** entry screen, we will see the lines in use and the ability to adjust the VAT values if required:

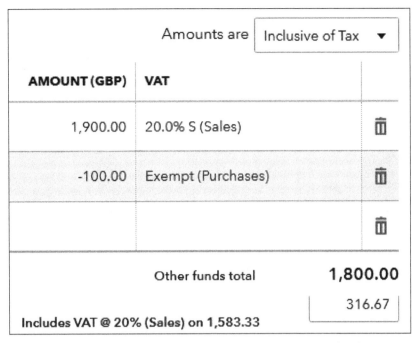

Figure 4.6 – Bottom-right section of the Bank Deposit screen with split entries

Using Sales Receipts

At the time of writing, although a sales receipt can be entered directly from the bank feed, it is not possible to select the product or service. A general default product/service code will be used instead:

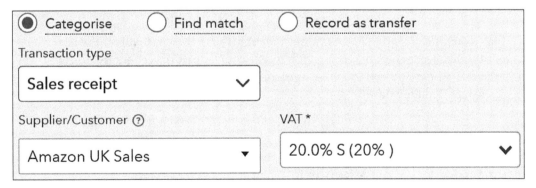

Figure 4.7 – Recording a sales receipt using bank feeds

As we can see, it is safe to say that if sales receipts are to be used, they will not be created from a bank feed due to the limitations on how they are recorded. Using the same total value received from the previous example, let's see how the sales receipt could be entered:

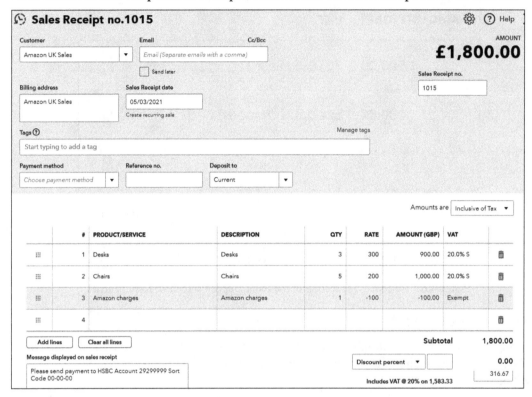

Figure 4.8 –Sales Receipt no.1015 – recording data

The **Sales Receipt** data entry screen is almost identical to that of an **Invoice**. The key difference is that a sales receipt requires you to select a **Deposit to** account to indicate where the cash or card payments are being recorded. Invoices are paid to terms, so they require an expected **Due date**.

Using the example in *Figure 4.8*, it is being recorded that 3 desks and 5 chairs have been sold, with sales totaling £1,900 including VAT. As per our example in *Figure 4.6*, there are Amazon charges of £100. Sales receipts require all the values to be recorded against a **Product/Service** item, so a **Service item** for Amazon charges is required.

Amazon charges should be set up as a **Cost of sales** in the chart of accounts. This is because the charge is directly associated with the sale:

NAME	TYPE ▲	DETAIL TYPE
Amazon charges	Cost of sales	Cost of Sales

Figure 4.9 – Chart of account settings for Amazon charges

When we create a **Service item** for Amazon charges, **Income account** used is the Cost of sales account that was created, as per *Figure 4.9*:

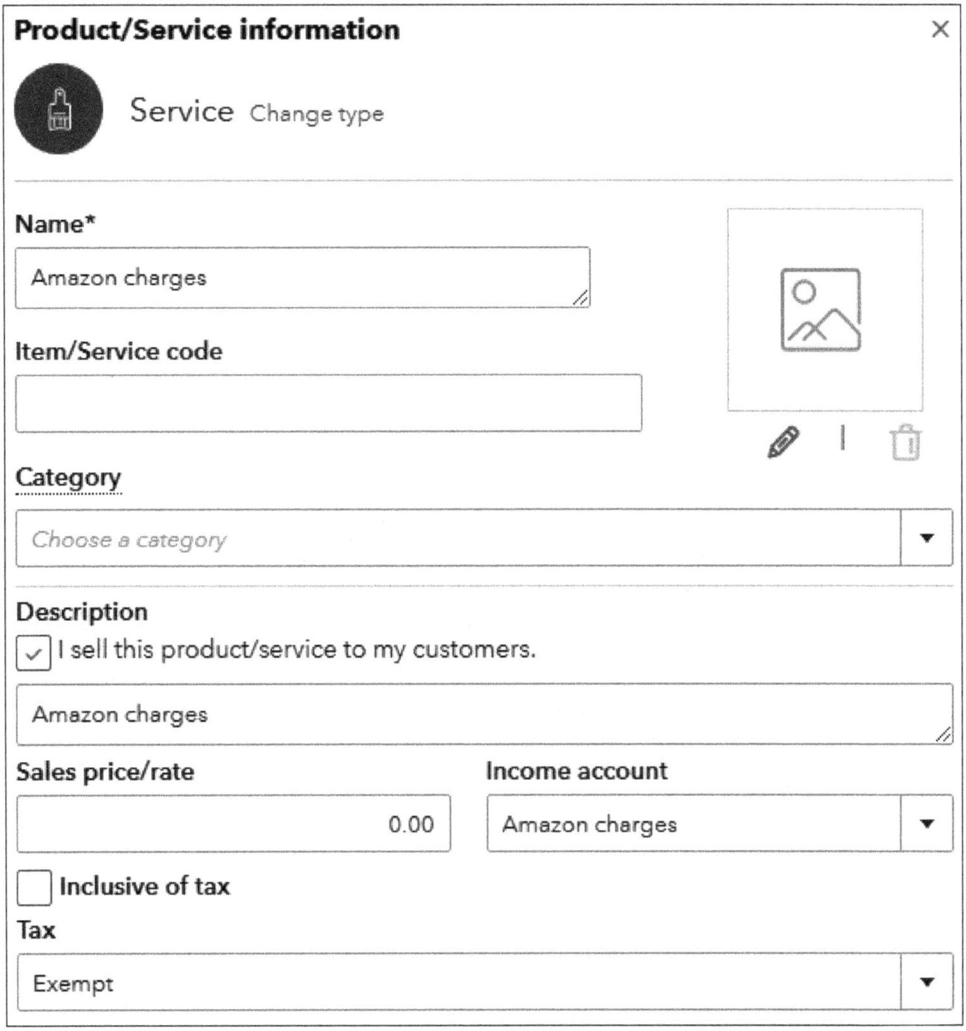

Product/Service information   ✕

Service Change type

Name*

Amazon charges

Item/Service code

Category

Choose a category   ▼

Description

☑ I sell this product/service to my customers.

Amazon charges

Sales price/rate   **Income account**

0.00   Amazon charges   ▼

☐ **Inclusive of tax**

Tax

Exempt   ▼

Figure 4.10 – Service item settings for Amazon charges

With **Sales receipt** open from *Figure 4.8* and using the **More** option at the bottom of the data entry screen, the **Transaction journal** option can be selected. This enables us to see all the entries that have been made as a result of recording the sales receipt:

ACCOUNT	DEBIT	CREDIT
Current	£1,800.00	
Cost of sales	£450.00	
Stock Asset		£450.00
Sales of Product Income		£750.00
Stock Asset		£375.00
Sales of Product Income		£833.33
Cost of sales	£375.00	
Amazon charges	£100.00	
VAT Control		£316.67
VAT Control	£0.00	
	£2,725.00	£2,725.00
	£2,725.00	£2,725.00

Figure 4.11 – Accounting entries made from a sales receipt

Here, we can see that with multiple products/services in use, all sales can be directed to credit the same chart of account category – Sales of Product Income. The Amazon commission charges will be debited to Amazon charges in the Profit and Loss report, and the total amount of payments will be logged to the Current bank account.

After looking at a couple of different ways in which sales can be recorded, what happens if different payment methods and sources are in use? If that is the case, using **Undeposited funds** and a selection of control accounts can make things a lot easier for us.

Undeposited funds

Within QuickBooks Online, it is possible to utilize an account with **Undeposited funds** as its type. It is a special account – so special you are only allowed to have one.

You can record payments received to **Undeposited funds** instead of using a bank – so it is essentially a temporary holding area. When the time comes, a **Bank deposit** is required to move funds out of the **Undeposited funds** account:

NAME	TYPE	DETAIL TYPE
Receipts not yet banked	Current assets	Undeposited Funds

Figure 4.12 – Undeposited funds

The default name of this type of account is `Undeposited funds` but you can change the name, as shown here – it is `Receipts not yet banked` in this example.

Before looking at how the **Undeposited funds** account is used, let's imagine that a business generates sales from a website. Due to the way that the website has been built, payments are routed through different payment mechanisms, such as the following:

- PayPal
- American Express
- Stripe
- Direct bank transfers

Direct bank transfers will arrive in our business bank account. For payments arriving via PayPal, American Express, or Stripe, additional control accounts can be set up as banks in QuickBooks Online:

NUMBER	NAME	TYPE ▲	DETAIL TYPE
1200	1200 Business Bank Account	Cash at bank and in hand	Current
1201	1201 American Express	Cash at bank and in hand	Cash on hand
1202	1202 PayPal	Cash at bank and in hand	Cash on hand
1203	1203 Stripe	Cash at bank and in hand	Cash on hand

Figure 4.13 – Bank accounts created for different payment options

To combine the use of **Undeposited funds** with the bank accounts that were created in the preceding screenshot, a **Sales receipt** will be used to record sales.

This will mean that a **Product/Service** item will be required for each of the bank accounts. Taking PayPal as an example, a service item should be created where **Income account** is directed to PayPal bank account:

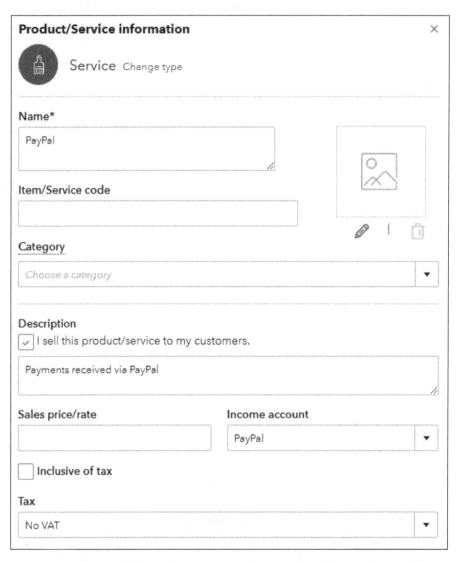

Figure 4.14 – Service item for payments received via PayPal

Tax is set to **No VAT**. This is important because this item is only being used to create an internal accounting adjustment. It will not affect sales or VAT.

Although not always necessary, we can create an additional chart of account category and service items to monitor the payments that are expected in the bank account:

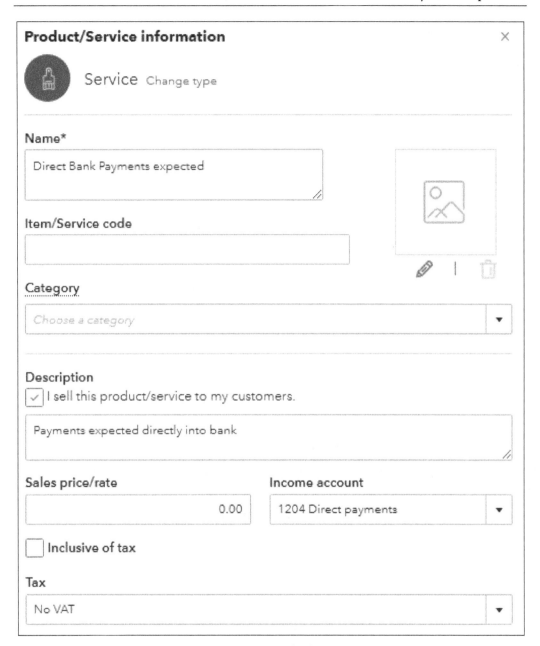

Figure 4.15 – Service item for direct payments

The benefit of creating this additional item for direct payments means that if the total of the direct payments is made up of multiple values, it will be easier to manage.

In the example **Sales receipt** shown here, we have sales that total £12,000, including VAT. Payments of sales have been made through PayPal, Stripe, and American Express, and a total amount of £9,800 is expected to be received directly into the bank account:

				Amounts are	Inclusive of Tax ▼
DESCRIPTION	**QTY**	**RATE**	**AMOUNT (GBP)**	**VAT**	
Web Sales	1	12,000	12,000.00	20.0% S	🗑
PayPal	1	-1,000	-1,000.00	No VAT	🗑
Stripe	1	-700	-700.00	No VAT	🗑
American Express	1	-500	-500.00	No VAT	🗑
Direct Bank Payments expected	1	-9,800	-9,800.00	No VAT	🗑
					🗑

Subtotal	0.00
	2,000.00
Includes VAT @ 20% on 10,000.00	
Total	0.00
Amount received	0.00
Balance due	0.00

Figure 4.16 – Sales receipt with multiple payment sources

In this example, we are not fully utilizing **Undeposited funds** as **Sales receipt** has been balanced back to £0.00, so there will be nothing left to deposit.

As we did previously, after checking **Transaction journal** within the **More** option, all the accounting double entries can be seen:

ACCOUNT	DEBIT	CREDIT
Receipts not yet banked	£0.00	
Sales		£10,000.00
1202 PayPal	£1,000.00	
1203 Stripe	£700.00	
1201 American Express	£500.00	
1204 Direct payments	£9,800.00	
VAT Control		£2,000.00
	£12,000.00	**£12,000.00**
	£12,000.00	**£12,000.00**

Figure 4.17 – Accounting entries from the sales receipt shown in Figure 4.15

The sales receipt has credited sales for profit and loss, and the VAT liability has been adjusted correctly. Debit entries have been made that reflect where the different payments will come in from.

Taking the entry for £9,800, after checking the bank account, only £8,760 has been received so far. After reviewing the **Business Account** bank feed, this can be entered as a transfer from the **1204 Direct payments** account:

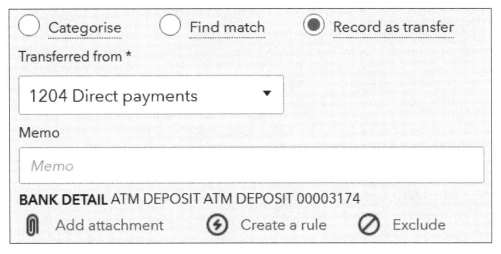

Figure 4.18 – Recording a transfer within the bank feed

After recording the transfer for the funds that have been received in the business bank account, we can check the details within the account for `Direct payments`:

DATE	TRANSACTION TYPE	ADJ	SPLIT	AMOUNT	BALANCE
▾ Direct Payments					
12/03/2021	Sales Receipt	No	Receipts not yet banked	9,800.00	9,800.00
12/03/2021	Transfer	No	Business Bank Account	-8,760.00	1,040.00
Total for Direct Payments				£1,040.00	
TOTAL				£1,040.00	

Figure 4.19 – Details of entries in the account for direct payments

The entries shown reflect the £9,800 adjusted on the sales receipt and the funds that have been received in the bank account; that is, £8,760. This has left a balance of £1,040, which should be received the following day.

Now, let's look at an example where the **Undeposited funds** account is fully utilized.

In this example, we have a small café that records sales daily. They are using a cloud-based point of sales till system. This does not integrate with QuickBooks, but we can still view and download daily sales figures. The following information is available from the **Electronic Point of Sale (EPOS)** system:

- Date of sales
- The sales details (food/drinks/takeaway)
- Sales tax information
- Gratuity
- Methods of payment

Using the information recorded in the EPOS system, it can be summarized and recorded in QuickBooks using a **Sales receipt**.

> **Tip**
> If the feature is available in your region, **Import data**, which can be found upon clicking the *gear icon*, provides you with an option to import **Sales receipts**. This can save you even more time on data input.

The following screenshot shows an excerpt of a sales receipt for the café:

DESCRIPTION	QTY	RATE	AMOUNT (GBP)
Food Consumed on Premises		120.50	120.50
Take-Away		140.20	140.20
Tips		5	5.00
Credit Card Receipts	1	-150	-150.00
Overs and Shorts - to adjust cash balance	1	-1.50	-1.50

Figure 4.20 – Café sales receipt excerpt

The preceding screenshot shows sales receipt being deposited to **Undeposited funds** and the use of multiple **Product/Service** items that reflect different sales items, as well as the fact that some payments were received by card – the rest would have been received in cash.

An additional item service item has been created here called `Overs/Shorts`. The purpose of this item is to adjust the cash balance to what was expected. If the total sales, including VAT minus amounts paid by card, left a balance of £115.70 but there is only £114.20 in the till, a negative adjustment of £1.50 will be required.

This item for **Overs and shorts** will require an **Expenses** chart of account category to be set up with the same name:

NAME	TYPE ▲	DETAIL TYPE
Overs and shorts	Expenses	Other Miscellaneous Service Cost

Figure 4.21 – Overs and shorts chart of account settings

The following screenshot shows the **Product/Service information**:

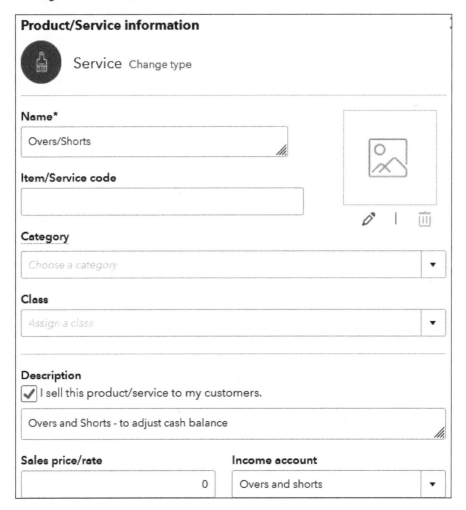

Figure 4.22 – Service item setting for Overs/Shorts

Depositing undeposited funds into a bank

When any payments are deposited to the **Undeposited funds** account, at a later point in time, funds should get paid into the bank account. In this example, sales receipts are being used, but payments of invoices and journal entries can also be coded to the **Undeposited funds** account.

When funds are paid into the bank account, a **Bank deposit** entry is required. Using the **New** button from the left navigation menu, the **Bank deposit** option can be found in the other column.

At the top of the **Undeposited funds** screen, all the payments that have been made to this account can be deposited into the bank account of your choice:

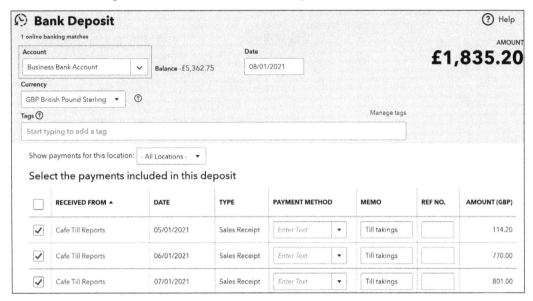

Figure 4.23 – Depositing undeposited funds into a bank

In the lower section of the **Bank Deposit** entry screen, adjustments can be made to the total amount being deposited into the bank. In the **Add funds to this deposit** area, positive or negative entries can be entered against a chart of account category, which will increase or decrease the total of the bank deposit:

▼ Add funds to this deposit

	#	RECEIVED FROM	ACCOUNT	DESCRIPTION
⣿	1		Insurance	Refund
⣿	2			

Add lines   Clear all lines

☐ Track returns for customers

Figure 4.24 – Adding additional funds to the deposit

Toward the lower right of the **Bank Deposit** screen, below the area for adding additional funds, is the **Cash back goes to** option, where you can select a balance sheet account where the cash balance can be adjusted:

Figure 4.25 – Using the Cash back feature

In this example, **Cash back goes to** is being used for the Petty cash account. It could also be used to adjust a Director's Loan or Drawings.

In this example, three sales receipts are being deposited that total £1,685.20. In addition, an insurance refund of £250 has been added, and £100 in cash has been held back to the Petty cash account. This gives us a total deposit of £1,835.20 for Business Bank Account.

One of the key benefits of recording receipts to **Undeposited funds** is the way it can simplify the bank reconciliation process. The bank deposit can be made up of multiple receipts and adjustments, and these are all reflected as one value on the bank statement:

	DATE	DESCRIPTION ▲	CATEGORY OR MATCH
☐	09/01/2021	Bank Deposit 000123	1 match found Deposit 08/01/2021 £1,835.20

Figure 4.26 – One match for the deposit from Undeposited funds

Using journal entries to record sales

Generally, journal entries are only used to create accounting adjustments to correct values that appear on the profit and loss report and balance sheet. A journal requires at least one debit and credit entry.

It can be useful to understand how journal entries are used because some third-party apps will create journal entries to reflect the sales recorded in an EPOS system, for example.

Taking the example we used for the bank deposit in *Figure 4.6*, let's look at how the same entry can be made as a *journal*.

A **Journal entry** can be made by accessing the **New** button from the left navigation menu in QuickBooks:

#	ACCOUNT	DEBITS (GBP)	CREDITS (GBP)	DESCRIPTION	NAME	VAT
1	Business Bank Account	1,800.00		Amazon Sales		
2	Sales		1,583.33	Amazon Sales	Amazon	20.0% S (Sales)
3	Amazon charges	100.00		Amazon Sales		
4						
5						
6						
7						
8						

Journal Entry no.Amazon Sales

GBP British Pound Sterling

Journal date: 05/03/2021

Journal no.: Amazon Sales

	Subtotal	1,900.00	1,583.33
	VAT @ 20% (Sales)		316.67
	Total GBP	1,900.00	1,900.00

Figure 4.27 – Using a journal entry

One advantage of using a **Journal entry** is that you can immediately see the accounts in use. If *sales tax* needs to be accounted for, the appropriate code must be used on the line accounting for sales. The sales tax value will appear as a separate value at the bottom of the journal.

However, you cannot use Product/Service items on a journal entry.

If you are not familiar with using journals, it can be helpful to create a template that you can use as and when you need it.

Recurring entries

At the bottom of most manual data entry screens, you will find the **Recurring** option. This can be used against **Invoices**, **Sales Receipts**, **Bills**, **Expenses**, **Journals**, and more.

The recurring feature can be used to automatically create an entry at a specified interval if **Scheduled** is selected for **Type**. If a recurring entry is saved as **Unscheduled**, you will be left with a template you can use as and when required:

Figure 4.28 – Unscheduled recurring journal entry

By clicking the *gear icon*, which can be accessed from the main menu screen in QuickBooks, you will find **Recurring transactions** below **LISTS**. Once selected, any saved templates will be displayed. You can **USE** a template at any time to create an entry:

TEMPLATE NAME ▼	TYPE	TXN TYPE	INTERVAL	PREVIOUS DATE	NEXT DATE	CUSTOMER/SUPPLIER	AMOUNT	ACTION
Cafe Till Reports	Unscheduled	Sales Receipt				Cafe Till Reports	0.00	Use ▼
Amazon sales	Unscheduled	Journal					0.00	Use ▼

Figure 4.29 – List of recurring templates

Using Customers

A retail-based business could be selling to hundreds or thousands of customers each week, so recording every single customer name in QuickBooks is not required. Depending on how income is recorded, you don't always need to record a customer name.

If income is recorded directly as a deposit to a chart of account category, it is not mandatory to use the **Supplier/Customer** field. It can be left blank:

Figure 4.30 – Deposit with the Supplier/Customer field left blank

When a sales receipt is recorded, it will be necessary to use the **Customer** field:

Figure 4.31 – Sales Receipt no.1014 requires the customer's name

The benefit of using a customer name means that Sales by Customer reports will be updated correctly.

> **Tip**
> The sales receipts for a café could simply be recorded to a customer named `Cash Sales`. If a different customer was created that reflected sales on different days, such as `Monday sales` or `Tuesday sales`, a Sales by Customer summary report would show which day of the week produced the most sales. This could help a business owner make informed decisions when it comes to the best days of the week to trade.

Within this section, we have looked at how retail sales can be recorded using either **Bank Deposits** or **Sales Receipts**. We can make adjustments if payments are being received via different sources. Where cash is received daily, we can make use of **Undeposited funds** and make appropriate adjustments when payments reach the bank account.

If the retail business is holding stock, what happens if it needs to be revalued? What if the retail price needs to be changed for a lot of items? How can we make adjustments that reflect those changes? Let's take a look.

Considerations for Inventory

At the beginning of this chapter, we discussed when tracking inventory might be appropriate for a retail-based business. If this feature is in use, at some point in time, the business will need to do the following:

- Update price lists

- Revalue inventory items

- Adjust stock quantities

Adjusting stock quantities was covered in *Chapter 3, QuickBooks Online for Manufacturing Businesses*, so please refer to the appropriate section within that chapter if you need help with that.

Updating Sales Prices

If you only have a few items where the default sales price needs to be increased or decreased, you can simply edit the **Product/Service** item and amend the price accordingly. However, if you have a lot of items, the last thing you want to do is spend a lot of time editing them individually. Thankfully, there is a much more efficient way to change a lot of values very quickly.

Toward the right of the **Products and Services** center, above the **Action** column for the list of Product/Service items, there is the option to export. Use this option to export the list of products and services to **Excel**:

> Tip
> If you filter the **Product/Service** list in QuickBooks Online before exporting it, the Excel file will only contain the items that reflect the filter. This filter option can be found toward the left of the screen, to the right of the search box.

Figure 4.32 – Filtering and then exporting the Product/Service list into Excel

Upon opening the Excel file, you will find a column for Sales Price / Rate. Change the values to reflect the new rates:

A	B	C	D	E	F
Product/Service Name	Sales Descrip	SKU	Type	Sales Price / Rate	Tax on Sales
Brown Brothers Whiteboard	Resistive technology 115 cm x 60 cm	QWD77NN	Stock	300	20.0% S
Coca-Cola (cans)	Coca-Cola		Stock	0.90	20.0% S

Figure 4.33 – Sales Price / Rate within the Excel export

Tip

If you needed to increase all the sales prices by 10%, you could use a spare column in the spreadsheet to create a formula. For example, within cell R2, the formula would be =e2*1.1. This will calculate the new rate. Using the **Copy** and **Paste Special** values in Excel, the amounts that are calculated could be used to replace the current sales/price rates:

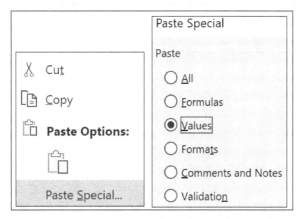

Figure 4.34 – Paste Special – Values within Excel

Save the Excel file with the updated Sales Price / Rate. Back in QuickBooks, at the top right-hand corner of the **Products and Services** center, you will find the option to **Import** if you click the arrow next to **New**:

Figure 4.35 – Importing Products and Services

With the **Import** feature selected, you will need to browse for the Excel file that has been updated. You don't need to download a template as you already have everything in place. Once the file is in place, click on the **Next** button twice until you see the **Import** option (all of the mappings will be correct):

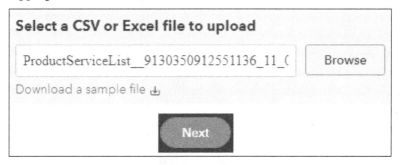

Figure 4.36 – Import File selected and the Next button

At the final stage of the import, you will need to tick the **Overwrite all values for each product or service that you import with the identical name. (This can't be undone.)** box:

SELL	BUY	TRACK	NAME	SKU	TYPE	SALES DESC	SALES PRICE/ RATE
✓	✓	✓					
✓	✓	✓	Brown Br	QWD77N	Stoc ▼	Resistive·	330
✓	✓	✓	Coca-Col		Stoc ▼	Coca-Col	0.90

2 products and services are ready to be imported   Filter by name

☑ Overwrite all values for each product or service that you import with the identical name. (This can't be undone.)

Figure 4.37 – The final import stage for overwriting values

With this box ticked, click the option to **Import** at the bottom right of the screen. All the sales prices will now be updated, and a message will briefly appear at the top of the screen to confirm this.

If the screen does not close after the import has been completed, click on the **X** button at the top right of the import screen to close. A message may appear that asks *Do you want to leave without saving?*. Click the **Yes** option to close the screen. You should find that the appropriate products and services reflect the new rates when you check them.

Now that you have learned how to update sales prices for items, what happens if you discover that some inventory items held on the balance sheet are now worth less than what was originally paid for them? Those items require a revaluation adjustment. We will look at this next.

Revaluating inventory (Stock)

To revalue inventory items, we need to utilize some of the features in QuickBooks Online that we used in the previous section.

We can run a report called **Stock Valuation Summary** (the name may differ slightly in other regions), which will provide the current valuation for all stock items:

	SKU	QTY	ASSET VALUE	CALC. AVG
Stock Valuation Summary				
As of July 11, 2021				
Brown Brothers Whiteboard	QWD77NN	5.00	800.00	160.00
Coca-Cola (cans)		1,200.00	300.00	0.25
▼ Educational Whiteboards				
AVM Interactive Whiteboard	WTI009X	5.00	1,995.00	399.00
Spruce Whiteboard	88UJ9	7.00	2,800.00	400.00
Total Educational Whiteboards			4,795.00	
IWB Whiteboard	PO87MN	3.00	450.00	150.00
Ultra Spec Whiteboard	UI888PO	2.00	1,218.00	609.00
Wireless Keyboards		100.00	1,000.00	10.00
TOTAL			£8,563.00	

Figure 4.38 – Stock Valuation Summary report

> **Tip**
> It is a good idea to see if the stock value is reflected correctly in the balance sheet.

The following screenshot shows the **Stock Asset** value:

▼ Current Assets	
Retentions	1,250.00
Stock Asset	8,563.00
Undeposited Funds	0.00
Total Current Assets	**£9,813.00**

Figure 4.39 – Checking the stock value on the balance sheet

In this example, we have 100 `Wireless Keyboards` at an original cost of £10 each, with a total value of £1,000. The keyboards are now only worth £6 each, so the stock should have a value of £600.

When the value of the stock is being reduced, the business incurs a cost that will affect its profit and loss. QuickBooks has a default chart of account category called `Stock Shrinkage` for this purpose. We shall use this account here.

To revalue the stock, first, the current quantity of stock needs to be adjusted to zero. For a single item, the **Adjust quantity** option can be selected from the drop-down **Action** menus in the **Product and Services** center. Batch actions are available for multiple items when adjusting stock quantities, as explained in the previous chapter:

Figure 4.40 – Adjusting the quantity against a single item

With this option selected, the quantity can be adjusted to zero in the **NEW QTY** column, and **Stock adjustment account** should be set to `Stock Shrinkage`:

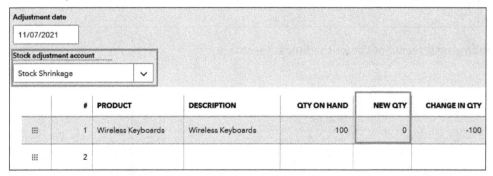

Figure 4.41 – Using the Stock adjustment account feature

With the stock adjustment saved, the effect of this entry should be checked within QuickBooks. This adjustment will reduce the value of the stock on the balance sheet by £1,000. The accounting double entries will be *Debit* `Stock Shrinkage` (increase the cost of sales in terms of profit and loss) and *Credit* `Stock Asset` (reducing the asset on the balance sheet).

At this point, we are left with zero quantity against `Wireless Keyboards`, but that is not correct. There are still 100, but they are worth less than what they had been valued at previously. What we must do now is adjust the stock quantity to £100 but with a different cost price.

QuickBooks values stock on a **first in first out** (**FIFO**) basis, so just editing the purchase cost alone will not create any accounting entries. Therefore, these stock movements are required.

Export the items that need to be revalued into Excel, as explained in the previous section.

Edit the columns for `Purchase Cost` (value per item), `Quantity On Hand`, and `Quantity as-of Date`:

J	K	L	M	N	O	P	Q
Purchase Cost	Tax on Purchases	Purchase Cost Expense Account	Quantity On Hand		Low Stock	Stock Asset Account	Quantity as-of Date
6	20.0% S	no	Cost of sales	100		Stock Asset	12/07/2021

Figure 4.42– Editing the Excel report for revised costs and quantities

Before this data is imported, make the item/s inactive. With the box to the left of the item ticked, **Batch actions** will be available if you need to delete more than one stock item:

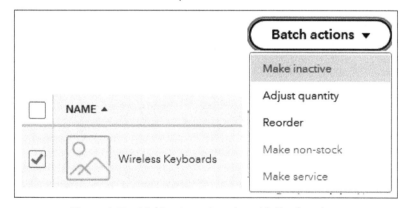

Figure 4.43 – Making items inactive with Batch actions

It is necessary to delete the item (make inactive) because of the FIFO principles that QuickBooks uses. Simply reimporting the stock will use the last cost price of £10 instead of the revised price of £6 per unit.

With the Excel spreadsheet updated, import the file in the same way as explained in the previous section. This time, it is not necessary to overwrite values because new items are now being imported.

With the file imported, we can check the last entry that QuickBooks has made by clicking on the magnifying glass icon for **Search and recent transactions**. The last import will show stock values with a starting value:

RECENT TRANSACTIONS	Stock Starting Value START | Wireless Keyboards | 12/07/2021 | £600.00
	Stock Qty Adjust 13 | Wireless Keyboards (deleted) | 12/07/2021 | £0.00

Figure 4.44 – Recent transaction for Stock Starting Value

Clicking on the transaction for **Stock Starting Value**, we can see which **Stock adjustment account** has been used. This is likely to default to Opening Balance Equity:

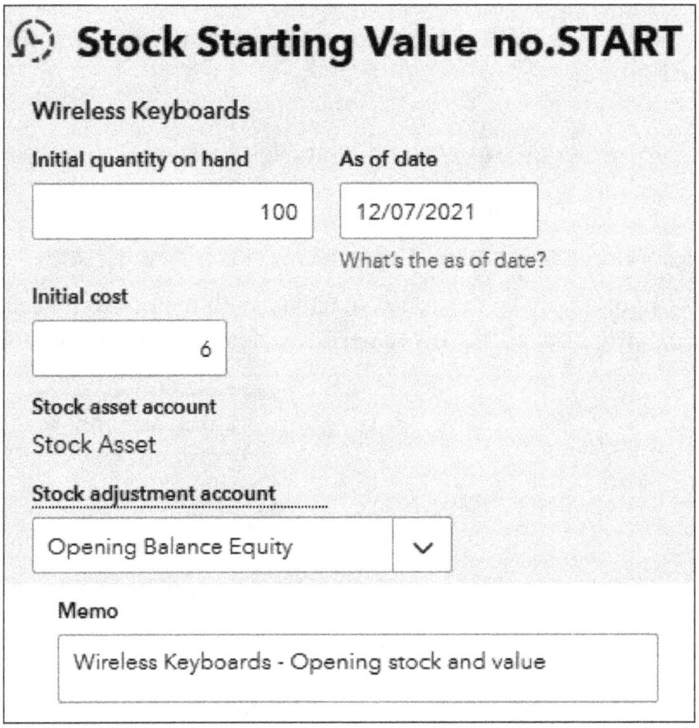

Figure 4.45 – Stock Starting Value

If only one item has been adjusted, simply edit the **Stock adjustment** account that was used for Stock Shrinkage. If a lot of items were revalued, look at the combined total adjustments that were made to the Opening Balance Equity account and create a journal entry to correct the profit and loss, as shown in the following screenshot:

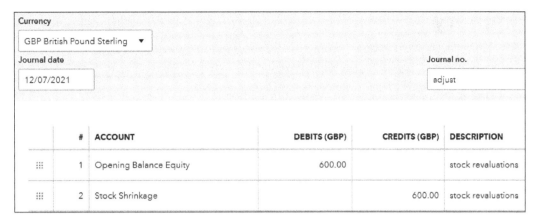

Figure 4.46 – Journal entry for stock reevaluations

This will mean that debits and credits are being made to the same account for the revaluation process.

During this revaluation process, stock to the value of £1,000 has been removed, and then £600 has been added back. These adjustments create an overall cost of £400 that will affect the Stock Shrinkage account within the cost of sales:

Figure 4.47 – Total adjustments made to Stock Shrinkage

Summary

In this chapter, we looked at how income can be recorded in QuickBooks Online for a retail-based business, the following areas have been covered:

- Using Sales Receipts, Bank Deposits, Journal Entries
- Recurring templates
- Using Undeposited Funds
- Use of Customer names
- Use of Product/Service Items
- Updating price-lists
- Revaluation of stock

QuickBooks Online offers a lot of flexibility when it comes to choosing how income is recorded. The level of complexity depends largely on the reporting requirements and the necessity to monitor inventory.

The next chapter looks at how a business might need to monitor how money that is not strictly theirs is handled – *client money*. Lawyers, realtors, and trusts often handle money on behalf of others. But how can we use QuickBooks to handle that? Read on to find out!

5
Handling Client Money

Some businesses will need to handle money that is not theirs. This is usually referred to as *Client Money*. Lawyers, Realtors, Investment Brokers, and other businesses that act as agents might need to handle funds on behalf of others.

This chapter is all about how QuickBooks Online can be used effectively to monitor funds held by a business that belong to other parties – usually clients.

Understanding how to fully separate standard business activities from those where receipts and payments are being made on behalf of others is important. Handling client funds often requires the need to comply with strict regulations.

There should never be any confusion between funds owed to clients and funds that belong to the business. Setting up QuickBooks correctly will help to avoid making unnecessary mistakes.

Throughout this chapter, you will learn how to do the following:

- Set up QuickBooks to account for Client Funds
- Record entries when funds are received for clients
- Record entries when payments are made to or on behalf of clients
- Adjust client account balances for disbursements payable to suppliers
- Adjust client account balances for any fees chargeable by the business
- Report against client transactions

Before we start recording any transactions that relate to funds received and paid on behalf of clients, we will need to have a QuickBooks Online file set up specifically for this purpose.

The next section of this chapter looks at those settings in detail, so let's dive in.

Setting up QuickBooks for Client Funds

It is highly recommended that if a business needs to monitor client funds, they use two separate QuickBooks Online files. One file would be used for the business, for office transactions. This is the file that is used to create invoices, pay employees, and record expenses – where the profit and loss for the business is reported.

A separate QuickBooks subscription should be used for the handling of client funds. Although, using options such as **Classes** and **Locations**, it is technically possible to use one QuickBooks Company file, it is not recommended.

These are the benefits of keeping the client funds area separate by using a separate QuickBooks Online company file:

- Users can be granted access to the *Client* QuickBooks only, restricting any visibility to the movements in the *Office* file.
- Reconciliation of the client funds will be made very much easier.
- Mistaking client funds for income or expenditure of the business is significantly reduced (especially useful for VAT registered businesses).

If the business needs to adjust for disbursements to be paid from client funds, the *Plus* version of QuickBooks Online will be required for the client file. If the file is only being used to record payments and receipts, the *Simple Start* subscription should be sufficient.

The office file is really like any other business, so we are just concentrating on the setup and operation of the QuickBooks file used for handling client money.

When setting up a brand-new QuickBooks file, selecting the business and industry type is not important. The screenshot in *Figure 5.1* displays the selections made in this example:

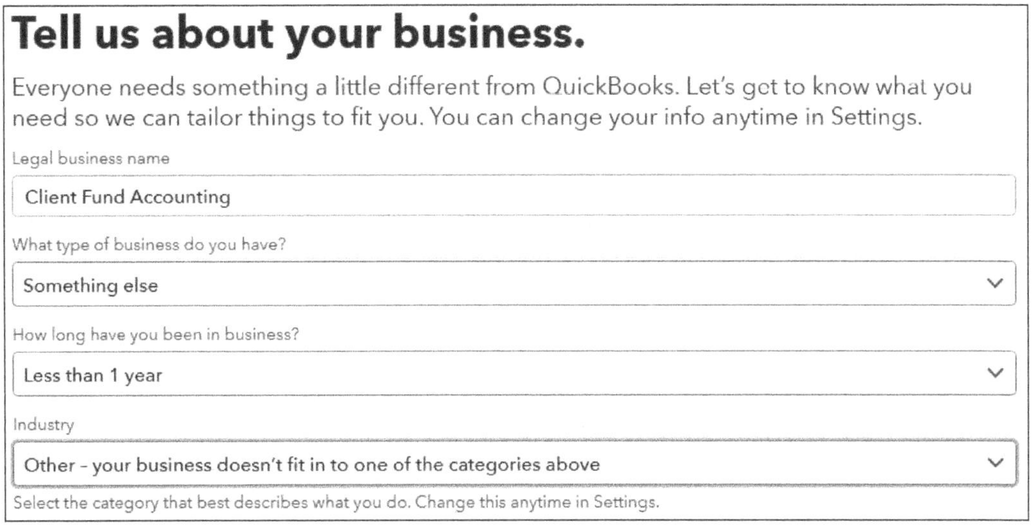

Tell us about your business.

Everyone needs something a little different from QuickBooks. Let's get to know what you need so we can tailor things to fit you. You can change your info anytime in Settings.

Legal business name

Client Fund Accounting

What type of business do you have?

Something else   ∨

How long have you been in business?

Less than 1 year   ∨

Industry

Other - your business doesn't fit in to one of the categories above   ∨

Select the category that best describes what you do. Change this anytime in Settings.

Figure 5.1 – Initial QuickBooks Settings

With the initial settings in place, we will now need to look at what further settings should be enabled before we record any transactions, starting with those we may need when paying suppliers on behalf of clients.

Settings for expenses

Within the **Expenses** area of **Account and Settings**, if the *Plus* subscription is in use, enable the **Track expenses and items by customer** and **Make expenses and items billable** options.

These settings will come into full use in a later section of this chapter, *Paying Suppliers on behalf of clients*:

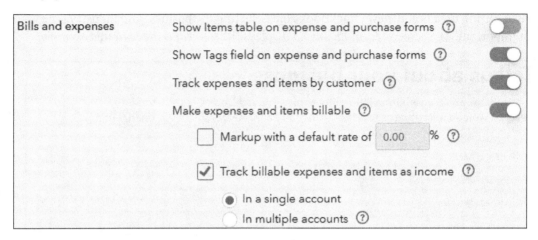

Figure 5.2 – Settings for Expenses

There are very few company settings required for this QuickBooks file used to record funds received and paid on behalf of clients. With those settings selected, it is time to check the chart of accounts.

Setting up the Chart of Accounts

The chart of accounts structure for the file that handles client money can be extremely basic. In its simplest structure, where only funds received for clients and payments made to clients are recorded, there could be just two categories that are required:

- A bank account used for holding client money

- Debtors/accounts receivable – **Customers** are the **Clients**

In addition to those two categories (a bank account and debtors), other categories might be required: a fees control account, a disbursements control account, and **Creditors/ Accounts Payable** where suppliers are paid from client funds.

Before setting up the chart of accounts, as explained in *Chapter 2, Useful Tips and Tricks Every QuickBooks User Should Know*, use the **Purge Company** option, or delete (make inactive) all the chart of accounts categories created by default.

> **Important Note**
>
> VAT (sales tax) should **not** be enabled within the client file. The transactions recorded in the client file form no part of the profit and loss of the business, so tax is ignored. All values are entered gross. Fees are transferred from the client bank and recorded in the client QuickBooks as per *Figure 5.19*. These funds would be received into the office bank account where business profits and VAT/ sales tax are calculated.

Figure 5.3 shows all the chart of accounts codes in use for this example. Notice there are no profit and loss categories in use – only balance sheet categories:

NAME	TYPE ▲	DETAIL TYPE
Client Bank Account	Cash at bank and in hand	Cash on hand
Client trust account	Cash at bank and in hand	Client trust account
Client Ledger Balances	Debtors	Debtors
Disbursements Control	Current liabilities	Current Liabilities
Fees Control	Current liabilities	Current Liabilities
Opening Balance Equity (DO NOT USE)	Equity	Opening Balance Equity
Retained Earnings (DO NOT USE)	Equity	Retained Earnings

Figure 5.3 – Chart of Accounts for Client Fund Accounting

The default sales account for `Sales` has been changed to `Fees Control`. The default account for `Billable Expense Income` has been changed to `Disbursements Control`. The account for `Debtors/Accounts Receivable` has been changed to `Client Ledger Balances`. You can edit the names to suit your own preferences.

Setting up Products and Services

In some instances, the use of products and services will not be required. However, sometimes it can be useful to create some invoices within this client QuickBooks file for internal use.

Reports can be produced to summarize the fees to be charged to clients and later recorded in the QuickBooks file that handles the office transactions.

We will take an example of a property management company. Commission is charged on rent received, and other ad hoc fees can be charged to landlords who own properties that are being managed.

The item that we are creating will be used later in this chapter in the *Managing fees deducted from client funds* section.

For any service items that will be used to create invoices for internal purposes, the chart of accounts category selected for **Income account** should always be **Fees Control**:

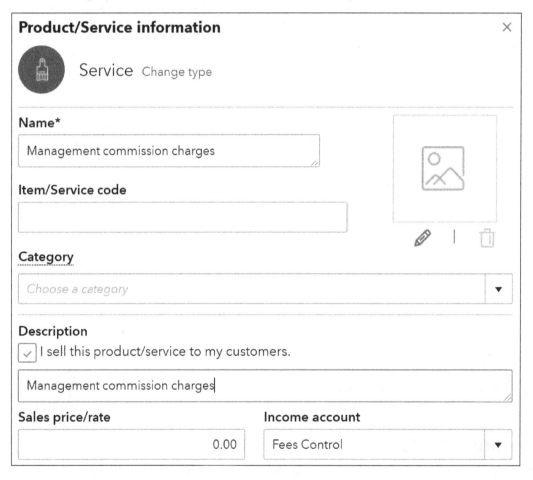

Figure 5.4 – Service Item used for internal invoices

This QuickBooks Company file is being set up specifically to record client funds. Clients are customers in QuickBooks. Let's see whether there are any specific features that can be applied within this area.

Settings for Customers

Settings for customers can really be the same as for any other business; however, the use of sub-customers can prove useful. Take the following information into consideration when creating a customer for a property management company:

- Landlord name
- Property name
- Tenant name

All this information could be entered into the **Display name as** field:

Figure 5.5 – Customer name with Landlord / Property / Tenant

Alternatively, the landlord could be entered as the main customer, and the property could be entered as a sub-customer of the landlord. The tenant could be entered as a sub-customer below the property:

Figure 5.6 – Property created as a sub-customer of the landlord

The decision of whether to use sub-customers or not will ultimately depend on the reporting requirements of the business. You might have questions such as *will reporting against the client alone be sufficient?*, or, as in this example, *are reports against properties and tenants also required?*. *Figure 5.7* shows how the use of the sub-customers will appear on the customer list within the customer center:

CUSTOMER ▲ / COMPANY	PHONE	OPEN BALANCE
Stephenson		£0.00
142 High Street		£0.00
Jefferies		£0.00
Stephenson / 142 High Street / Jefferies		£0.00

Figure 5.7 – Sub-customers in the customer list

You could use projects for the different properties held against a landlord. However, you cannot create a *sub-project* if you wished to have that level of nesting:

Figure 5.8 – Using Projects for Properties held by a landlord

The profitability reporting options of a project would not be required in this example of a client file, but the feature does provide a neat alternative to sub-customers. This could be useful for recording time against clients.

> **Tip**
> This example is based on a property management company. A law firm has clients, and the different types of work being done for those clients are referred to as *matters*. *Client matters* could be created as either a sub-customer or a project.

We shall be looking at the use of projects in more detail in the next chapter of this book.

Settings for Suppliers

There are no specific settings for suppliers. However, there are specific ways in which the supplier charges (client disbursements) need to be created, and those will be covered later in this chapter, in the *Paying suppliers on behalf of clients* section.

So far, we have covered all the key settings required for this QuickBooks file used for client account transactions. We have checked and edited the following:

- Basic company settings
- The Chart of Account categories required
- Product and Service items required
- Customer settings (using sub-customers or projects)
- Suppliers (added as normal)

Now that our QuickBooks company file is set up and ready to use, let's look at how we record funds received and paid out on behalf of clients.

Recording Client Account Transactions

When it comes to recording funds received or payments made on behalf of clients, it is straightforward. There is only one chart of accounts code that is required, and in this example, it is **Client Ledger Balances**. The account was re-named from the default, **Debtors (Accounts Receivable)**; see *Figure 5.3:*

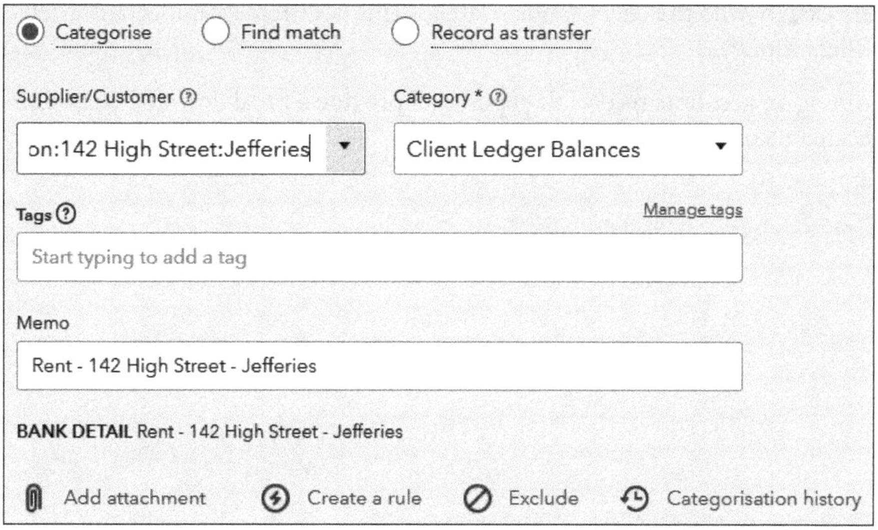

Figure 5.9 – Recording client funds received using bank feeds

In *Figure 5.9*, a receipt for £1,000 of rent has been recorded to a sub-customer named **Jefferies** using the bank feeds within QuickBooks Online. If sub-customers are in use, it is important that a payment or receipt is coded to the lowest nesting level to which it relates. This entry is being recorded as a bank deposit.

Tip

You can create a rule for these bank entries to help automate regular client receipts, which can save a huge amount of time.

After recording various receipts on behalf of clients, the trial balance for this QuickBooks file for client funds will generate a report as shown in the following figure:

Client Fund Accounting		
Trial Balance		
As of August 31, 2021		
	DEBIT	CREDIT
Client Bank Account	4,900.00	
Client Ledger Balances		4,900.00
TOTAL	£4,900.00	£4,900.00

Figure 5.10 – Trial balance with client receipts recorded

The true benefit of using this separate QuickBooks file for client funds is how easily we can identify exactly who the client funds relate to. This is extremely important when handling client money.

Simply running an accounts receivable report will provide a breakdown of client funds so no complicated reconciliation process is required:

Client Fund Accounting						
A/R Ageing Summary						
As of August 31, 2021						
	CURRENT	1 - 30	31 - 60	61 - 90	91 AND OVER	TOTAL
▾ Deposits						£0.00
The Grange (Deposit - O'Sulliv...			-3,000.00			£ -3,000.00
Total Deposits			-3,000.00			£ -3,000.00
▾ Stephenson						£0.00
▾ 142 High Street						£0.00
Jefferies			-1,000.00			£ -1,000.00
Total 142 High Street			-1,000.00			£ -1,000.00
▾ 148 High Street						£0.00
Jameson			-900.00			£ -900.00
Total 148 High Street			-900.00			£ -900.00
Total Stephenson			-1,900.00			£ -1,900.00
TOTAL	£0.00	£0.00	£ -4,900.00	£0.00	£0.00	£ -4,900.00

Figure 5.11 – Accounts Receivable report for Client Funds

If you wish, you can customize the report shown in *Figure 5.11*. The following figure shows the exact same report with the title changed and with negative numbers displayed in red and in brackets.

These changes can be made easily using the customization options found in the top right-hand corner of the screen when a report is in view:

Client Funds Held						
As of August 31, 2021						
	CURRENT	1 - 30	31 - 60	61 - 90	91 AND OVER	TOTAL
▾ Deposits						£0.00
The Grange (Deposit - O'Sulliv...			(3,000.00)			£ (3,000.00)
Total Deposits			(3,000.00)			£ (3,000.00)
▾ Stephenson						£0.00
▾ 142 High Street						£0.00
Jefferies			(1,000.00)			£ (1,000.00)
Total 142 High Street			(1,000.00)			£ (1,000.00)
▾ 148 High Street						£0.00
Jameson			(900.00)			£ (900.00)
Total 148 High Street			(900.00)			£ (900.00)
Total Stephenson			(1,900.00)			£ (1,900.00)
TOTAL	£0.00	£0.00	£ (4,900.00)	£0.00	£0.00	£ (4,900.00)

Figure 5.12 – Customized Accounts Receivable Report

The values in this report should always display negative. A positive value would indicate that more money had been paid on behalf of a client than what had been received.

> **Tip**
>
> In the example in *Figure 5.12*, a customer has been created with the name **Deposits**. A sub-customer can be created for all the different deposits received and they will be grouped together on the report.

When funds are paid to the client, the coding of the transaction is the same as the deposit. It is important to use the appropriate sub-customer and the category will be **Client Ledger Balances**:

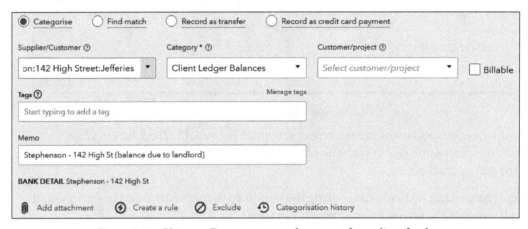

Figure 5.13 – Using an Expense to record payment from client funds

It is not necessary to use the **Customer/Project** field with the expense when paying funds to the client. Using the **Supplier/Customer** name field alone is sufficient.

So far, we have looked at how payments and receipts are recorded against client funds and how a simple report helps us reconcile those client balances. Let's look next at how fees charged to the client can be accounted for.

Managing fees deducted from client funds

The profits of a management company will ultimately be reported within the QuickBooks company file for office transactions. However, where commission is being charged on rent payments collected, this will be deducted from the final balance owed to the client. Adjustments can be made in the client file first.

As an example, a business may charge 10% plus VAT as a management charge. First, a **Transaction Detail by Account** report can be run in QuickBooks and then filtered by the bank account. The following example shows a customized report with the columns that were not required removed:

Transaction Detail by Account All Dates		
DATE	**NAME**	**AMOUNT**
▾ Client Bank Account		
12/07/2021	Deposits:The Grange (Deposit - O'Sullivan)	3,000.00
12/07/2021	Stephenson:142 High Street:Jefferies	1,000.00
15/07/2021	Stephenson:148 High Street:Jameson	900.00
Total for Client Bank Account		**£4,900.00**

Figure 5.14 – Customized Transaction Detail by Account Report

As with nearly all reports in QuickBooks, this data can be exported into Excel, and formulas could be created to calculate the commission due on rent received. Ignoring the deposit, two rent payments for £1,000 and £900 have been received.

A management charge of 10% plus VAT of 20% would result in fees of £120 and £108 including VAT due from clients in this example.

Using the **Import Data** options within QuickBooks Online, invoices can be imported (the function may not be available in all regions). The import option provides a sample template that you can download:

Upload your CSV file

⬇ Download an example

Select .csv   (Browse)

Your CSV file can have no more than 1000 rows.

☐ Add new contacts that don't already exist in QuickBooks.
☐ Add new products/services that don't already exist in QuickBooks.

Figure 5.15 – Download an example template to import invoices

Some of the data exported from the report in *Figure 5.14* can be copied into the template – the date and customer name. The sample in *Figure 5.16* displays the minimum amount of information required when importing customer invoices:

	A	B	C	D	E	F	G
1	*InvoiceNo	*Customer	*InvoiceDate	*DueDate	Item(Product/Service)	Memo	*ItemAmount
2	1000	Stephenson:142 High Street:Jefferies	15/07/2021	15/07/2021	Management Commission Charges	Commission charges	120
3	1001	Stephenson:148 High Street:Jameson	15/07/2021	15/07/2021	Management Commission Charges	Commission charges	108

Figure 5.16 – Data in an Excel file to import invoices

If we take a look at the lowest-level sub-customer (the tenant), if only the rent had been recorded and the commission invoice was imported, the transaction list against the customer would appear as shown in *Figure 5.17*:

	DATE ▼	TYPE	NO.	MEMO	DUE DATE	TOTAL
☐	15/07/2021	Invoice	1000	Commission charges	15/07/2021	£120.00
☐	12/07/2021	Deposit		Rent - 142 High Street - ...	12/07/2021	-£1,000.00

Figure 5.17 – Transaction list against the tenant

The invoices on the client file are for internal use only. At a desired frequency, the income will need to be recorded in the office QuickBooks file. A **Sales by Product/Service Detail** report could be produced that will detail the commission recorded for the chosen period:

Client Fund Accounting

Sales by Product/Service Detail
1-15 July, 2021

DATE	NO.	CUSTOMER	AMOUNT
▼ Management commission charges			
15/07/2021	1000	Stephenson:142 High Street:Jefferies	120.00
15/07/2021	1001	Stephenson:148 High Street:Jameson	108.00
Total for Management commission charges			£228.00

Figure 5.18 – Sales by Product/Service Detail report

In the QuickBooks company file for office transactions (where income and expenditure are recorded for the business – *not client funds*), a single invoice can be recorded. The invoice could be created against a single customer set up with a generic name – `Management Fees`, for example:

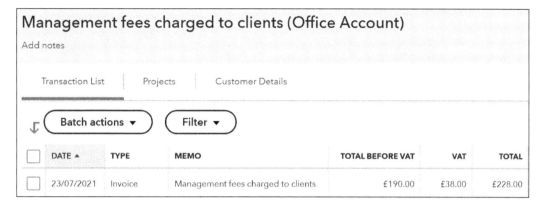

Figure 5.19 – Invoice for Commission within an office account

> **Note**
>
> In this example, we are transferring fees across that relate to multiple clients. An alternative would be to create a single invoice against a customer in the client file (gross including VAT) and a single invoice in the office file (net plus VAT) for a specific customer. This is useful if a VAT receipt is required or more detailed reporting is required in the office QuickBooks file.
>
> Although VAT is not split in the client file, the invoice template within the client file could be adapted. The VAT number of the business could be added within the footer and a note included on an invoice that fees are inclusive of VAT at a specified rate.

At this point in time, the fees calculated are still held in the client bank account. When funds are transferred, in the QuickBooks client company file, the amount due to the business can be entered as a transfer to **Fees Control**:

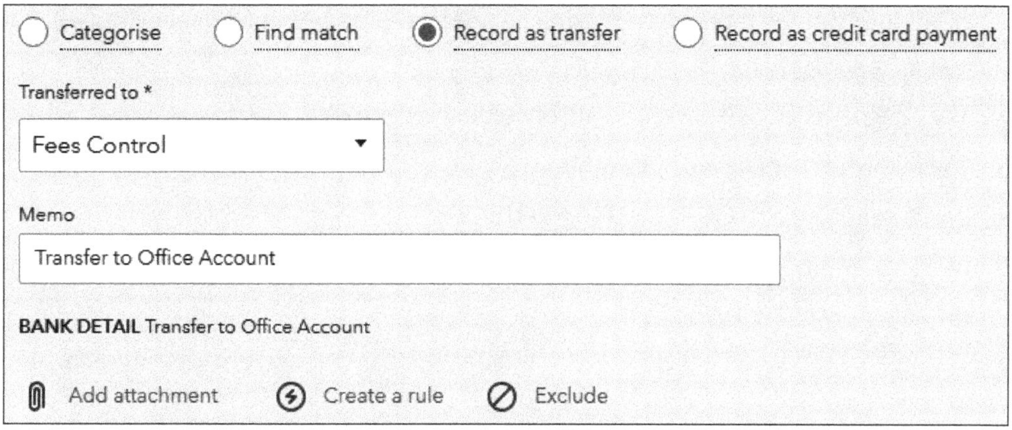

Figure 5.20 – Transfer entered to Fees Control

Tip

It is useful to attach the reports generated for fees using the **Add attachment** option – both to the transfer and the invoice created within the office QuickBooks file.

If we look at the **Fees Control** account in detail, we can see the movements included the charges applied to the client balances and the transfer to the office account. The account should regularly balance back to zero:

				Client Fund Accounting			
				Transaction Detail by Account			
				All Dates			
DATE	TRANSACTION TYPE	NO.	NAME	MEMO/DESCRIPTION	SPLIT	AMOUNT	BALANCE
▾ Fees Control							
15/07/2021	Invoice	1000	Stephenson:142 High Street:Jeff...		Client Ledger Balances	120.00	120.00
15/07/2021	Invoice	1001	Stephenson:148 High Street:Ja...		Client Ledger Balances	108.00	228.00
22/07/2021	Transfer			Transfer to Office Account	Client Bank Account	-228.00	0.00
Total for Fees Control						£0.00	

Figure 5.21 – Report against the Fees Control account

So far, we have looked at how we can record payments and receipts against client funds, but what happens when we need to pay a supplier on behalf of the client, using funds that we are holding? Let's look at that in the next section.

Paying Suppliers on behalf of clients

As we have already learned, the QuickBooks file used to handle client funds does not need to use many chart of accounts categories. The priority of the file is to record the receipts and payments made on behalf of clients and ensure everything balances.

Supplier bills that are going to be paid from client funds can be entered just like any other supplier bill in any other company, but using the method in this book, the following will apply:

- The category used will always be **Disbursements Control**.

- The bill will always be made **Billable**.

- It will be assigned to **CUSTOMER/PROJECT**:

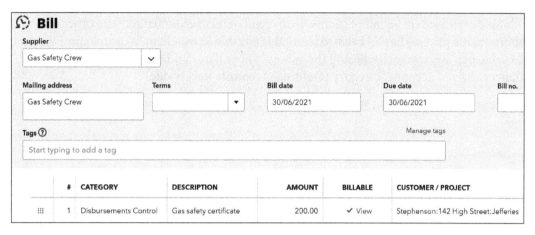

Figure 5.22 – Recording the supplier bill to be paid from Client Funds

Recording the supplier bill in this way will create a billable expense charge against the customer. From this, we can create an invoice that will adjust the customer balance further:

DATE ▼	TYPE	NO.	PROJECT	MEMO	DUE DATE	TOTAL	STATUS	ACTION
15/07/2021	Invoice	1000		Commission charges	15/07/2021	£120.00	Open	Receive payment ▼
12/07/2021	Deposit			Rent - 142 High Street - ...	12/07/2021	-£1,000.00	Overdue	Print
30/06/2021	Billable Expense Charge			Gas safety certificate wit...	30/06/2021	£200.00	Open	Create invoice

Figure 5.23 – Billable expense charge against a customer account

As shown in *Figure 5.23*, all that is required is to click on the **Create invoice** option and then click **Save and close**.

When the supplier bill was created, the `Disbursements Control` account would have been **debited**. When the invoice was generated to update the customer balance, the `Disbursements Control` account will have been **credited**:

DATE	TRANSACTION TYPE	NO.	NAME	MEMO/DESCRIPTION	SPLIT	AMOUNT
Transaction Detail by Account						
All Dates						
▼ Disbursements Control						
30/06/2021	Bill		Gas Safety Crew	Gas safety certificate	Creditors	-200.00
15/07/2021	Invoice	1002	Stephenson:142 High Street:Jeff...	Gas safety certificate	Client Ledger Balances	200.00
Total for Disbursements Control						£0.00

Figure 5.24 – Disbursements control account movements

With funds received on behalf of clients, management fees accounted for, and other disbursements paid we have a balance left that is payable to the client. As shown in *Figure 5.13*, an expense is categorized using the sub-customer name and the **Client Ledger Balances** chart of accounts category (**Debtors/Accounts Receivable**).

In this example, the payment made to the landlord brings the balance of the account back to zero:

	DATE ▾	TYPE	NO.	MEMO	DUE DATE	TOTAL
☐	18/07/2021	Payment			18/07/2021	£0.00
☐	18/07/2021	Expense		Stephenson - 142 High St	18/07/2021	£680.00
☐	18/07/2021	Invoice	1003	Gas safety certificate	18/07/2021	£200.00
☐	15/07/2021	Invoice	1000	Commission charges	15/07/2021	£120.00
☐	12/07/2021	Deposit		Rent - 142 High Street - Jefferies	12/07/2021	-£1,000.00
☐	30/06/2021	Billable Expense...		Gas safety certificate with no markup	18/07/2021	£200.00

Figure 5.25 – Transaction list against the tenant (sub-customer)

Billable Expense Charge is a *non-posting* entry on the customer account – a memo entry to remind us to charge the client. The entries for the deposit, the two invoices, and the expense balance to £0.00.

Now that all the client account entries have been made, we may need to consider the following:

- How to report against client movements
- How client balances need to appear within the *office* QuickBooks file

We will learn about this in the next section.

Reporting Against Client Funds

There are multiple ways to report against customers within QuickBooks, but using the default reports provided, you are unlikely to find exactly what you are looking for. In this section, we are going to build a custom report from scratch, starting with the trial balance:

		Client Fund Accounting			
		Trial Balance			
		All Dates			
			DEBIT		**CREDIT**
Client Bank Account			0.00		
Client trust account			3,000.00		
Client Ledger Balances					3,000.00
Creditors					0.00
Disbursements Control					0.00
Fees Control					0.00
TOTAL			£3,000.00		£3,000.00

Figure 5.26 – Trial Balance

In this example, we are left with £3,000 that relates to a deposit received against a property. We are interested in looking at the movements against a particular tenant account, so the next step is to click on the value against **Client Ledger Balances**:

DATE	TRANSACTION TYPE	SPLIT	AMOUNT	BALANCE
▼ Client Ledger Balances				
12/07/2021	Deposit	Client Bank Account	-3,000.00	-3,000.00
12/07/2021	Deposit	Client Bank Account	-1,000.00	-4,000.00
15/07/2021	Payment	-Split-		-4,000.00
15/07/2021	Deposit	Client Bank Account	-900.00	-4,900.00
15/07/2021	Invoice	Fees Control	120.00	-4,780.00
15/07/2021	Invoice	Fees Control	108.00	-4,672.00
18/07/2021	Payment	-Split-		-4,672.00
18/07/2021	Invoice	Disbursements Control	200.00	-4,472.00
18/07/2021	Expense	Client Bank Account	680.00	-3,792.00
19/07/2021	Expense	Client Bank Account	792.00	-3,000.00
Total for Client Ledger Balances			£ -3,000.00	
TOTAL			£ -3,000.00	

Figure 5.27 – Detailed transactions against Client Ledger Balances

At this point, we have a report showing entries against every single client, property, and tenant, but we are only interested in one. Our next step is to use the **Customise** option found in the top right of the screen:

Figure 5.28 – Using the Customise option

Within the customization area, the **Filter** option is selected. **Distribution Account** will automatically be filtered. The **Customer** option needs to be ticked, and then the customer or sub-customer name is selected. In this example, the **Stephenson:142 High Street:Jefferies** sub-customer has been selected:

Figure 5.29 – Filter by Customer

You can also use the **Rows/Columns** options to add or remove columns used on the report. Tick or untick the boxes as desired. The grid box to the left of each option can be used to click and drag to change the position of the column on the report: top = left and bottom = right:

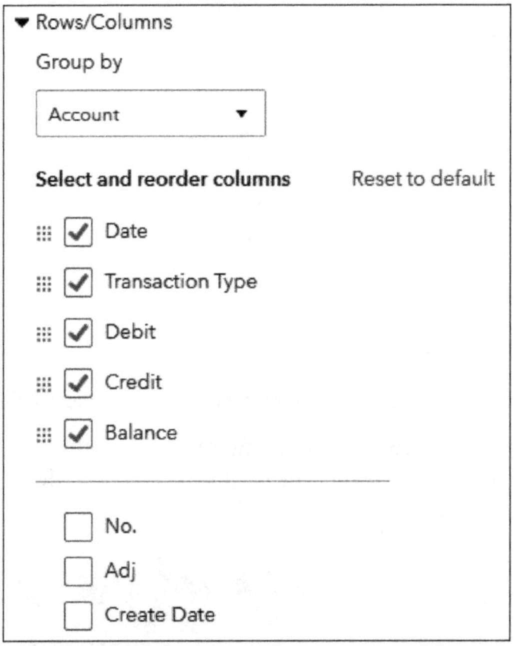

Figure 5.30 – Edit the Rows/Columns options

After customizing the report, the title can be edited by just clicking in the title area. You should be left with a report that is more usable:

Client Fund Accounting

Report - 142 High Street - Jefferies
All Dates

DATE	TRANSACTION TYPE	DEBIT	CREDIT	BALANCE
▾ Client Ledger Balances				
12/07/2021	Deposit		£1,000.00	(1,000.00)
15/07/2021	Invoice	£120.00		(880.00)
15/07/2021	Invoice	£200.00		(680.00)
18/07/2021	Expense	£680.00		0.00
Total for Client Ledger Balances		£1,000.00	£1,000.00	
TOTAL		£1,000.00	£1,000.00	

Figure 5.31 – Final report against the tenant

If the report is to be used in the future, use **Save customization**. The report will be added to the list of custom reports you can access any time, and if you wish, you can schedule the report to be sent out every month using the **Edit** function:

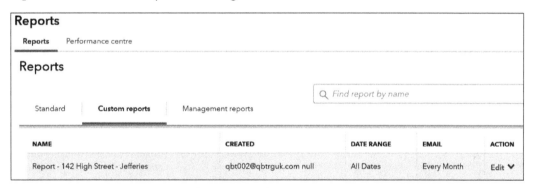

Figure 5.32 – Custom reports

On a day-to-day basis, there is no need to reflect any client-related transactions in the office account, apart from when the value of fees raised is transferred from the client bank account to the office bank account.

Periodically though, the total balance of client funds held may need to be reported within the accounts of the business. Let's look at how that can be done.

Reporting Client Balances within the Office Company File

During the year, there is usually no need to record any transactions that involve the use of client money in the office account, except when funds are transferred from the client account for the fees raised.

NAME	TYPE ▲	DETAIL TYPE
Client Account Bank Balances	Cash at bank and in hand	Client trust account
Funds owed to Clients	Current liabilities	Client Trust Accounts - Liabilities

Figure 5.33 – Chart of accounts codes for client balances in the office company file

With the chart of accounts codes in place, a simple two-line journal can be created to account for the cash held and the liability owed. Using our worked example, we were left with £3,000 held as a deposit:

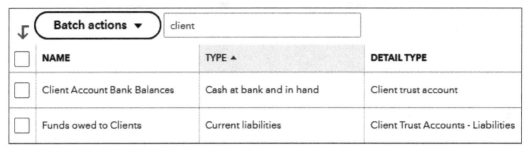

Figure 5.34 – Journal to account for client balances

With the journal entry saved, it could be reversed and replaced with another journal when the amounts need to be reported – this could be every month if regular management reports are being prepared.

That is really the final adjustment that is required, so let's recap what we have covered.

Summary

Throughout this chapter, we have looked at how we can use QuickBooks Online to monitor funds received and paid on behalf of clients. Essentially, it is advised to use a separate QuickBooks subscription for this.

This results in having two QuickBooks subscriptions: one for the business, and another dedicated to handling client funds. The client QuickBooks file is used to do the following:

- Receive money on behalf of clients.

- Make payments on behalf of clients.

- Create adjustments for fees and client disbursements.

A very basic setup is required for the client file.

The office QuickBooks file is used for everything else, such as this:

- Accounting for all income and expenditure of the business

- Accounting for VAT and other taxes

This keeps a clear division between transactions that have an impact on the business and those that relate to clients.

If specialist third-party software is in use, you may only need one QuickBooks file as the third-party software is likely to create journals to ensure everything is being accounted for accordingly. However, it is important to ensure the use of such software is cost-effective. The next chapter is all about getting the most out of using projects. This feature can be useful to all business types, including those that monitor client funds.

6

The Secret to Success with Projects in QuickBooks Online

Projects are a fantastic way of checking the profitability of separate jobs that are being worked on for customers. Many people often associate the use of projects in QuickBooks with the construction industry, but in fact, there are a lot of business types that can benefit from using the feature.

Marketing agencies, lawyers, graphic designers, and even accountants and bookkeepers may have different types of work they do for the same customer/client. Using projects to keep track of those jobs separately makes reviewing the profitability of a particular job much easier.

In this chapter, you will learn how to do the following:

- Check and enable the required settings to use Projects
- Create a Project
- Record income and expenditure against a Project
- Record time against a Project
- Create a budget against a Project
- Manage Unbilled Expenses
- Run various Project-related reports
- Allocate other costs to a Project
- Differentiate between Projects and Sub-Customers

It is important to fully understand how a Project works within QuickBooks. As an accountant or bookkeeper, you can ensure clients are using the software correctly. As a business owner, having clear visibility on the profitability of a job can assist with future decision-making. This can include whether to take on new jobs and how much needs to be charged for any work undertaken.

Before we look at the settings required for projects, the lowest level of subscription required for this feature is the QuickBooks Online *Plus* subscription.

Settings for Projects

In this section, we'll look at the key settings needed to help us get the most out of using Projects in QuickBooks Online. This will include settings to track expenses by a customer/project and enabling the Progress Invoicing feature if we need to raise multiple invoices against a single estimate.

To begin with, let's check that the Projects feature itself has been enabled.

Enabling Projects

The Projects feature is usually enabled by default within QuickBooks Online and is accessed from the *Left Navigation* panel. If a *Plus* subscription is in place, and **Projects** is not immediately visible, the feature can be enabled within the **Advanced** area of **Account and settings**.

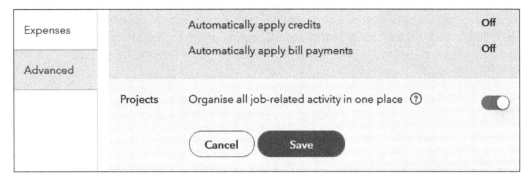

Figure 6.1 – Enabling the Projects feature in Account and settings

> **Tip**
> Clicking on your *company name* that is displayed when viewing the Dashboard
> will take you directly into **Account and settings**.

The purpose of using Projects is to track the profitability against a specific job. We cannot
do that accurately unless we choose to Track expenses and items by customer. So, let's
ensure those settings are in place.

Settings to track expenses by customer

After enabling Projects, there are some additional settings that we are likely to require
when using this feature. The next settings to check are found within the **Expenses** tab.

Enabling the settings as shown in the following screenshot will ensure that any costs
incurred for a project can be allocated appropriately:

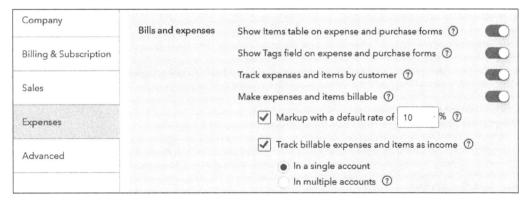

Figure 6.2 – Settings to track expenses by customer

In addition to allocating a cost to a customer, there are options to **Make expenses and items billable** and add a **Markup with a default rate** if desired. These functions can be useful if a customer needs to be recharged costs in addition to an estimate that may have already been sent.

Before we leave **Account and Settings**, we have another setting to check, one that will be useful if any of our projects will be invoiced at different stages of work being completed.

Progress Invoicing

The **Sales** tab of **Account and settings** contains the option to use **Progress Invoicing**. This feature allows you to create a large, single estimate that can be invoiced at different stages of work once completed.

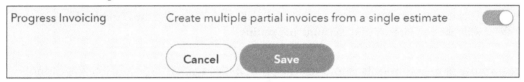

Figure 6.3 – Progress Invoicing enabled

We shall use this feature later in the *Recording Income and Expenditure against a Project* section of this chapter.

Now that we have all the appropriate settings enabled for projects, let's move forward and get a project in place for one of our customers.

Creating a Project

Using a project for a customer provides a distinct separation between different jobs you could be working on for a single customer. We'll take an example of an advertising and marketing agency.

The agency has a customer that supplies health food supplements, and they have a new protein shake that they are trying to promote. There will be design work involved to produce leaflets and website advertising banners (time costs), and the agency will use suppliers for printing and other advertising costs (bills and expenses).

The agency will produce an estimate for the work to be done. When the initial concept has been put together, 50% of the work will be invoiced, and the remainder will be charged when the job has been completed.

Before we can do any of the preceding, we need to create our project, and this is very easy to do. From the *Left Navigation panel*, select **Projects**. If this is the first project, there will be a guide to help you get started. If any projects have been created previously, there will be an option visible for **New project** on the right-hand side of the screen.

With either option selected, all that is required is a project name and the name of the customer that the project relates to; additional notes can be added if necessary.

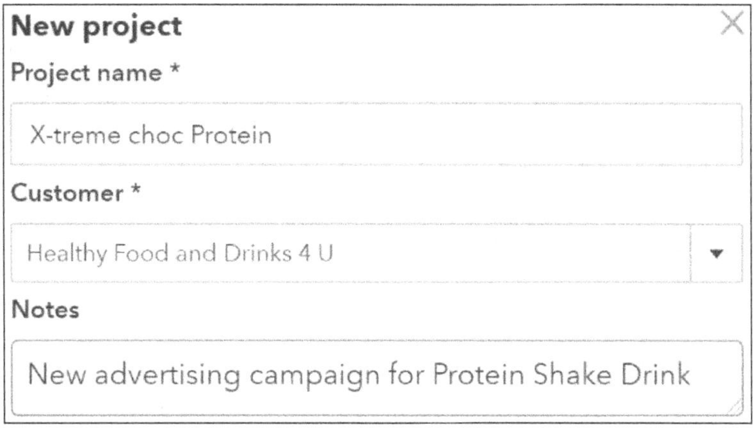

New project   ✕

Project name *

    X-treme choc Protein

Customer *

    Healthy Food and Drinks 4 U   ▼

Notes

    New advertising campaign for Protein Shake Drink

Figure 6.4 – New project information

Upon saving the newly created project, you are taken directly to the **Overview** area of the Project. This will correctly display a summary of **£0.00** against **INCOME**, **COSTS**, and **PROFIT** as no transactions would have been made at this point:

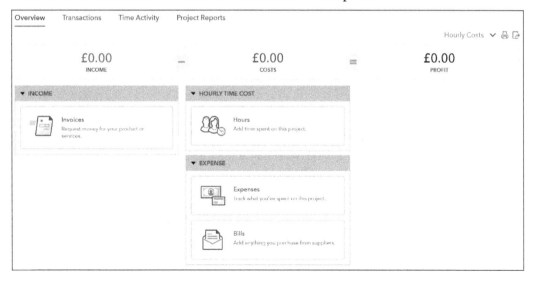

Figure 6.5 – Project overview

Below the **INCOME** and **COSTS** values within **Overview** are some shortcuts that can be used to create entries against the Project. The shortcuts can be used to raise invoices, record Bills and Expenses, or record Hours of time spent by either employees or sub-contractors.

Before we start to record any income or expenditure against this project, we need to send an estimate to the customer for the proposed work that is required. Let's look at how to do that first.

Recording Income and Expenditure against a Project

In this example, we will create an estimate that will be sent to the customer that can later be marked as accepted within QuickBooks. It's not mandatory to use estimates, but they are useful and a great place to start, so let's get stuck in.

Creating an Estimate

With a project open, click on the *drop-down action menu* labeled **Add to project**. From here, the option to create an estimate will be found:

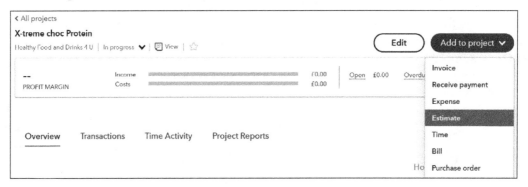

Figure 6.6 – Creating an Estimate for a Project

If you've never used estimates before, the screen is almost identical to that of an invoice. The only difference is that an invoice will have payment terms and an expected due date, while estimates can be saved with an Expiration date.

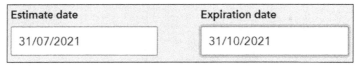

Figure 6.7 – Expiration date

An estimate is a non-posting entry. This essentially means that creating an estimate will not have any impact on the financial records of a business until it is converted into an invoice.

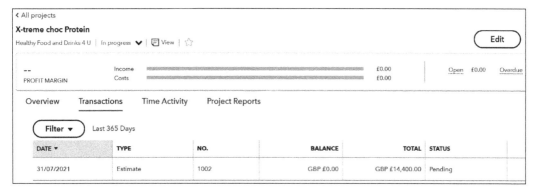

Figure 6.8 – Transactions within a Project after an Estimate is created

Figure 6.8 shows the transactions added to the project, which at this point is only the estimate. The estimate has not affected the income of this project.

You can change the status of an estimate at any time by clicking on the *drop-down action menu* against an estimate. The status options are **Pending**, **Accepted**, **Closed**, and **Rejected**. The status of an estimate will automatically change to **Closed** once it has been invoiced in full.

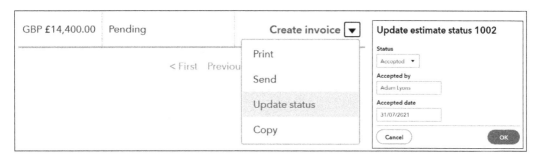

Figure 6.9 – Changing the status of an estimate

When the status is changed to **Accepted**, you can add details of the person that approved the estimate within the **Accepted by** field, along with an accepted date. However, this is not mandatory. Just changing the status alone is sufficient.

With our estimate accepted, work on the project will begin and this may involve incurring costs on behalf of the customer. Let's see what happens when we've received a couple of supplier bills that need to be associated with a project.

Allocating Bills and Expenses to a Project

Figure 6.2 displayed the settings we needed to enable if costs incurred are to be associated with a *customer/project*. With these settings in place, additional fields are available to use when either a bill, expense, or check is created.

If a cost is to be associated with a project, only the **CUSTOMER/PROJECT** field needs to be completed. However, if this is a cost that needs to be charged in addition to an original estimate, it should be marked as **BILLABLE** with a **MARKUP %** value if appropriate.

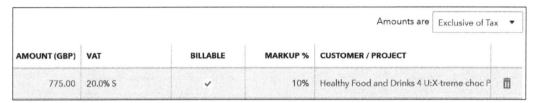

Figure 6.10 – Allocating costs to a project

> **Tip**
>
> If you are not sure whether a cost should be made Billable, it's sometimes a good idea to tick the box just in case. There is a tool that can be used to tidy up any outstanding unbilled expenses. We will look at this in the *Managing Unbilled Expenses* section.

Another cost has been added to the project we are working on, but this time the **BILLABLE** and **MARKUP %** fields have been left blank:

AMOUNT (GBP)	VAT	BILLABLE	MARKUP %	CUSTOMER / PROJECT	
2,500.00	20.0% S			Healthy Food and Drinks 4 U:X-treme choc Protein	🗑

Figure 6.11 – Allocating costs but not marking them as billable

At this stage, we have created an estimate for the project and incurred costs that have been associated with the project. Let's look at how the transactions appear within the project:

DATE ▼	TYPE	NO.	BALANCE	TOTAL	STATUS
03/08/2021	Bill		GBP £930.00	GBP £930.00	Open
03/08/2021	Billable Expense Charge		GBP £0.00	GBP £852.50	Open
01/08/2021	Bill		GBP £3,000.00	GBP £3,000.00	Open
31/07/2021	Estimate	1002	GBP £0.00	GBP £14,400.00	Pending

Figure 6.12 – Transactions against the Project

The transaction values are displayed as gross (inclusive of any VAT/Sales Tax) on this view except for the billable expense charge. This reflects the proposed recharge to the customer from the cost incurred in *Figure 6.10*. The amount of £775, plus a 10% markup of £77.50, gives a total recharge of £852.50.

It's time to create an invoice for the first 50% of our original estimate. So, let's see how that works.

Creating invoices against a Project

As with many things in QuickBooks, there are different routes you can take that will ultimately lead to the same input screen.

Figure 6.8 shows an estimate visible within the **Transactions** area of a project. On the far right, there will be the **Create invoice** option, as per *Figure 6.9* – that is the option used in this example.

With **Progress Invoicing** enabled, the screen will appear as shown in the following screenshot:

How much do you want to invoice?

○ Remaining total of all lines

◉ 50%   of each line =   £7,200.00

○ Custom amount for each line

Create invoice

Figure 6.13 – Converting an estimate to an invoice with Progress Invoicing

After selecting the option to invoice for 50% of the original estimate, we select **Create invoice**. This will open the invoice screen, where we can make edits if necessary.

Within this example, we created a billable expense, and this will appear on the right of the screen, giving us the option to add to the invoice.

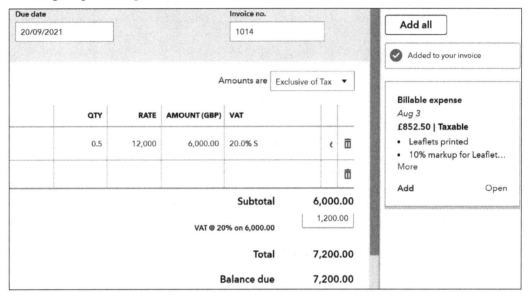

Figure 6.14 – Billable expenses appear on the invoice screen

In our current example, we should not be charging any costs in addition to the original estimate, so for now, this Billable expense will be ignored.

With some income and expenditure added to QuickBooks for our project, the **Overview** screen will look a little different.

Figure 6.15 – Project Overview

> **Note**
> All values on the overview appear as net (excluding VAT/sales tax).

At this stage, our project is reflecting a profit of £2,725. How accurate is this figure? What if we have employees working on this project? Time is money, so we should ensure that any time an employee has spent working on a project is recorded so that a realistic profit figure is reported.

Let's look at what is involved when it comes to recording employee time against a project.

Recording Time against a Project

Having employees or sub-contractors record time in QuickBooks has a few benefits. Not only will it help produce a more realistic profit figure for a project but it can also help a business owner decide how much should be charged for future similar projects. In addition, if a fixed charge hasn't been agreed against a project, time can be marked as billable and charged to the customer when it's time to raise an invoice.

Who can record time?

Anybody with access to QuickBooks can record time against a project. It's possible to create a user that can access **Time tracking only** features. New users are added from within the *gear icon*, selecting the **Manage users** option:

Add a new user

Select user type

These count toward your user limit.

○ Standard user
    You can give them full or limited access, without admin privileges.

○ Company admin
    They can see and do everything. This includes sending money, changing passwords, and adding users. Not everyone should be an admin.

These don't count toward your user limit.

○ Reports only
    They can see all reports, except ones that show payroll or contact info.

● Time tracking only
    They can add their own time sheets.

Figure 6.16 – Adding a Time tracking only user

Time tracking only users don't count toward user limits, which is a great bonus.

Before we look at how time is recorded, first we need to ensure employees and sub-contractors have been set up appropriately.

Employees and Sub-Contractors

Employees and sub-contractors can record time in QuickBooks if they have been granted access. Even without using QuickBooks Online payroll software, employees can still be listed within the **Payroll** area of QuickBooks.

The **Payroll** area is accessed from the *left-hand navigation* panel in QuickBooks. If an employee is added from here, there are options to include the cost rate (/hr) and the billing rate (/hr) for an employee:

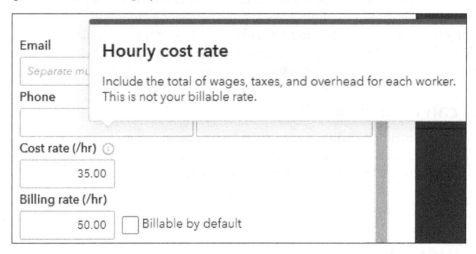

Figure 6.17 – Hourly Billing and Cost rates of an employee

It is also possible to add hourly cost rates from within the **Projects** Center where all projects are listed. In the top right-hand corner of the screen, you will find the option for **Hourly cost rate**. With that option selected, **+ Add Employee** will allow you to add further employees if they are not visible.

Figure 6.18 – Employees added from the Project Center

If an employee is listed within the project area without a **COST RATE** in place, the option to add one is available. The *pencil icon* will allow you to edit the rates. After selecting either option, the **Hourly cost rate calculator** icon is available to help put together a proposed hourly cost rate for an employee.

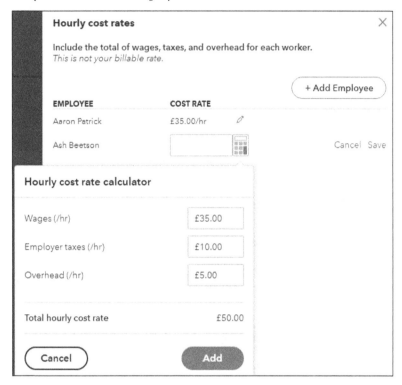

Figure 6.19 – Hourly cost rate calculator

Sub-contractors are simply suppliers/vendors in QuickBooks. When you add or edit supplier details, it is possible to edit the hourly cost and billing rates for the supplier. If bills are allocated to a project, it shouldn't be necessary to use the cost rate, as the bill itself reflects the cost of the sub-contractor.

Title	First name	Middle name	Last name	Suffix	Email		
					Separate m...		

Company
J G Web Designs

Phone

Need to add cost rates?
Cost rates help you track time costs for your projects (without touching your books). But, if you pay suppliers through bills or expenses, don't add a cost rate.

* Display name as
J G Web Designs

Other

Address map
Street

Cost rate (/hr) ⓘ   **Billing rate (/hr)**
75.00

Figure 6.20 – Hourly rates for suppliers

> **Tip**
>
> Recording time is especially useful for businesses where most of the cost relates to hours worked on a project. Service-based businesses such as accountants, lawyers, and consultants, there will be no material spend. With costs displayed that relate to the time spent, it's possible to get a much more accurate picture of any profit made on a project.

Now that we have learned how to set up hourly rates for both employees and sub-contractors, let's look at how time can be recorded.

TimeSheet Entries

Within the overview of a project, there is a shortcut below the **COSTS** value for **Hours**. It's possible to just click on this option to start recording time.

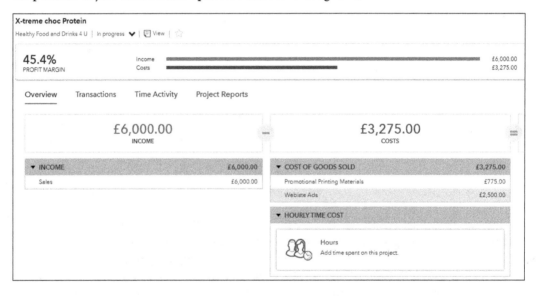

Figure 6.21 – Adding hours from the overview of a project

After selecting the option to add hours from the project overview, you will be presented with a screen where time can be recorded for a single day. The name of an employee or supplier/vendor is entered, along with cost rates and the name of the project the work done relates to. Time can be entered either as a number of hours or by using start and end times.

If work is being charged by the hour (instead of a fixed amount per an estimate), the time can be marked as billable. In the following screenshot, the **Billable** box has been left unticked as the time is not chargeable in addition to the agreed estimate:

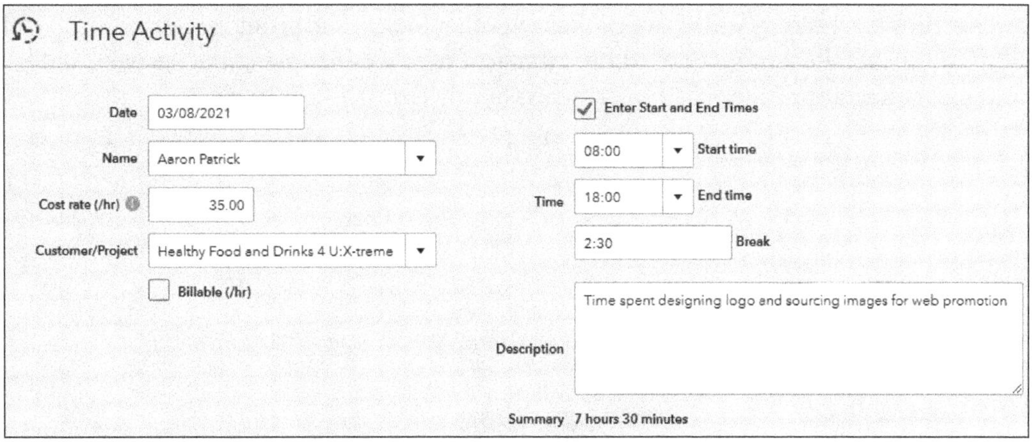

Figure 6.22 – Recording time against a project

From the **New** button found within the *left-hand navigation* panel in QuickBooks, there are time recording options found in the column for **EMPLOYEES**. **Single time activity** is the exact same option as shown in *Figure 6.22*. **Weekly Timesheet** allows all time worked in a week to be recorded on one screen.

Figure 6.23 – Using Weekly Timesheet

Now that time has been recorded, we can take another look at the profit values shown against the project. Recording time will not impact the profit and loss of the business, but it will impact the profitability of a project when hourly cost rates are in place.

Figure 6.24 – Project Overview after time recorded

Recording time for an employee has reduced the profit on this job by £612.50, because that reflects the cost of employees for the number of hours worked.

> **Note**
>
> It's not possible to record time using the QuickBooks Online mobile app. However, there are some third-party apps available that will integrate with QuickBooks that do allow for time to be recorded on a mobile device.
>
> *QuickBooks Time*, previously known as *T-Sheets*, is part of the Intuit family. Details of this app to record time and many others can be found by visiting the website www.apps.com and searching for the keyword *time*.

So far, we've created a project, raised an estimate for the project, recorded costs and time against this project, and raised an invoice for 50% of the original estimate value. If we need to keep a more watchful eye over our anticipated costs and income, creating a budget may be useful.

Let's look at how that works in QuickBooks.

Creating a Budget against a Project

To create the budget, we need to look outside the project area. By clicking the *gear icon* (top right of the main screen), **Budgeting** is found below the **TOOLS** options.

If it is the first budget, there will be a button within the center of the screen to create a budget. If a budget has been created previously, the **Add budget** option will be visible in the top right-hand corner of the budget screen.

Creating a budget is relatively straightforward. When creating the budget, the following options will be visible at the top of the screen:

- **Name***: You must give the budget a name.

- **Financial Year**: Choose the year the budget relates to.

- **Interval**: Enter budget values on either a **Monthly**, **Quarterly**, or **Yearly** basis (all options will provide pro-rata monthly values for reporting).

- **Pre-fill data?**: You can choose to bring in actual values (not usually required for projects).

- **Subdivided by**: To create a budget for a project, select **Customer**.

- **Add subdivided budget for**: Select the Project you are creating the budget for.

With the appropriate settings selected for the budget, you will be able to click **Next** in the bottom right-hand corner of the first budget screen.

On the second screen, you can add the expected income and expenditure values against the desired categories. When creating a budget for a project, there shouldn't be too many categories in use. (All amounts are entered with positive values.)

While editing a budget, there is a *list cog* on the far right of the screen. Within this option, you can change how the budget is viewed and hide any rows that are not in use.

Figure 6.25 – Hiding blank rows in a budget

Once you've added all the values for the expected income and expenditure against a budget, your screen will appear as per the following screenshot. If you are happy with the values, the budget can be saved:

ACCOUNTS	JAN-MAR	APR-JUN	JUL-SEP	OCT-DEC	TOTAL
▾ INCOME					
Sales			6,000.00	6,000.00	12,000.00
Total Income	0.00	0.00	6,000.00	6,000.00	12,000.00
▾ OTHER INCOME					
Total Other Income	0.00	0.00	0.00	0.00	0.00
▾ COST OF SALES					
Labour	0.00	0.00	500.01	499.97	999.98
Promotional Printing Materials	0.00		750.00	750.00	1,500.00
Webiste Ads	0.00		750.00	750.00	1,500.00
Total Cost of sales	0.00	0.00	2,000.01	1,999.97	3,999.98
▾ EXPENSES					
Payroll expenses	0.00		1,500.00	500.00	2,000.00
Total Expenses	0.00	0.00	1,500.00	500.00	2,000.00
▾ OTHER EXPENSE					
Total Other Expense	0.00	0.00	0.00	0.00	0.00
TOTAL NET INCOME	0.00	0.00	2,499.99	3,500.03	6,000.02

Figure 6.26 – Completed budget

All budgets that have been saved will appear on a list of budgets created. Different actions are available against saved budgets, but the one that we are most interested in is the **Run Budgets vs. Actuals report** option.

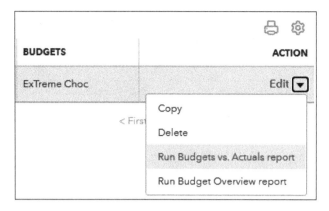

Figure 6.27 – Action menu against a budget

Selecting the **Run Budget vs. Actuals report** option will help us see how we are performing against our expectations. You will find that simply selecting this option alone will not produce the desired report we are looking for, so a little bit of customization will be required.

After selecting **Run Budgets vs. Actuals report**, we will need to select the **Customize** option found in the top right-hand corner of the screen.

In this example, two changes are being made initially:

- **Rows/Columns**: Changing **Show Grid** to display **Accounts vs. Total**
- **Filter**: Selecting **Customer**, which is the project name.

Figure 6.28 – Customizing the Budget versus Actuals report

Customizing the report in this way will provide us with a Budget versus Actuals report that will make a lot more sense visually. The following screenshot shows how the report will display with those two changes alone, but of course, there are lots of options available:

			TOTAL	
	ACTUAL	BUDGET	OVER BUDGET	% OF BUDGET
▾ Income				
Sales	6,000.00	12,000.00	-6,000.00	50.00%
Total Income	£6,000.00	£12,000.00	£ -6,000.00	50.00%
▾ Cost of Sales				
Labour		999.98	-999.98	
Promotional Printing Materials	775.00	1,500.00	-725.00	51.66667%
Webiste Ads	2,500.00	1,500.00	1,000.00	166.66667%
Total Cost of Sales	£3,275.00	£3,999.98	£ -724.98	81.87541%
GROSS PROFIT	£2,725.00	£8,000.02	£ -5,275.02	34.06241%
▾ Expenses				
Payroll expenses		2,000.00	-2,000.00	
Total Expenses	£0.00	£2,000.00	£ -2,000.00	0.00%
NET OPERATING INCOME	£2,725.00	£6,000.02	£ -3,275.02	45.41652%
NET INCOME	£2,725.00	£6,000.02	£ -3,275.02	45.41652%

Budget vs. Actuals: ExTreme Choc - FY21 P&L Customers
January - December 2021

Figure 6.29 – Completed budget versus actuals report

The report in *Figure 6.29* shows that we have invoiced 50% of our income, which is as expected. But there are other areas that are not really in line with our budget. It's not wildly out and could simply be due to timing differences or costs missed.

For now, we'll accept the figures as good, and we can check the report again in the future to make sure there has not been any significant overspend.

> **Tip**
> If you produce and customize your reports, don't forget to select **Save customization**. That way, you will be able to run the report again quickly from the **Custom reports** area within **Reports**.

Earlier on in this chapter, we incurred costs that were marked as billable. *Figure 6.10* shows a cost incurred for a project of £775 that is flagged to be recharged to the customer with a 10% markup.

If this has been marked as billable by mistake, we could simply edit the transaction and remove the tick from the **BILLABLE** box. That's fine if there is only one, but what if lots of transactions had been created incorrectly for different customers and projects?

Well, there is a little hidden tool you can use to quickly update a lot of transactions in bulk. Let's find out how.

Managing Unbilled Expenses

If you have created a bill, expense, or check and marked it as **BILLABLE**, the entry will always appear on the right-hand side of the screen when you are creating an invoice – prompting you to add the cost to your invoice.

The unbilled charge will also appear within the **Unbilled time and expenses** report that can be found within the **Project Reports** area of a project. That will only display values for the one project.

By accessing **Reports** from the *left-hand navigation* panel and searching for Unbilled charges, the report will display unbilled charges for all customers.

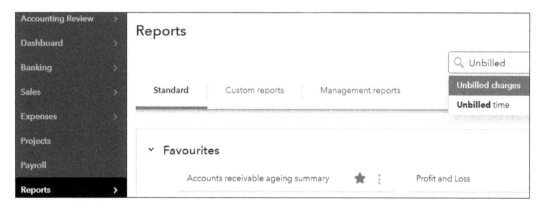

Figure 6.30 – Searching for the Unbilled charges report

After selecting the **Unbilled Charges** report, the following screenshot shows the report will default to displaying unbilled charges for all customers for all dates:

Unbilled Charges						
All Dates						
DATE	**TRANSACTION TYPE**	**NO.**	**POSTING**	**MEMO/DESCRIPTION**	**AMOUNT**	**BALANCE**
▾ Charlie Whitehead Construction						
▾ The White Horse						
01/02/2021	Billable Expense Charge		No	10% markup	150.00	150.00
01/02/2021	Billable Expense Charge		No		1,500.00	1,650.00
01/02/2021	Billable Expense Charge		No		1,500.00	3,150.00
01/02/2021	Billable Expense Charge		No	10% markup	150.00	3,300.00
Total for The White Horse					£3,300.00	
Total for Charlie Whitehead Construction					£3,300.00	
▾ Healthy Food and Drinks 4 U						
▾ X-treme choc Protein						
03/08/2021	Billable Expense Charge		No	Leaflets printed	775.00	775.00
03/08/2021	Billable Expense Charge		No	10% markup for Leaflets printed	77.50	852.50
04/08/2021	Time Charge		No		210.00	1,062.50
Total for X-treme choc Protein					£1,062.50	
Total for Healthy Food and Drinks 4 U					£1,062.50	
TOTAL					£4,362.50	

Figure 6.31 – Unbilled Charges report

The report in *Figure 6.31* shows two customers with a few Billable Expenses. Even with just these few, it would be a pain having to edit the entries and remove the tick from the billable expense box. Imagine how long that would take with a few hundred!

Using the manage billable expense tool

The tool to manage billable expenses is not found within any menus. It is only accessed by changing the address bar within the browser. Any text after the word app needs to be removed and replaced with managebillableexpense, as shown in the following screenshot:

Figure 6.32 – Changing the browser address to manage unbilled expenses

Once the browser address has been changed, a different screen will display, where you simply need to enter a date up to which QuickBooks will hide any unbilled expenses.

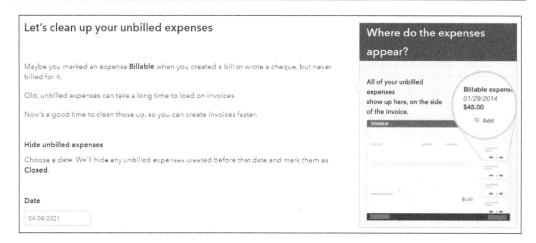

Let's clean up your unbilled expenses

Maybe you marked an expense **Billable** when you created a bill or wrote a cheque, but never billed for it.

Old, unbilled expenses can take a long time to load on invoices.

Now's a good time to clean those up, so you can create invoices faster.

Hide unbilled expenses

Choose a date. We'll hide any unbilled expenses created before that date and mark them as **Closed**.

Date

04/06/2021

Where do the expenses appear?

All of your unbilled expenses show up here, on the side of the invoice.

Billable expense
01/29/2014
$45.00

Add

Figure 6.33 – Hiding unbilled expenses

Once the date has been selected, simply click the **Save** option that will be at the bottom right of the screen. This tool simply removes the **BILLABLE** tick from the transactions that had previously been created.

Now that we've recorded transactions against a project and tidied up any expenses that were marked as billable in error, let's look at what other reports are useful when running projects.

Useful reports for Projects

Within the **Project Reports** area of a project, there are just three reports listed. These reports are handy as they are automatically filtered to report only against the project that is being viewed.

Before we look at any of the default reports, there are other reports that can be useful when using projects and can be searched for within the **Reports** Center. The search option is shown in *Figure 6.30*.

Here are a few extra reports that you can search for that may be helpful when using projects:

- **Estimates & Progress Invoicing Summary by Customer**: This report displays a list of estimates raised and the percentage invoiced against each.

- **Estimates by Customer**: This report displays a list of estimates raised, the status, who accepted the estimate and when, and the expiry date.

- **Income by Customer Summary**: This report will display a summary of the income and expenditure recorded against all customers and projects.

> **Tip**
> All these reports can be customized and filtered to display specific projects.
> This way you could show information that relates to several projects in a single
> report.

The great thing about using projects is that there are reports already in place that will
produce information specifically for the project being viewed.

Let's take a look at those now.

Default Project Reports

Within the **Project Reports** area of a project, the following three reports are available:

- **Project profitability (without time costs)**
- **Time cost by employee or supplier**
- **Unbilled time and expenses**

We looked at the last report on this list in the *Managing Unbilled Expenses* section. The
Project profitability (without time costs) report is simply a profit and loss report that
has been automatically filtered to only display values that relate to the project. However,
time costs are not included within that report so to match the values that appear on
the overview, values within the **Time cost by employee or supplier** report need to be
considered.

Let's look at what we can do to avoid having to run both reports and combine the values.

Allocating other costs to a Project

It's possible that a business could have purchased costs and materials that will be used for
multiple projects. When costs are initially incurred, they may not have been purchased for
a specific project, but as items are consumed, adjustments can be made to ensure that the
costs are reflected against a project.

First, we'll use a journal to adjust for employee time.

Using journals to adjust a project

If our project overview displays £762.50 of **HOURLY TIME COST**, this will not be visible in the **Project profitability (without time costs)** report. We can make the value appear on both the overview and the report with the following journal entry:

Currency						
GBP British Pound Sterling ▼						

Journal date					Journal no.	
05/08/2021					adjust	

	#	ACCOUNT	DEBITS (GBP)	CREDITS (GBP)	DESCRIPTION	NAME
⠿	1	Payroll expenses	762.50		charge time to project	Healthy Food and Drinks 4 U:X-treme choc Protein
⠿	2	Payroll expenses		762.50	charge time to project	

Figure 6.34 – Using a journal to adjust payroll costs on a project

Both lines 1 and 2 of the journal entry are coded to the same account category, **Payroll expenses**. This ensures the overall profit of the business is not affected. However, line 1, posting the Debit entry, contains the project details in the **NAME** column.

When viewing the Overview of a project, there is an option to switch between using **Hourly Costs** or **Payroll Expenses**, as shown in the following screenshot. With **Payroll Expenses** selected, **Hourly Time Cost** is no longer displayed:

Figure 6.35 – Using Payroll Expenses within the project overview

With our Overview, using **Payroll Expenses**, the project is showing a current profit of £7,962.50. If we run the **Project profitability (without time costs)** report, the same values are displayed.

Project Profitability for Healthy Food and Drinks 4 U's X-treme choc Protein (without time costs) All Dates	TOTAL
▾ Income	
Sales	12,000.00
Total Income	£12,000.00
▾ Cost of Sales	
Promotional Printing Materials	775.00
Webiste Ads	2,500.00
Total Cost of Sales	£3,275.00
GROSS PROFIT	£8,725.00
▾ Expenses	
Payroll expenses	762.50
Total Expenses	£762.50
NET OPERATING INCOME	£7,962.50
NET INCOME	£7,962.50

Figure 6.36 – Project profitability report agrees with the overview

So, we can see that using a journal can adjust the profit displayed on a project, but what if we need to take items out of stock or make them billable? That's not possible with a journal entry so we'll need to use a zero-total bill or expense for that.

Using a zero-total Bill to adjust a project

It's possible for us to use a bill or expense that has the same effect as a journal. By creating an entry that has a total of zero, there is no impact on the supplier or bank balance. Only the accounts used on the line items are affected.

In the following example, negative values have been recorded against **PRODUCT/ SERVICE** within **Item details**, which will reduce stock levels. A positive value has been entered against **CATEGORY**, and the **CUSTOMER/PROJECT** field is used to enter the project details:

▼ Category details

	#	CATEGORY	DESCRIPTION	AMOUNT (GBP)	BILLABLE	MARKUP %	CUSTOMER / PROJECT
⠿	1	Promotional Printing Materials	Photo paper charged to job	20.00	✓	10%	Healthy Food and Drinks 4 U:X-treme choc Protein
⠿	2						

[Add lines] [Clear all lines]

▼ Item details

	#	PRODUCT/SERVICE	DESCRIPTION	QTY	RATE	AMOUNT (GBP)	BILLABLE	MARKUP %	SALES AMT
⠿	1	High Quality Photo Paper	Quality Photo Paper	-100	0.20	-20.00			

Figure 6.37 – Zero-total bill

The supplier's name used in this example was `Contra adjustments`. With a £20 positive entry and a £20 negative entry, the total balances to £0.00. The **No VAT** VAT code can be used as this entry is being used as an internal adjustment.

The entry can be made in the exact same way using an expense. It's not mandatory to use a supplier name with an expense, but a payment account will be required. The payment total will be £0.00.

This chapter has all been about using projects; however, before this feature was available, sub-customers could be used. What are the main differences?

Well, let's find out about these differences in the next section.

Sub-Customers versus Projects

Projects provide great visibility when checking the profitability of work done for a customer without the need to customize any reports. *Figure 5.6* in the previous chapter, *Chapter 5, Handling Client Money*, shows how sub-customers can be created.

There are no limits on how many sub-customers you can create, but *nesting* is restricted to five levels: the main customer and up to four sub-levels.

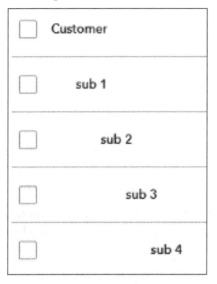

Figure 6.38 – Maximum nesting of customers

This sort of nesting that will associate the lowest level with those above is not available when using a project. Add-ons or revisions of projects need to be treated separately, or just contained within the one project.

Also, when using sub-customers, it is possible to use a different address for each sub-customer by changing the option from **Bill with parent** to **Bill this customer**.

Figure 6.39 – Using a different address with a sub-customer

This option can be useful if you just want to group customers for reporting purposes. A training event could be set up as the main customer. All those that are due to attend could be set up as sub-customers and all will have invoices sent to their own address.

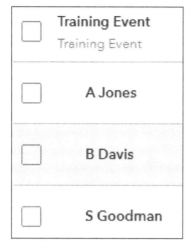

Figure 6.40 – Different customers attached to an event

As you can see, QuickBooks offers a lot of flexibility when it comes to working with customers and how they can be grouped. You could choose to use a combination of sub-customers and Projects.

A construction company could have several site offices that all have different addresses, and a project could be linked to one of those offices.

Figure 6.41 – Using projects with sub-customers

The screenshot in *Figure 6.41* shows AA Construction Services as the customer. London Branch is the sub-customer, and Red Square Housing Development is the project.

We've covered a lot of ground throughout this chapter, so let's have a quick recap.

Summary

Projects can make it easy to check the profitability of work carried out for a customer that relates to a specific job or task. Throughout this chapter, we have done the following:

- Created a project
- Recorded income and expenditure against a project
- Prepared a budget for a project
- Recorded time and adjusted other costs against our project
- Run various reports
- Looked at how sub-customers compare with projects

As you've learned, there are lots of options available, so you can really tailor QuickBooks so that it meets the needs of a business.

What if one of your customers operates in a different country and they wish for invoices to be sent in a currency used by that country? The next chapter, *Chapter 7, Handling Foreign Currencies in QuickBooks Online*, looks at all of the settings required, and how transactions are recorded using the **Multicurrency** feature.

7
Handling Foreign Currencies in QuickBooks Online

If you are working within a business that needs to deal with customers and suppliers located in different countries, there is a high chance those other businesses will operate in a different currency to that of your own.

It could be that although a business has customers based in different countries, the policy of the business is to always raise invoices using the currency of their country only. For example, a UK-based business may charge all customers in GB Pounds Sterling, regardless of where the customer is based.

However, if a business raises invoices using the currency of the customer, the value of an invoice that's sent in a foreign currency can fluctuate by the time it is paid.

Let's say an invoice has been raised for 30,000 USD and that the rate was 0.67. This would give a GBP value of £20,000 against the invoice. If the rate were to change to 0.77 by the time it was paid, the same amount in dollars would be worth £23,100. The business would gain on this transaction.

However, it works both ways, and variable exchange rates could harm a business and could sometimes cause it to lose money. Therefore, businesses need to monitor exchange gains and losses. In some instances, this can dictate how the sales of products and services are priced for foreign customers.

This will be the same for suppliers too; if the exchange rates are working against a business, further negotiations may be required before future purchases are made.

For users of QuickBooks Online *Essentials* and above, the **Multicurrency** feature can be enabled, which can simplify the process of dealing with foreign customers and suppliers.

Throughout this chapter, you'll learn how to:

- Enable the Multicurrency settings
- Set up banks, customers, suppliers (vendors) in foreign currencies
- Edit foreign currency exchange rates
- Record transactions using foreign currencies
- Check gains and losses on foreign currency transactions
- Use extra control accounts for foreign currencies and why
- Revalue foreign currency balances
- Edit reports for foreign currency transactions

Ensuring that you fully understand how multicurrency works within QuickBooks Online is important. Businesses that operate with several foreign bank accounts, as well as with customers and suppliers using different currencies, might find that things will get a little bit untidy if transactions have not been matched or allocated correctly. Before we start recording any foreign currency transactions, we need to check that the relevant settings are in place. Without further ado, let's start by looking into Multicurrency settings.

Enabling Multicurrency settings

In this section, you will learn how to do the following:

- Enable **Multicurrency**
- Set up customers and suppliers that operate in foreign currencies
- Set up a bank account in QuickBooks that uses a foreign currency

Within the **Advanced** section of **Account and Settings**, you will find the option to enable **Multicurrency** using a little slider button. With the toggle enabled, the **Multicurrency** settings will appear, as shown in the following screenshot:

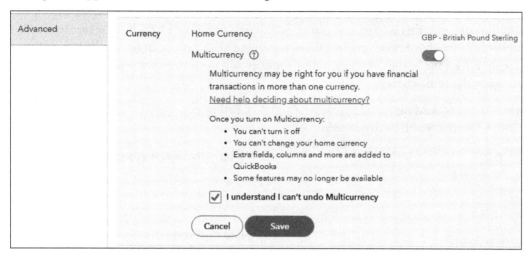

Figure 7.1 – Multicurrency settings

Check that your **Home Currency** is correct before saving the settings – this is the currency your company generally operates in and needs to report against. It cannot be changed later.

> **Important Note**
> Multicurrency is a permanent setting that cannot be disabled once the feature has been enabled. If you don't have many foreign currency transactions throughout the year, you may find that manually converting values so that they reflect your currency will be sufficient.

Now that **Multicurrency** has been enabled, our customers and suppliers that operate in foreign currencies need to be set up appropriately.

Settings for Customers, Suppliers (Vendors), and Banks

Once customers, suppliers, and other balance sheet categories have been set up using a specific currency, this is fixed and can't be changed later. If you have been recording supplier bills that have been sent in a foreign currency but have been manually converting values to reflect the home currency, a new supplier will need to be created if you wish to start using the **Multicurrency** feature.

If you choose to **Add new** while creating a supplier **Bill** or customer **Invoice**, the option to choose a **Currency** will be displayed:

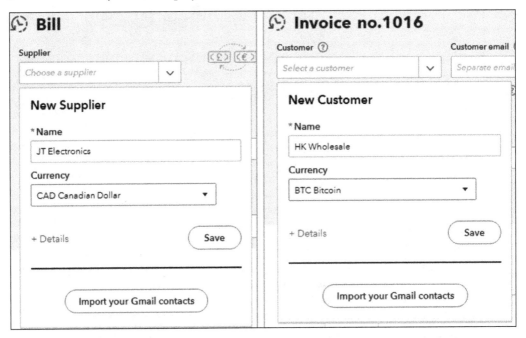

Figure 7.2 – Adding a new supplier and customer using different currencies

If you're adding customers from within *Customer Center*, the **Currency** option can be found within the **Payment and billing** tab of the customer record. When adding a supplier from within the *Supplier Center*, the **Currency** field will be visible at the bottom right of the screen.

Some businesses may deal with foreign customers and suppliers but choose to only operate with a bank account in their home currency. However, others may have bank accounts set up in different currencies.

We can create bank accounts in QuickBooks Online that use foreign currencies that can make reconciling a foreign bank account much easier. Let's look at how they are created.

Setting up Bank Accounts

When you create a new bank account within the chart of accounts for QuickBooks, you will also have the option to use a specific currency:

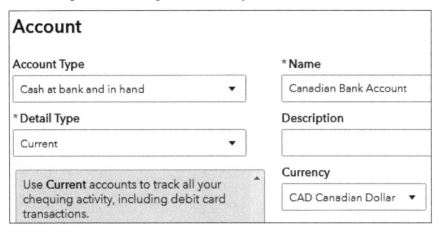

Figure 7.3 – New bank in a foreign currency

> **Tip**
>
> This setting is not just for banks. Other assets and liabilities can be set up in a different currency if required.

At this point, we have all our settings in place. But what exchange rate is being used to calculate gains/losses on foreign currency transactions? Let's find out next.

Editing Foreign currency Exchange Rates

In this section, you will learn how:

- Exchange rates are updated automatically
- Exchange rates can be edited from the list of currencies in use
- Exchange rates can be edited while creating a transaction

Once the **Multicurrency** feature has been enabled, **Currencies** will become visible within the **LISTS** column, which can be accessed from the *gear icon*:

CURRENCY	GBP	LAST UPDATED	ACTION
USD - United States Dollar	0.720812	07/08/2021 at 08:01 am British Summer Time	Edit currency exchange ▼
CAD - Canadian Dollar	0.574345	07/08/2021 at 08:01 am British Summer Time	Edit currency exchange ▼
EUR - Euro	0.847817	07/08/2021 at 08:01 am British Summer Time	Edit currency exchange ▼

Figure 7.4 – List of currencies in use

Most exchange rates are automatically updated daily or every 4 hours. If you don't wish to use the rates that are automatically provided, you can use the **Edit currency exchange rate** option, where you can choose to apply **Your rate**.

When creating any transaction that involves using a foreign currency, you can choose to override the rate provided. This can be seen in the following screenshot:

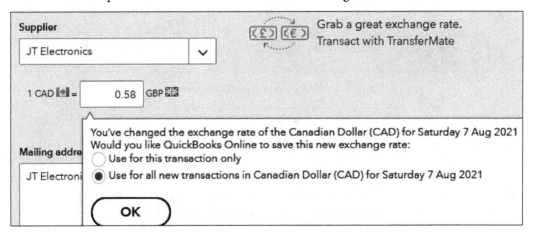

Figure 7.5 – Editing the exchange rate within a transaction

When you do override a rate, you can choose if the exchange rate applies only to that transaction. If further entries are going to be made on that day, you can ensure that they will also use the same rate. This will update the currency list shown in *Figure 7.4*.

Now that multicurrency has been set up and we understand how rates are applied, let's start entering some transactions. We will look at some basic entries first.

Recording Transactions in Foreign Currencies

When transactions are recorded using a foreign currency, we don't usually need to do anything differently compared to when we are creating an entry in our home currency. However, some additional information will be displayed on the screen. This includes the following:

- The foreign currency in use

- The exchange rate in place (which can be edited)

- The foreign value and home currency value

Let's take an example of a customer invoice. The *home currency* is in **Great British Pounds Sterling** (**GBP**), while the customer operates in **Canadian Dollars** (**CAD**). This invoice will be sent in Canadian Dollars – all the details will be entered to reflect this. In this example, the sales total is 2,000 CAD.

Toward the top left of the input screen of an invoice, you will see the currency and rate, as shown in *Figure 7.5*. At the bottom right of the screen, where the summary totals are displayed, the home currency and foreign currency values will be visible:

Subtotal	2,000.00
VAT @ 0% on 2,000.00	0.00
Total (CAD)	2,000.00
Total (GBP)	1,152.33
Balance due (CAD)	2,000.00

Figure 7.6 – Home currency and foreign currency values on an invoice

This entry is the first for this customer. The balance shown within the customer center will reflect the foreign currency (CAD):

CURRENCY	OPEN BALANCE ▼	ACTION
CAD	$2,000.00	Receive payment ▼

Figure 7.7 – Foreign customer displayed within the customer center

If we run the `Accounts Receivable Ageing Summary` report, the home currency value will be displayed:

	CURRENT
T J Import and Exports	1,152.33

Figure 7.8 – Home currency value shown on the accounts receivable aging summary report

It is possible to produce a report that will display both home currency and foreign currency values on a single report. We will look at how that can be done toward the end of this chapter, in the *Editing reports for multicurrency transactions* section.

The current example has used an exchange rate of `0.576165` as of `July 31, 2021`. This has resulted in `$2,000` equating to `£1,152.33`. *Take a note of this value as we will refer to this again shortly.*

Keeping things simple, the customer paid this invoice in full on `August 8, 2021`. At this stage, the business has no foreign bank accounts in place, and the funds have come into the home currency (GBP) bank account. The exchange rate has changed to `0.573808`. A payment of `$2,000` has a value of `£1,147.62`. This will result in a small loss due to exchange rate variances.

Using the **Receive payment** option to mark the invoice as paid (accessed from the **New** button or *customer center*), a loss of `£4.71` (`£1,152.33` less `£1,147.62`) will automatically be adjusted for the **Exchange Gain or Loss** category, which will appear on the **Profit and Loss** reports for the business.

At this point, all the entries have been created manually. Now, let's look at what we'd do if the payment from the customer had appeared within the bank feed.

Matching Foreign Currency Transactions in the feed of the Home Currency Bank Account

Our customer, `T J Imports & Exports`, has paid the business `$2,000`, but this appears on the bank feed as `£1,150`:

	DATE	DESCRIPTION ▲	CATEGORY OR MATCH	VAT	AMOUNT	ACTION
☐	08/08/2021	T J Imports Exports	Materials		£1,150.00	Add

Figure 7.9 – Foreign payment received in the home currency bank account

Receive payment has already been entered, so we need to use the option to **Find match**, which can be accessed when clicking on the entry that appears on the bank feed.

Once this has been done, it's necessary to select the **Foreign currency** option:

Show	Search	From	To
All ▾	🔍	10/05/2021	18/08/2021

○ Home currency ● Foreign currency

Select transaction to match

	DATE	TYPE		REF NUMBER
●	08/08/2021	Payment		

Matching this payment to the downloaded bank item will update the home currency amount to £1,150.00 and the exchange rate to 0.575.

Figure 7.10 – Matching foreign currency transaction

In the example, the bank has applied an exchange rate of 0.575. Matching this transaction will override the rate that was used when the entry was manually created and will reduce the loss on exchange rate differences to £2.33 (£1,152.33 less £1,150) *These are the GBP values that were calculated previously.*

So far, we have looked at creating an invoice in a foreign currency but receiving payment into our main home currency bank account. Now, let's look at what happens if the payment is received directly into a bank using the same foreign currency as the customer.

> **Note**
> If a transaction on a bank feed relates to a single **Invoice** or **Bill**, the *open balance* could be matched without you having to use **Receive Payment** first.

Matching foreign currency transactions with a foreign currency bank account

In the following example, we have $2,000 showing as funds received in our Canadian bank account. This could either match an outstanding open balance or match a payment if it's already been entered manually:

☐	DATE ▲	DESCRIPTION	CATEGORY OR MATCH	VAT	AMOUNT	ACTION
☐	08/08/2021	T J Imports Exports	1 match found Payment 08/08/2021 $2,000.00 T J Import and Exports		$2,000.00	Match

Figure 7.11 – Foreign payment received in a bank account of the same currency

That's nice and easy – one click, and we are all sorted.

With that, we've looked at a customer where a payment has been received against one invoice. But what happens if a foreign customer sends one payment that is for several invoices? Let's look at what we need to do.

Matching a single payment for multiple foreign invoices

Again, in this example, the home currency is GBP and the customer is using CAD, but this time, there are four unpaid invoices:

☐	DATE ▼	TYPE	BALANCE
☐	30/07/2021	Invoice	$500.00
☐	15/07/2021	Invoice	$500.00
☐	30/06/2021	Invoice	$500.00
☐	15/06/2021	Invoice	$500.00
		Total (GBP)	£1,158.77

Figure 7.12 – Multiple foreign invoices unpaid

We've received $2,000 on August 8, 2021, but regardless of whether the funds come into the Canadian or UK GBP bank account, we will need to enter the transaction manually first. We can only match the payment and not the combined unpaid balances.

This is because of the following reasons:

- If a foreign payment is received in the home currency bank account, when the foreign currency option is selected, it is only possible to select one transaction at a time.

- If the payment is received in the foreign bank account, the **Find match** option is not available.

Using this example, $2,000 will need to be entered using the **Receive payment** option from the **New** button or from within the *Customer center*. All the invoices will be marked as paid on this entry:

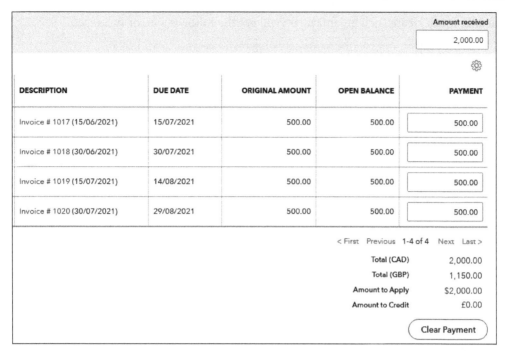

Figure 7.13 – Multiple invoices paid using the Receive payment option

With the manual **Receive payment** recorded, this would **Match** the bank feed value if funds were paid into the foreign bank account. When payment is received in the home currency bank account, a **Find match** that's using a **Foreign currency** would be used.

> **Note**
> The examples we've looked at are related to customers. The same principles apply to suppliers/vendors when matching foreign currency bills and expenses.

Let's imagine that our Canadian customer was given the wrong bank account details when we advised them on how to make a payment. Instead of the payment coming into the Canadian bank account, funds have been received into the USD bank account.

This creates a further complication, so let's look at how we can resolve it.

Receiving a foreign payment in a different foreign currency bank account

QuickBooks Online does not allow you to use two foreign currencies at the same time. If the home currency is GBP, you will not be able to record the payment for a CAD customer in a USD bank account.

If you attempt to create such an entry, you will get the following error message:

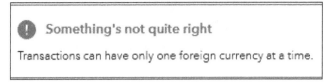

Figure 7.14 – Error message when attempting to use two foreign currencies

In scenarios like these, you will need to use an additional *Control account*. This will be used both against the customer and as an entry as it appears on the bank account.

An extra chart of account category will need to be set up with **Account Type** set to **Cash at bank and in hand** and **Detail Type** set to **Current**. In the following example, **Name** has been set to FX Control Account:

Figure 7.15 – FX Control Account

> **Note**
> This account must be created using the *home currency* of the business.

Using our earlier example, the customer that owes 2,000 CAD has made a payment into our USD bank account. This equates to 1,600 USD. As our home account is using **GBP**, we cannot mix the **USD** and **CAD** currencies on the same entry.

First of all, we will record the invoice, as paid in full, in our FX Control Account, which is set up in our home currency of **GBP**:

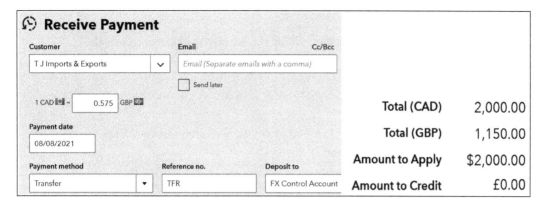

Figure 7.16 – Receiving payment in the control account

Here, we can see that by receiving the payment in our GBP FX Control Account, a rate of 0.575 has been applied that results in a GBP value of £1,150 marked as received.

We need to make note of the GBP value as we can ensure that the same is applied when accounting for the funds that have been received in the USD bank account:

08/08/2021	T J Imports Exports		08/08/2021	T J Imports Exports
○ Categorise ● Record as transfer			○ Categorise ● Record as transfer	
Transferred from *			Transferred from *	
Select an account ▼			FX Control Account ▼	
Memo			Memo	
T J Imports & Exports			T J Imports & Exports	
Currency exchange conversion ⑦			Currency exchange conversion ⑦	
1153.62 GBP 0.721012 1600 USD			1150 GBP 0.71875 1600 USD	
BANK DETAIL T J Imports & Exports			**BANK DETAIL** T J Imports & Exports	

Figure 7.17 – Recording the funds received in the wrong foreign bank account

The preceding figure displays two screenshots. The funds that have been received must be recorded as a **Transfer**. The left screenshot shows how an entry will appear before any edits are made. The right screenshot shows how the edited entry will appear before accepting the entry within the bank feed. We have made the following changes here:

- Selected FX Control Account within **Transferred from***
- Changed the home currency value in **GBP** to that received in *Figure 7.16*

> **Note**
>
> Amending the home currency value within the transfer, to ensure it reflects the same as that recorded against the payment, will ensure the balance within the FX Control Account is £0.00.
>
> This avoids the need to create journal entries to correct the balance due to exchange rate differences.
>
> Changing the value in this way is useful when you're creating any transfers between home currency and foreign currency bank accounts.

Although this entry is being created from a bank feed, the same entry can be made using **Transfer**. This can be found below the **OTHER** options, which can be accessed from the **New** button:

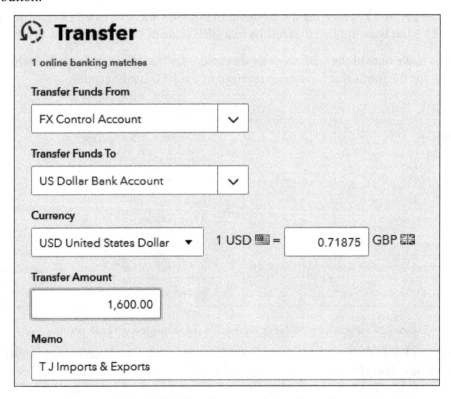

Figure 7.18 – Transfer screen (manual entry)

> **Reminder**
>
> As we mentioned previously, although a foreign customer is being used in the examples shown, the same adjustments can be made when working with foreign suppliers.

So far, we've only considered the different exchange rates that are applied when creating entries using foreign currencies. Sticking with the same example, what would we do if our bank had deducted a bank charge from the payment?

Let's see what adjustments are required.

Making further adjustments when working with Foreign Currencies

Figure 7.9 showed that we received £1,150 relating to the unpaid balance of our Canadian customer, who owed $2,000. In this example, we have received £1,140 because our bank has deducted a charge of £10 to handle this transaction.

There are a couple of ways that we can deal with this. If we were not originally aware of this charge, we may already have matched the payment, as shown previously, but the value that was adjusted for the **Exchange Gain or Loss** account would be incorrect by £10.

A journal entry will be the quickest way to adjust for this. In the following screenshot, £10 has been added to the **DEBITS** column against **Bank charges**, and £10 has been added to **CREDITS** against **Exchange Gain or Loss**:

Currency

GBP British Pound Sterling ▼

Journal date						Journal no.	
08/08/2021						adjust	

	#	ACCOUNT	DEBITS (GBP)	CREDITS (GBP)	DESCRIPTION	NAME
⠿	1	Bank charges	10.00		Bank charge - TJ Imports / Exports	T J Import and Exports
⠿	2	Exchange Gain or Loss		10.00	Bank charge TJ Imports / Exports	T J Import and Exports

Figure 7.19 – Adjusting for bank charges

Adding details within the **DESCRIPTION** and **NAME** fields of a journal is not mandatory, but it can be useful when you're running reports and reviewing data later.

> **Tip**
>
> Journal entries can be created in different currencies. If you know that a charge of 20 Canadian Dollars has been applied, **Currency** can be changed, and the appropriate **Journal entry** can be created.

If it's known that a charge has been deducted before the receipt against the customer has been recorded, we can adjust it there and then. When working with entries on the bank feed for funds received from a customer, we will need to create a **Deposit**. Before coding the transaction, we also need to use the option to **Split**. The following screen will appear:

Figure 7.20 – Splitting the transaction into different accounts for bank charges

Creating the entry shown in the preceding screenshot will create a payment on account against our customer and account for any charges that are deducted at the same time. The following edits are required when creating this entry for a foreign customer:

- Amend **Currency** to reflect that used by the customer.

- Add the customer to **RECEIVED FROM**.

- Add details to **DESCRIPTION** (not mandatory but can be useful).

- No VAT/Sales Tax should be applied to the amount received.

- Apply VAT/tax coding to the bank charge if appropriate.

- Enter the full amount to be allocated to the customer before any charges were deducted in the foreign currency in the **AMOUNT** column, on the first line, using the Debtors **CATEGORY**, along with the relevant currency; for example, Debtors - CAD.

- Enter a negative value to reflect the bank charge that was deducted on the second line in the **AMOUNT** column by using a relevant **CATEGORY**, such as Bank Charges.

> **Important Note**
>
> At time of writing this book, it was discovered there is a bug in QuickBooks. When splitting a deposit, the negative line may be saved with a sales tax code even if a purchase tax code is selected. Please check these entries carefully - opening and editing will correct the entry.

Once saved, this entry will correct the customer balance, but it will not mark invoices as paid. The following screenshot shows the outstanding balances against the customer:

Transaction List	Projects	Customer Details	

Batch actions ▼   Filter ▼

	DATE ▲	TYPE	BALANCE	TOTAL
☐	15/06/2021	Invoice	$500.00	$500.00
☐	30/06/2021	Invoice	$500.00	$500.00
☐	15/07/2021	Invoice	$500.00	$500.00
☐	30/07/2021	Invoice	$500.00	$500.00
☐	08/08/2021	Deposit	-$2,000.00	-$2,000.00

Figure 7.21 – Unmatched balances against the customer

Selecting the option to receive payment against any of the unpaid invoices will open the **Receive Payment** screen. All unallocated amounts will automatically be ticked.

Invoices and any other debit entries appear in the top half of the screen. Credit notes and deposits will appear at the bottom of the screen.

The total of the entry must be zero. If there were any unpaid invoices ticked that hadn't been paid, you must remove them from the selection until the total equals 0.00.

As this entry should total zero, it's a good idea to record the transaction in **FX Control Account**:

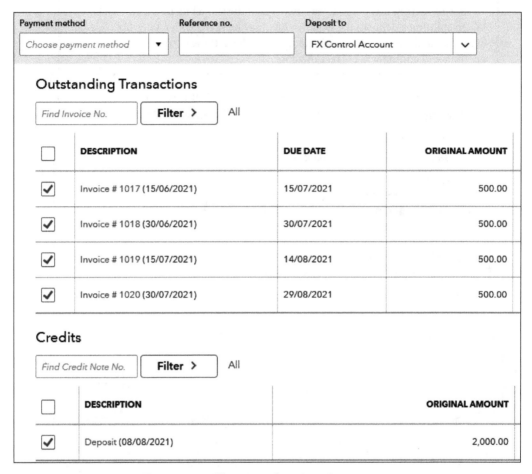

Figure 7.22 – Allocating a deposit against invoices

Once the entry has been made, you will see that a **Payment** of $0.00 has been recorded, the **BALANCE** details against **Invoices**, and that **Deposit** has been adjusted to $0.00:

DATE ▼	TYPE	BALANCE	TOTAL
09/08/2021	Payment	$0.00	$0.00
08/08/2021	Deposit	$0.00	-$2,000.00
30/07/2021	Invoice	$0.00	$500.00
15/07/2021	Invoice	$0.00	$500.00
30/06/2021	Invoice	$0.00	$500.00
15/06/2021	Invoice	$0.00	$500.00

Figure 7.23 – Balances matched against a zero payment

When reviewing foreign currency balances in QuickBooks, we may come across unpaid balances that reflect entries that were made many months ago. The rate of exchange that was in place may have changed a lot since. In such instances, a revaluation exercise may be useful.

Revaluation of Foreign Currency Balances in QuickBooks

All foreign currency exchange rates are held historically in QuickBooks, and as we have learned already, these rates may change daily. Exchange gains/losses are calculated automatically at the point of payment.

When an invoice has been created for a foreign customer, a rate stored in QuickBooks will be used to calculate the *Home Currency Value*. If several months have passed, and the balance of that invoice remains unpaid, the value of that invoice in the home currency may have increased or decreased.

In this section, you will learn how to use the tools within QuickBooks to revalue foreign currency balances and how those revaluations impact the financial reports.

Within the *drop-down* **ACTION** menu of any currency listed within **Currencies**, you will find the option to **Revalue currency**:

Figure 7.24 – The Revalue currency option

Let's take an example where our home currency is GBP, and we are going to revalue any balances held in Canadian dollars. There are two Canadian balances in place, both of which were created on April 1, 2021:

- $5,000 transferred into the Canadian bank account

- $5,000 owed against a Canadian customer invoice

The exchange rate on April 1 was 0.576283, which meant each balance equated to a value of £2,881.42.

The date of the revaluation is August 9, 2021, and the exchange rate is now 0.574289. It is possible to use a **Custom rate** instead of the **Market rate** value held in QuickBooks:

NAME	CAD BALANCE	BALANCE (GBP)	REVALUED (GBP)	EXCHANGE GAIN/LOSS (GBP)
Canadian Bank Account	5,000.00	2,881.42	2,871.45	-9.97
Debtors - CAD	5,000.00	2,881.42	2,871.45	-9.97

Figure 7.25 – Revaluing the currency

Using the tool to **Revalue currency**, the current **BALANCE** and **REVALUED** balances are displayed, along with the calculated **EXCHANGE GAIN/LOSS**. Both **Debtors – CAD** and **Canadian Bank Account** held the same balances as were created on the same day, so as expected, the **GAIN/LOSS** calculations are also the same.

Let's see what happens when the option to **Revalue and save** is selected.

A **Journal Entry** is automatically created because of the revaluation. You will find that where bank or credit cards held in a foreign currency are revalued, the journal will contain values to reflect the revised balances.

Where debtors or suppliers/vendors are revalued, a placeholder **Journal Entry** of 0.00 will be made:

Currency				
GBP British Pound Sterling 1 CAD ▮▮ = 0.574289 GBP ▮▮				
Journal date				Journal no.
09/08/2021				

	#	ACCOUNT	DEBITS (GBP)	CREDITS (GBP)	DESCRIPTION
⠿	1	Exchange Gain or Loss	9.97		
⠿	2	Canadian Bank Account		9.97	
⠿	3	Debtors - CAD	0.00		This is a placeholder for you to keep track of the date you revalued a currency and the exchange rate you used. Reports use this exchange rate to calculate unrealised gains and losses.

Figure 7.26 – Journal created from the currency revaluation

The reason why a placeholder entry is made against a customer or supplier is because at this stage, we are calculating what the gain or loss on that balance may be in the future. Gains/losses are always calculated at the point of payment. Until payment is received against a customer balance, or a supplier bill is paid, we will not truly know what the actual gain or loss on a foreign balance will be.

However, because the journal entry displays 0.00, we can run reports that will display our **unrealized gain or loss**.

When we run either a **Profit and Loss Report** or a **Balance Sheet Report**, the option to **Show unrealized gain or loss** will become available to us:

Figure 7.27 – The Show unrealized gain or loss option

When a **Balance Sheet Report** is viewed, `Debtor balances` will reflect the revalued amounts if the option to **Show unrealized gain or loss** is selected. **Profit and Loss Report** will display both **Exchange Gain or Loss** and **Unrealized Gain or Loss** on separate lines:

▼ Other Expenses	
Unrealised Gain or Loss	9.97
Exchange Gain or Loss	9.97

Figure 7.28 – Separate entries for the gains and losses reported in P&L

> **Note**
> The Trial Balance Report will only display actual **Exchange Gain or Loss** values. Should you wish to account for the unrealized values when preparing year-end accounts, you may need to create journal entries to adjust for any provisions required.

When running reports in QuickBooks, in most instances, only the home currency values are displayed. If you need to pay suppliers/vendors that use foreign currencies, it can make life easier to have the foreign balance values visible.

Now, let's look at how we can customize a report so that we can see all the information that we need.

Editing reports to display Foreign Currency values

When it's time to review reports that include entries that have been recorded in a foreign currency, balances report in the home currency by default. Imagine that you have suppliers in different currencies. Customizing reports can make life so much easier when checking the foreign amounts that are due to be paid.

It's not possible to customize all reports, and reports that display a summary will often only be reported in the home currency. If we run an **Accounts Payable Ageing Summary** report, we are limited regarding the customizations we can make.

However, if we run an **Accounts Payable Ageing Detail** or **Unpaid Bills** report, a lot more options become available when it comes to customization.

Let's take the **Unpaid Bills** report as an example. Using the **Customize** option, we can make some simple changes, as follows:

- **Filter**: Select the supplier/vendor you wish to generate a report against.
- **Rows/Columns**: Add columns for **Currency** and **Foreign Open Balance** (remove any unwanted columns).
- **Header/Footer**: Change the title of the report.

These options and many more can be found when you wish to **Customize** a report. This option is always shown in the top right-hand corner of the screen when viewing a report. With our customizations in place, we can **Run report**:

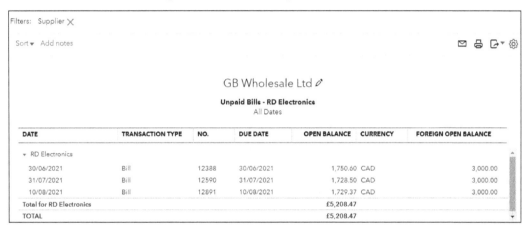

Figure 7.29 – Customized Unpaid Bills report with foreign currencies

The preceding screenshot clearly shows the **CURRENCY** type used by the supplier, together with **FOREIGN OPEN BALANCE** owed against each **Bill** and **OPEN BALANCE** owed in the home currency.

The same levels of customization are available in the following reports:

- **Profit and Loss Detail**
- **Supplier Balance Detail**
- **Open Invoices**
- **Sales by Customer Detail**
- **Transaction Detail by Account**

If a report provides details on a line-by-line basis for a transaction, a significant amount of customization options are available.

Hopefully, this chapter has helped provide you with a better understanding of how the Multicurrency feature works within QuickBooks Online. Let's quickly recap what has been covered in this chapter.

Summary

The Multicurrency feature in QuickBooks Online can save you a lot of time when you're working with foreign customers and suppliers on a regular basis. In this chapter, we learned how:

- To put the required settings in place to use the multicurrency feature
- Gains/Losses are calculated when payments are made or received
- Rates of exchange can be edited
- To create a work-around when trying to account for two foreign currencies simultaneously
- The revaluation of foreign currency balances work
- Reports can be customized to display both home currency and foreign currency balances

The Multicurrency feature is just one of many tools you can use to help you get the most out of QuickBooks Online. In the next chapter, we'll be looking at a few reports that will help you follow the best practices when reviewing financial records.

Section 3 – Reviewing and Reporting Data in QuickBooks Online

Whatever type of organization is using QuickBooks, there will come a time to check whether the information recorded in QuickBooks is correct. This could be just once a year when it's time to prepare tax returns, or much more frequently.

Regularly reviewing and reporting in QuickBooks will help to spot any errors being made in the way data is being entered, and hopefully prevent mistakes from happening in the future. When financial information is checked regularly, producing accounts and tax returns at the end of a financial period is made easier.

This section comprises the following chapters:

- *Chapter 8, Best Practices When Reviewing Financial Records*
- *Chapter 9, Enhancing the Consistency of Your Financial Statements*
- *Chapter 10, Reconciling the Balance Sheet*
- *Chapter 11, Closing the Year-End, the Audit Log, and More*

8
Best Practices When Reviewing Financial Records

The first two chapters of this book covered topics that could be useful to all business types. These included checking that opening balances had been set up correctly, and a few small tips that can be useful when using QuickBooks day to day.

In chapters 3-7, we looked at specific business types and provided some detailed advice on the use of the Projects and Multicurrency features.

The last four chapters of this book are useful for all business types. Entering information into QuickBooks can be pretty easy, and if we are using any automated tools such as Bank Rules, it is really important to check that entries are being made exactly as expected.

In this chapter, we are going to start reviewing the data held in our QuickBooks Online company file. You will learn the following:

- How frequently, and when is the best time, to review financial records
- Standard accounting principles and concepts
- What reports to check regularly and what to look out for
- Common errors to check that can affect income and expenditure reported
- How to fix some common errors affecting income and expenditure

It's important to understand what we are looking for when reviewing different reports in QuickBooks. Errors made in either data entry, or the initial setup of QuickBooks, can really distort the values that are produced on the profit and loss report.

Let's talk about the frequency and best time to review your reports.

How frequently should we review our financial records in QuickBooks Online?

Before we can fully answer this question, we must really take the following into consideration:

- The size of the business
- The number of employees
- The volume of transactions that flow through the business
- The number of bank accounts in place
- Who is ultimately responsible for the day-to-day bookkeeping?

As a bare minimum, it would be advisable to review figures within QuickBooks monthly. Without going into detail at this stage, this would, at the very least, involve performing a full bank reconciliation. This means agreeing that the bank balance shown in QuickBooks fully ties back to a balance shown on a bank statement at a specified date.

> **Important Note**
> The reconciliation of bank accounts and other areas of the balance sheet are covered in *Chapter 10, Reconciling the Balance Sheet*.

It's possible that statutory requirements, such as the filing of sales tax or VAT returns monthly or quarterly, will dictate the frequency at which different financial reports are checked in QuickBooks Online.

Sometimes, when banks or other third parties are providing financial assistance to a business, it will be necessary to provide them with management information periodically. Before we can provide this, it's important to review the information to check that it's as accurate as possible to the best of our knowledge.

Let's start by thinking about some of the basic reports we need to review, and the sort of things we should be looking out for.

Checking Financial Reports

Whichever version of QuickBooks Online you are using, the number of different reports available by default is usually ample to meet the needs of most businesses. Considering the ease with which a report can be customized, you should find that you are well catered for.

Let's look at four of the most used reports in QuickBooks. If we are running reports with a specific date in mind (such as the financial year end that has just passed), we may also need to make comparisons to the previous year, against how balances appear now.

The four main reports we are going to run and review are as follows:

- The Profit and Loss Report
- The Balance Sheet
- The Accounts Receivable Ageing Summary Report
- The Accounts Payable Ageing Summary Report

When it comes to reviewing reports, there are various accounting principles and concepts that a business should follow. The terminology may vary slightly in different countries, but overall, everybody is trying to achieve the same goals.

Let's explain a few of these concepts.

The Matching Concept

The matching concept requires that when income is recorded, any cost that was incurred to generate that income should be recorded within the same period that is being reported.

The Accruals Concept

The accruals concept can sometimes be linked to the matching concept, but we are accounting for a cost not simply by the date when a supplier sends a bill, but the date on which the services were provided or to which they relate.

Accountancy fees are one of the most common *accruals* found in accounting. Accounting reports and tax returns prepared for a period that has passed usually include an accrual to adjust for fees that will be invoiced later.

Income Recognition

It's important to understand the dates when income is to be fully recognized. It's not always going to be the date an invoice was raised or when a payment is received; there are often other factors to consider.

Imagine a cleaning company raises an invoice once a year in advance against an annual service agreement. For monthly management reporting, it would be incorrect to fully recognize all the income in one month (even if all of it was paid). The costs associated with income, such as staff salaries and cleaning materials, will be purchased and consumed over the course of the agreement. In this instance, we must *defer income* and create adjustments to spread the income over the appropriate financial periods.

On the flip side, a consultant may have introduced a lot of business to one of their clients and could be due some sort of payment, which could either be an introductory fee or commission. A lot of time and effort could have been spent building relationships without any fees raised. In this instance, it could be sensible to *accrue income*.

We will look at how we'll make these types of adjustments in *Chapter 9, Enhancing the Consistency of Your Financial Statements*.

The Going Concern Concept

Basically, under this concept, the business will trade indefinitely for the foreseeable future when there is no evidence to the contrary. Fixed assets are recorded at cost and depreciated over their estimated useful lives to the business.

There are other concepts, but for the purposes of this book, the ones discussed here should keep you going for now. However, now is a good time to mention some accounting principles, starting with *materiality*.

Materiality

When the accounts are being reviewed, sometimes there can be a question mark over the treatment of a particular transaction. An accountant may ask themselves, *What is the impact of a particular business expense if disallowed?* Or, if the totals on the profit and loss report for sales do not agree exactly with those on the sales by customer summary report.

A large difference would be deemed material and would need to be investigated. A small difference may simply be ignored. Due to the different ways in which income can be recorded (bank deposits, invoices, sales receipts, and journals), all entries will affect the profit and loss, but not all require a customer name so will not affect the customer-based report.

Prudence

When producing a financial report, it's very important that we paint a picture that is *true and fair* and not clouded by any speculation. A good example is when valuing stock/inventory. Stock is always valued at whatever is the lower of the original cost and current net realizable value.

So, just because we purchased 10 items at £20 each, and we are going to easily sell them for £50 each, we must not adjust the value of stock in the balance sheet to reflect the future profit we expect to make. This profit is only realized when the sale is made.

Consistency

When accounts are prepared for a particular reporting period, they will usually be compared to another. This is often going to be the current year compared to last year, but for larger businesses, comparisons may be made on a month-by-month basis. Irregularities need to be investigated and explained.

Now that we have an idea of some of the accounting principles and concepts to be considered when reviewing accounts, let's start by taking a close look at the Profit and Loss Report.

Reviewing the Profit and Loss Report

The location of the profit and loss report in QuickBooks is not hard to find. You'll find that in the **Business Overview** area of the **Dashboard**, there is a **PROFIT AND LOSS** tile, and just clicking on this alone will open the report.

The report can also be found easily within the **Reports** center accessed from the left navigation menu bar. It's usually flagged as **Favorite** by default, but you can also search for the report easily from here.

When we're reviewing the profit and loss, to begin with, we are looking at *consistency* and *materiality*. To do this, we may need to do the following:

- Check or change the dates of the report.
- Check or change the way that columns are being displayed.
- Check or change the way that a report is being sorted.
- Compare the report to a previous financial period.

Let's begin by choosing the date range that we need to review and report against.

Report dates

Starting with the dates, selecting the period for review is relatively straightforward. You can choose to use **Custom** dates, meaning you must select two dates, one being the start date and the other being the end date:

Figure 8.1 – Using custom dates

Alternatively, you can select one of the default date ranges using the drop-down selection. The **Since 365 Days Ago** date option will automatically report 1 year back from today's date.

> **Tip**
> Saving the profit and loss report or other sales reports with the **Since 365 Days Ago** date option can be really useful if you need to keep an eye on turnover on a *rolling* annual basis.

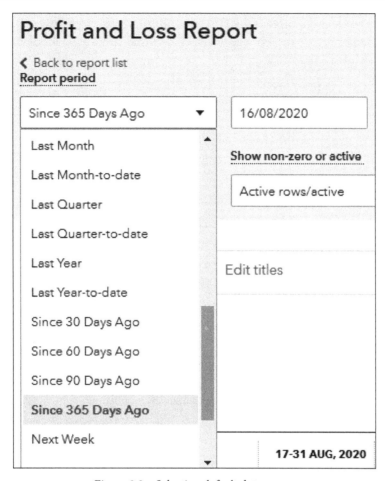

Figure 8.2 – Selecting default date ranges

Now that we've selected the dates we are reporting against, we can choose how the data will be displayed.

Changing the way that Columns are Displayed

Part of this review of our profit and loss report is to check for consistency. If we are presented with a **Total Only** value for a period of a year, we are not getting much of a story when it comes to the financial movements of the business, so we need to dig a little deeper.

Just below the date selection, there is the **Display columns by** option. This will usually default to **Total Only**, but we will choose to select **Months**. There are a lot of different options to choose from:

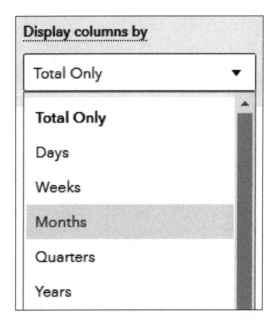

Figure 8.3 – Display columns by months

After customizing a report in any way, you will need to click **Run report** before the changes come into place.

As part of our effort to start reviewing figures entered in our profit and loss categories, we have checked the dates and changed the way that columns are displayed. Next, we may want to change the way a report is *sorted*. Let's look at how and why we might need to customize our report in this way.

Changing the order in which a Profit and Loss Report is sorted

In QuickBooks Online, the default order in which any report is sorted is alphabetical within a specified group or section. So, if we take a profit and loss report, different sections will always report in a particular order that can't be changed. These are as follows:

1. Income
2. Cost of sales
3. Expenses

4. Other income

5. Other expenses

> **Tip**
>
> Although you can't change the order in which key sections appear on the profit and loss report and balance sheet, you can choose the **Edit titles** option. You will find this option just above the title of the report. You could replace `Income` with `Turnover`, and `Expenses` with `Overheads`.

If we look at the section for **Expenses**, all the charts of accounts in use will appear alphabetically by default, as shown in the following figure:

Expenses	
Depreciation Expense	399.96
Dues and Subscriptions	650.00
Insurance Expense-General Liability Insurance	4,250.00
Interest expense	1,425.00
Janitorial Expense	404.83
Rent Expense	17,500.00
▼ Utilities	
Utilities - Electric & Gas	2,555.04
Utilities - Water	818.03
Total Utilities	**3,373.07**
Total Expenses	**£28,002.86**

Figure 8.4 – Expenses section of the profit and loss report

In *Chapter 2, Useful Tips and Tricks Every QuickBooks User Should Know*, within the section that covers the chart of accounts, we looked at the use of *account numbers* – see *Figure 2.17* and *Figure 2.18*.

When account numbers are in use, reports that summarize data held within chart of accounts categories, such as the profit and loss and balance sheet reports, will instead be sorted in account number order within the different sections.

It is possible to override the way a report is sorted by selecting the **Sort** option that is found just above the title of the report when on screen. How the data is sorted will vary on the report being viewed, but for profit and loss, the options are **Default**, **Total in ascending order**, and **Total in descending order**.

Applying the **Total in descending order** option can be very useful when reviewing a profit and loss report. The income categories with the largest values will appear at the top of the **INCOME** section, and the expense categories with the highest spend will appear at the top of the **EXPENSE** section.

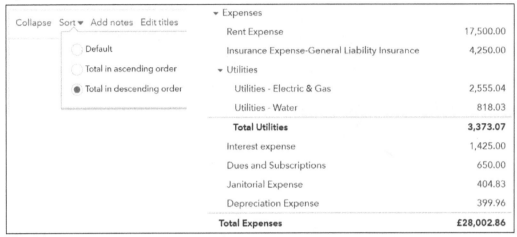

Figure 8.5 – Profit and loss sorted by total in descending order

Having the report sorted in this way can make it easier to draw the eye to areas of interest when carrying out financial reviews of the business.

So, when reviewing our profit and loss report for a quarter, or year, it's a good idea to make use of all these techniques at the same time – selecting a date range, viewing columns by months, and sorting in descending order.

By doing this, we are well on our way to checking for consistency and any possible material differences from month to month.

Before we start looking at the financial data in more detail, there is another useful reporting feature to help us check consistency and increases/decreases in revenue and expenditure. Let's use that feature now.

Comparing Values to Previous Financial Periods

Whether we are reviewing the profit and loss report or Balance Sheet, comparing values between different financial periods is important for many reasons, but in particular the following:

- Checking the consistency of standard fixed overheads
- Reviewing the spend against all other expense categories
- Checking that income is reported as expected

Within the top section of the report screen, just below the date selection boxes, you will find the **Compare another period** option:

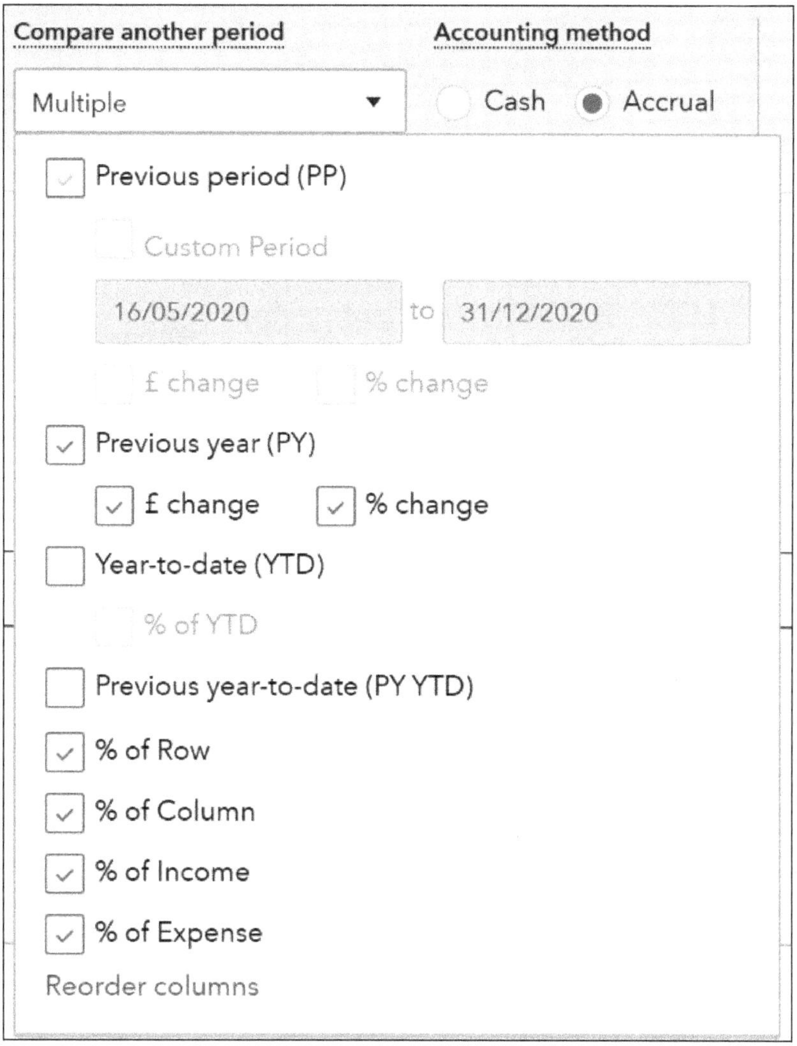

Figure 8.6 – Compare another period

Important Note

The **Compare another period** feature is not available in *QuickBooks Online Simple Start*.

If we run the profit and loss report and choose the **Compare another period** option, selecting only **Previous year (PY)** with **£ change** and **% change**, it will appear as follows:

	TOTAL			
	JAN - AUG, 2021	JAN - AUG, 2020 (PY)	CHANGE	% CHANGE
▼ Income				
Billable Expenses Income	28,547.75	11,012.50	17,535.25	159.23042%
Sales of Product Income	8,747.45		8,747.45	
Markup	8,609.55		8,609.55	
Sales	4,994.91	2,000.00	2,994.91	149.7455%
Services	1,200.00		1,200.00	
Total Income	**£52,099.66**	**£13,012.50**	**£39,087.16**	**300.38163%**

Figure 8.7 – Profit and loss compared to a prior period

> **Tip**
> To reduce the decimal places on the **% CHANGE** column, use the **Customize** option, selecting the **Without pence/cents** option in the **General** customize options.

The customization suggested within the tip has been applied to the report shown in *Figure 8.7*, so that it now displays as per the following figure:

	TOTAL			
	JAN - AUG, 2021	JAN - AUG, 2020 (PY)	CHANGE	% CHANGE
▼ Income				
Billable Expenses Income	28,548	11,013	17,535	159%
Sales of Product Income	8,747		8,747	
Markup	8,610		8,610	
Sales	4,995	2,000	2,995	150%
Services	1,200		1,200	
Total Income	**£52,100**	**£13,013**	**£39,087**	**300%**

Figure 8.8 – Profit and loss compared to a prior period without pence

Now that we understand how to apply some basic customizations that can assist with the review of our financial records, let's start looking out for some common errors that can occur within QuickBooks and how to fix them.

Looking Out for Errors and Inconsistencies

Reviewing our figures on a month-by-month basis, or comparing prior periods, makes it so much easier to check income and expenditure against what we are expecting. Let's look at some expenses of our business.

Take Rent Expense as an example category in our profit and loss report. If we know as a business our monthly rent costs are £1,250, that is the figure we expect to see on our report each month. What do we do if our report is displaying different amounts?

| Rent Expense | 2,500.00 | 2,500.00 | 2,500.00 | 1,250.00 | 2,500.00 | £11,250.00 |

Figure 8.9 – Monthly profit and loss figures for rent

Figure 8.9 shows a total rent cost of £11,250 for five months but in fact, the total cost should have been £6,250, as there should only be £1,250 paid each month. We will need to dig a little deeper.

With our profit and loss report open, we'll click on £11,250 to drill down to see what makes up that cost:

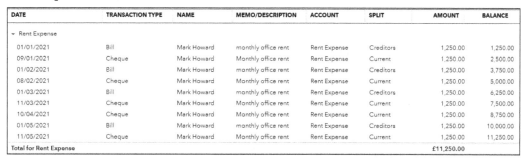

DATE	TRANSACTION TYPE	NAME	MEMO/DESCRIPTION	ACCOUNT	SPLIT	AMOUNT	BALANCE
▼ Rent Expense							
01/01/2021	Bill	Mark Howard	monthly office rent	Rent Expense	Creditors	1,250.00	1,250.00
09/01/2021	Cheque	Mark Howard	Monthly office rent	Rent Expense	Current	1,250.00	2,500.00
01/02/2021	Bill	Mark Howard	monthly office rent	Rent Expense	Creditors	1,250.00	3,750.00
08/02/2021	Cheque	Mark Howard	Monthly office rent	Rent Expense	Current	1,250.00	5,000.00
01/03/2021	Bill	Mark Howard	monthly office rent	Rent Expense	Creditors	1,250.00	6,250.00
11/03/2021	Cheque	Mark Howard	Monthly office rent	Rent Expense	Current	1,250.00	7,500.00
10/04/2021	Cheque	Mark Howard	Monthly office rent	Rent Expense	Current	1,250.00	8,750.00
01/05/2021	Bill	Mark Howard	monthly office rent	Rent Expense	Creditors	1,250.00	10,000.00
11/05/2021	Cheque	Mark Howard	Monthly office rent	Rent Expense	Current	1,250.00	11,250.00
Total for Rent Expense						£11,250.00	

Figure 8.10 – Detailed transactions against rent expense

Reviewing the transactions entered in Rent Expense, it appears that we are incurring a cost twice every month against our supplier Mark Howard. Are we paying this supplier double what we are supposed to? We need to review the supplier account to investigate.

After running an accounts payable report and looking into the supplier account in detail, QuickBooks is reporting that we owe the supplier £6,000. So that's good news; we've not actually paid the supplier twice. What has happened is that instead of marking a bill as paid, checks have been created and posted directly to `Rent Expense`:

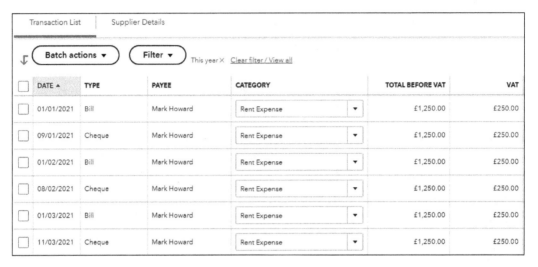

	DATE ▲	TYPE	PAYEE	CATEGORY	TOTAL BEFORE VAT	VAT
☐	01/01/2021	Bill	Mark Howard	Rent Expense ▼	£1,250.00	£250.00
☐	09/01/2021	Cheque	Mark Howard	Rent Expense ▼	£1,250.00	£250.00
☐	01/02/2021	Bill	Mark Howard	Rent Expense ▼	£1,250.00	£250.00
☐	08/02/2021	Cheque	Mark Howard	Rent Expense ▼	£1,250.00	£250.00
☐	01/03/2021	Bill	Mark Howard	Rent Expense ▼	£1,250.00	£250.00
☐	11/03/2021	Cheque	Mark Howard	Rent Expense ▼	£1,250.00	£250.00

Figure 8.11 – Bills not marked as paid

Before we correct these entries, we should understand the impact this error alone would have made:

- It appears we owe £6,000 more than we do (4 x £1,500 including VAT).
- Rent costs are overstated by £5,000 (4 x £1,250).
- Profit is understated by £5,000.
- £1,000 input VAT may have been claimed in error (4 x £250).

This sort of error may occur if the bookkeeping is left for several months and then all entries are made directly from the bank statement. Later, the bills were added instead of putting bills first and matching open balances from the bank feed.

This is only one category and one supplier. If this had happened throughout the year, with a lot of other suppliers, the impact on the accounts and tax calculated could be considerable. Therefore, it's important to keep bookkeeping up to date and review regularly.

To correct the balance against the supplier and the profit figures overall, it's a simple fix. First, click on one of the checks. This will open the check screen, and the unpaid bills will appear on the right-hand side of the screen:

Figure 8.12 – Check open with unpaid bills on the right

With the check open, we can choose to add the bill from the right of the screen. This will change the transaction type to **Bill Payment**. When making this change, it's important that the **Amount** box is checked and agreed to the original check value:

Figure 8.13 – Check converted to bill payment

Once edited, the bill payment should be saved, and all other checks edited and converted to bill payments where necessary.

After making these simple changes, the balance against the supplier account is now £0.00, and the **Transaction List** field will contain **Bills** and **Bill Payments** values.

	DATE ▼	TYPE	PAYEE	CATEGORY		TOTAL BEFORE VAT	VAT
☐	11/06/2021	Bill Payment (Ch...	Mark Howard			-£1,500.00	£0.00
☐	01/06/2021	Bill	Mark Howard	Rent Expense	▼	£1,250.00	£250.00
☐	11/05/2021	Bill Payment (Ch...	Mark Howard			-£1,500.00	£0.00
☐	01/05/2021	Bill	Mark Howard	Rent Expense	▼	£1,250.00	£250.00

Figure 8.14 – Updated supplier record

> **Important Note**
>
> In this example, checks had been created. It works in the exact same way if expenses had been used instead of creating bill payments.

Now that we've made the correction that has overstated our expenses, very similar errors can be made when recording income. Again, reviewing our profit and loss on a month-by-month basis, our income is not reported as expected, so we need to investigate.

Reviewing Income values in the Profit and Loss Report

Just as we've already done with expenses, we've noticed that `Sales of Product Income` looks unusually high. After drilling down into the account for more details, we are presented with the following information:

DATE	TRANSACTION TYPE	NO.	NAME	AMOUNT
▼ Sales of Product Income				
16/03/2021	Invoice	1010	Benjamin Yeung	5,000.00
16/03/2021	Invoice	1010	Benjamin Yeung	1,500.00
15/04/2021	Invoice	1013	Adwin Ko	1,500.00
22/04/2021	Deposit		Adwin Ko	7,300.00
25/04/2021	Invoice	1009	Abercrombie International Group	747.45
Total for Sales of Product Income				**£16,047.45**

Figure 8.15 – Detailed transactions within sales of product income

Looking at the transactions listed, within the **TRANSACTION TYPE** column, we can see that both **Invoice** and **Deposit** have been used. This doesn't automatically mean anything is wrong, as some businesses will use a mixture. Before we investigate further, just a quick reminder on the different ways income is recorded:

- **Invoice** – Credit terms given to a customer to pay in a specified number of days.

- **Sales Receipt** – The sale of **Product/Service** items is recorded, but payment is received immediately and recorded to a **Deposit to** field.

- **Deposit** – Income is recorded directly to a chart of accounts code when payment has been received (the use of a **Customer** or **Product/Service** item is not required).

- **Journal entry** – Not often used during normal business activities but required when adjusting to *accrue* or defer *income*.

If we have a bank feed connection or have at the very least used the option to upload a bank statement, it is always very useful to click on a transaction to check how it was initially created. If we have opened the **Bank Deposit** entry, at the top right-hand corner of the screen will be a link for **online banking matches**:

Figure 8.16 – An online banking match within a transaction

Figure 8.16 shows the screen before and after the **online banking match** option has been clicked on. It contains details that appear on the bank statement feed. The value received was £8,760 (gross including VAT), which results in the net value £7,300 entered into sales on April 22, 2021.

It could be that all is okay, but the **Payee** details show as ATM DEPOSIT. This usually means cash or checks were paid in at the bank, and the total deposited could be made up of multiple values.

We will need to investigate this further. Obtaining the paying-in book used is likely to help, but if we don't have it immediately to hand, there are other things we can do.

If we are reviewing our income and it appears out of line, we can also check the following:

- The accounts receivable aging summary (unpaid customers)
- The bank reconciliation report
- The balance sheet (the undeposited funds balance in particular)

Let's say we've reviewed balances owed by customers, and at this stage, there are no balances that immediately tie in with the total received for £8,760. So, now we move on to look at our bank balance in more detail.

In the following screenshot taken from a bank reconciliation, there is an unreconciled entry for £7,800 dated April 22, 2021. If today's date was June 30, 2021, it would be expected that this entry should have cleared the bank and been marked as reconciled:

Figure 8.17 – An unreconciled entry

This amount of £7,800 is different from the amount deposited on this date by £960 (£8,760 – £7,800). If we use the **Search** or **Advanced Search** feature (as covered in *Chapter 2, Useful Tips and Tricks Every QuickBooks User Should Know*, within the *General Tips for Daily Use* section), we can try and search for this value of £960:

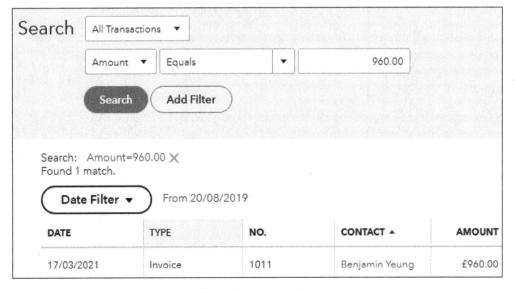

Figure 8.18 – Advanced search for a value

As we can see, the search for £960 has reported an invoice unpaid for that total value. Let's imagine that we are now in possession of the paying-in book. Details written in this book show that two checks were paid in on April 22, one for £960 and the other for £7,800.

To resolve our discrepancy in reported income, the deposit for £8,760 will need to be deleted. The bank should be reconciled again to account for the £7,800 previously left as unreconciled with a receipt of £960, marking the invoice in *Figure 8.18* as paid.

> **Important Note**
> Deleting and voiding transactions is explained in detail within *Chapter 11* of this book, *Closing the Year-End, the Audit Log, and More.*

Other Considerations

Here are some other things to look out for when reviewing the profit and loss report and when things don't look quite right:

- Have any entries for personal use, such as large bank transfers or payments for holidays, been recorded to expense categories in error?

- Have items of capital expenditure been recorded to the profit and loss report in error?

- Has any capital introduced been recorded as income in error?

- Have any loans been recorded as income in error?

- Have any chart of account types been used incorrectly?

> **Important Note**
> The incorrect use of chart of account types can drastically distort financial reports. An inexperienced QuickBooks user could create a `Wages and Salaries` category and set it up as a **Bank**. This would result in the balance sheet reporting a higher value of assets, lower expenses, and increased profits. We shall be looking into this area in more detail in *Chapter 9, Enhancing the Consistency of Your Financial Statements.*

We've really concentrated on looking at the profit and loss report so far, but as part of our review, it's important to look at the balance sheet. Entries recorded to undeposited funds can impact turnover if the process has not been handled correctly. Let's understand why.

Reviewing the Balance Sheet (Undeposited Funds)

In *Chapter 4, Recording Income for Retail Businesses*, we demonstrated the use of undeposited funds. The account can be used to initially record a payment, either against an invoice or for a sales receipt, and then later, the funds are transferred to the actual bank account using the deposit feature.

If care is not taken, when funds are received into the bank account, there is a danger that these amounts are not treated correctly. Instead of creating a deposit, as shown in *Figure 4.22*, a QuickBooks user might do the following:

- Record a receive payment against a customer.
- Record a deposit directly to a chart of accounts of income.

The first won't affect our profit and loss at all, but it will initially record that a customer has overpaid, possibly reporting their account is in credit. If not checked thoroughly, funds could be sent back to the customer in error, resulting in negative cash flow.

The first error could only be corrected by deleting any receive payments created in error and then creating the deposits correctly as they should have been. If this has happened a lot, it can be quite labor-intensive to fix.

The second type of error would be like the scenario shown in *Figure 8.16*, where we would be reporting more income than we have received. This would overstate our income, profit, and sales tax if applicable.

The second error could be a much quicker fix. If we know that we've double-counted income by recording against undeposited funds, and then again when amounts are received in the bank account, we can create a zero total deposit to fix.

In our balance sheet, a total of £4,380 is shown as sitting in **Undeposited Funds**. Normally, this means we have received payment and are waiting for funds to be paid into the bank account:

▼ Current Assets	
Stock Asset	8,411.93
Undeposited Funds	4,380.00
Total Current Assets	**£12,791.93**

Figure 8.19 – Undeposited Funds balance

After investigation, we've found that we have double counted income, treating funds that have cleared the bank account as deposits directly entered to an income category.

It could be possible to delete all the entries left in **Undeposited Funds**, but that could take some time if there are a lot. We can adjust by using one entry for a deposit that totals zero:

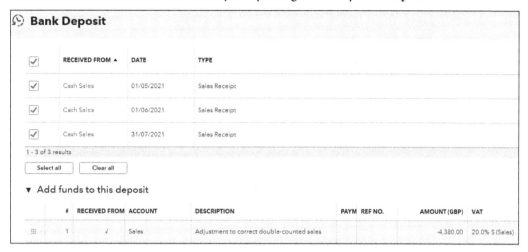

Figure 8.20 – Zero total sales receipt

Selecting to deposit all the entries in the top section of the screen totals £4,380. In the lower section of **Bank Deposit**, using the **Add funds to this deposit** area, we can enter a *negative* value of £4,380 inclusive of Tax. Overall, the transaction will total £0.00.

The accounting entries will be as follows:

- *Credit* Undeposited Funds – £4,380
- *Debit* Sales – £3,650
- *Debit* VAT – £730

This results in undeposited funds balancing to £0.00, and sales and VAT have been reduced accordingly.

What if sales are correct, but the cash has gone?

This scenario is very common within cash-based businesses. Sales have been recorded, but cash expenses or drawings of cash made by the businesses owner have been overlooked.

This can result in the balance sheet showing a value of cash held in Undeposited funds or Petty cash, but the money is nowhere to be found.

Where the cash is still showing as sitting within **Undeposited Funds**, we can repeat what we've done within *Figure 8.20*, but instead, we can create a negative value against an expense category and use the **Cash back amount** field to adjust `Drawings`:

				Selected Payments Total		4380.00
					Amounts are	Exclusive of Tax ▾
ACCOUNT	**DESCRIPTION**	**PAYMENT METHOD**	**REF NO.**	**AMOUNT (GBP)**	**VAT**	
Cost of sales	Materials purchased using cash	Cash		-500.00	20.0% S (Purchases)	🗑
Postage and Delivery	Stamps purchased using cash	Cash		-20.00	Exempt (Purchases)	🗑
						🗑
				Other funds total		**-520.00**
						-100.00
				VAT @ 20% (Purchases) on -500.00		

Cash back goes to	Cash back memo	Cash back amount
Drawings ▾	Cash taken out of business	3,760.00

	Total	**0.00**
	Total (GBP)	**0.00**

Figure 8.21 – Adjusting undeposited funds for drawings and expenses

The bookkeeping entries that will be created from the entry made in *Figure 8.21* will be:

- *Credit* Undeposited Funds – £4,380
- *Debit* Drawings – £3,760
- *Debit* Cost of sales – £500
- *Debit* Postage and Delivery – £20
- *Debit* VAT – £100

The total debits are the same as the total credits, so the amount deposited shows as £0.00. This has the same effect as creating a journal entry. If there were a balance of £4,380 within `Petty cash`, we would use a journal entry to make the correction:

#	ACCOUNT	DEBITS (GBP)	CREDITS (GBP)	DESCRIPTION	NAME	VAT
1	Petty cash		4,380.00	Adjust balance to £nil		
2	Cost of sales	500.00		Materials purchased with cash		20.0% S (Sales)
3	Postage and Delivery	20.00		Stamps purchased with cash		Exempt (Purchases)
4	Drawings	3,760.00		Cash drawings taken from business		
5						
6						
7						
8						
Subtotal		4,280.00	4,380.00			
VAT @ 20% (Sales)		100.00				
VAT @ 0% (Purchases)		0.00				
Total GBP		4,380.00	4,380.00			

Figure 8.22 – Using a journal to correct the cash balance

> **Tip**
> VAT codes are required on a journal entry if the values need to be included on a VAT return. Any VAT calculated is shown separately at the bottom of the journal against any of the rates used.

So far, we've looked at some areas of our profit and loss report and balance sheet. Any balances shown as owed from customers or owed to suppliers are going to be included on our balance sheet. Let's look at what we might need to consider when reviewing these values.

Reviewing Accounts Receivable

Any balances that appear on an accounts receivable report normally reflect the fact that a customer owes the business money. If the standard credit terms given to customers are 30 days from the invoice date, and there are a few balances that are 61 days overdue or more, these amounts should be investigated.

It could simply be that a customer is behind with payments and they need constant reminders before they pay. However, it's important to consider what else might have happened that means a business is reporting overdue customer balances. Here are some things to check:

- Has the business owner been paid in cash and not banked it?

- Is the bank fully reconciled, up to date, and all payments recorded?

- Has the customer transaction list been checked to see whether an invoice is a duplicate raised in error?

- Have any payments been received that have been incorrectly recorded?

  - Allocated to the wrong invoice/customer.

  - Recorded as a deposit in error.

  - Recorded as a sales receipt in error.

- Is a credit note required to clear the balance?

  - If the customer has gone out of business (bad debt).

  - The customer is not happy with the service and credit is due.

- If the customer is also a supplier and there is an agreement to offset the balance owed using a *contra*.

A lot of the preceding are not specific to using QuickBooks Online. It's important that when using QuickBooks or any accounting software, that we don't just accept a value as it appears on a report. All values should be checked carefully.

A few emails and phone calls may be required to resolve some of these issues, but we can look at how to deal with some of those that are *known*.

Business Owner Paid by Customer

If the business owner has been paid by the customer, we need to make sure the customer record is updated and marked as paid. First, we can create a bank in QuickBooks that we'll use a little bit like a control account:

Account

Account Type

| Cash at bank and in hand | ▼ |

* Name

| Ash - Personal Cash and Cards |

* Detail Type

| Cash on hand | ▼ |

Number

| |

Figure 8.23 – A bank created for adjustments

Creating the Chart of Account category, as shown in *Figure 8.23*, means that we now have an extra bank that we can use for customer or supplier-based transactions.

If it transpires that a customer with an old outstanding balance had actually paid the business owner in cash, we can now create an entry to mark as paid using the bank created:

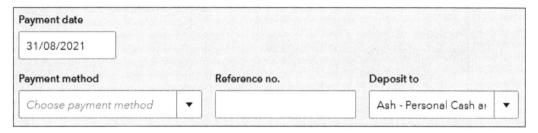

Figure 8.24 – Receiving payment using a personal bank account

Recording the entry in this way will result in the balance sheet showing an extra bank exists in the business and is holding cash. We know that is not the case, and we will need to make a journal entry to adjust `Drawings` or `Director's Loan`, depending on the structure of the business.

We shall make an adjustment for this balance at the end of the next section when we look at supplier balances. Next, we'll look at when the invoice is no longer payable.

Crediting Customer Invoices no Longer Payable

If a customer invoice is not payable because maybe goods were returned, or it's just a bad debt, we can create a credit note to clear. The credit note screen is almost identical to that of an invoice. Products and service items are required when a credit note is created.

If goods were returned, or it's simply been agreed that the charge should have been reduced, usually we would use the same product/service item like that on the original invoice.

If this is a true bad debt, then we should create a specific product/service item for this purpose, which is linked to a Chart of Accounts category for Bad Debts:

Figure 8.25 – Bad debt product and service item

It's important to note that just because a product/service item uses an **Income account** field, the Bad Debts chart of accounts category in use has been set up using the **Expenses** option from the **Account Type** field with the **Bad debts** option from the **Detail Type** field:

Figure 8.26 – Chart of account code for bad debts

Now that we've looked at our unpaid customer balances and adjusted where necessary, we can do something very similar with our unpaid supplier balances.

Reviewing Accounts Payable

In very much the same way as reviewing our unpaid customers, we are now doing the exact same thing with our unpaid suppliers. If our business usually pays suppliers on time, we shouldn't expect to find too many unpaid balances on our accounts payable reports.

It could be that our business is struggling and cash flow is not great. If that is the case, it would be of no surprise to find that we are late paying suppliers. However, we know from experience that all may not be as it seems, so we must check thoroughly.

Things to consider when reviewing unpaid supplier balances include the following:

- Has the business owner paid the supplier from personal funds?
- Has the transaction list been reviewed against the supplier to check for possible duplications?
- Are all banks fully up to date and reconciled?
- Have any payments been recorded in error?

  - An expense recorded instead of a bill payment.
  - An incorrect allocation against the wrong supplier.

- Is the balance payable in dispute?
- Has the amount been cleared using a hire purchase loan or similar?
- The supplier is also a customer and we've agreed to adjust the amount to reduce what is owed to us.

So, we can see there are a few similarities when reviewing unpaid suppliers compared to our unpaid customers. If you think about it, it's just the other side of the same coin. Some queries will require an email or phone call, but again, let's concentrate on fixing what we can, starting with amounts that have been paid by the business owner.

Supplier bills already paid by the business owner

It's very common that a small business owner will pay for things directly, using either cash they have or their own personal debit or credit card. These cash movements are going to be picked up by the business bank account, and it's not until we investigate old unpaid balances that we discover what has happened.

We already have a bank set up for use, as shown in *Figure 8.23*. We can use this to mark all old bills as paid using personal cash or cards where appropriate:

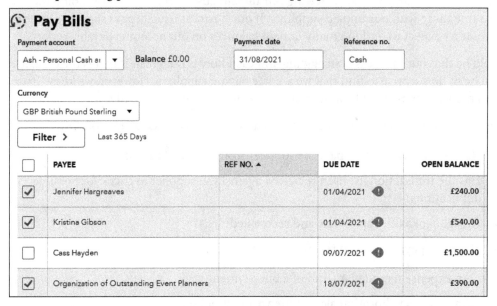

Figure 8.27 – Bills marked as paid using personal cash/cards

After adjusting customers and suppliers by marking amounts as paid using this extra bank, the entries against the chart of accounts category would appear as follows:

DATE	TRANSACTION TYPE	NO.	NAME	SPLIT	AMOUNT
▾ Ash - Personal Cash and Cards					
31/08/2021	Payment		Adwin Ko	Debtors	1,800.00
31/08/2021	Bill Payment (Cheque)	Cash	Organization of Outstanding Event Pla...	Creditors	-390.00
31/08/2021	Bill Payment (Cheque)	Cash	Kristina Gibson	Creditors	-540.00
31/08/2021	Bill Payment (Cheque)	Cash	Jennifer Hargreaves	Creditors	-240.00
Total for Ash - Personal Cash and Cards					£630.00

Figure 8.28 – Entries against an account for personal/cash cards

At this point in time, our balance sheet would display a value of £630 as being held in a bank account. As that is not actually the case, we can create a journal that will move this amount to either a director's loan or adjusted drawings:

#	ACCOUNT	DEBITS (GBP)	CREDITS (GBP)	DESCRIPTION
1	Drawings	630.00		Entry to correct cash balance
2	Ash - Personal Cash and Cards		630.00	Entry to correct cash balance

Figure 8.29 – Journal to correct cash balance

Now that we've adjusted amounts that were paid by the business owner, let's look at how we can adjust for an amount that has been settled by somebody else, a good example being a hire purchase agreement.

Supplier Bills settled by Hire Purchase Agreements

Amounts payable under finance agreements should not appear as a trade creditor on your accounts payable reports. They need to be shown separately on the balance sheet and, to start with, will need their own chart of accounts code:

Figure 8.30 – Chart of account category for loans

> **Tip**
> Some loans need to be split between current liabilities and non-current liabilities (long-term loans). Dealing with this split and interest charges are covered in *Chapter 9, Enhancing the Consistency of Your Financial Statements*.

Imagine we have a supplier, RR Motors, on our accounts payable aging summary report, and it shows that we owe £30,000. Although we purchased a vehicle from this company, a finance agreement is in place that will be repaid over 36 months.

The £30,000 needs to be removed from Creditors and adjusted to Hire Purchase Loan - Car. We can use a journal entry for this:

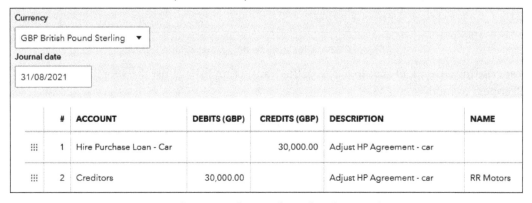

	#	ACCOUNT	DEBITS (GBP)	CREDITS (GBP)	DESCRIPTION	NAME
⠿	1	Hire Purchase Loan - Car		30,000.00	Adjust HP Agreement - car	
⠿	2	Creditors	30,000.00		Adjust HP Agreement - car	RR Motors

Figure 8.31 – Journal entry to adjust creditors for a hire purchase agreement

The entry in *Figure 8.31* alone will correct the balance sheet, but the supplier account will be left a `Bill` and `Journal Entry` that both have a balance that will need to be offset:

	DATE	TYPE	NO.	CATEGORY		BALANCE
☐	31/08/2021	Journal Entry	adjust			£30,000.00
☐	31/08/2021	Bill		Vehicles	▼	£30,000.00
		Total				£0.00

Figure 8.32 – Outstanding balances left on a supplier account

After choosing to make a payment against the `Bill`, both boxes within **Outstanding Transactions** (`Bill`) and **Credits** (`Journal Entry`) will be ticked, giving a total amount payable of zero.

Figure 8.33 – Allocating credit against a bill

After creating a payment that totals zero, the transaction list against the supplier's record will appear as follows:

	DATE	TYPE	NO.	BALANCE	TOTAL BEFORE VAT
☐	31/08/2021	Bill Payment (Cheque)	contra	£0.00	£0.00
☐	31/08/2021	Journal Entry	adjust	£0.00	-£30,000.00
☐	31/08/2021	Bill		£0.00	£25,000.00
		Total		£0.00	

Figure 8.34 – A supplier account updated after a journal is allocated to a Bill

Adjusting Amounts Between Suppliers and Customers

If one of our unpaid customers is also a supplier with an outstanding balance, we can use a journal to adjust values between debtors and creditors.

> **Important Note**
> QuickBooks will not allow a supplier and customer to have the exact same name. They must be different, even if it means just adding a full stop to the end of one of the names.

The most important thing to understand is where to put the debit and credit. If the customer owes us money, they are a *debtor*. This means that the balance they currently owe is a *debit* balance. When we create a journal entry, we will need to *credit* the amount:

#	ACCOUNT	DEBITS (GBP)	CREDITS (GBP)	DESCRIPTION	NAME
1	Debtors		480.00	Adjust to supplier account	Jordan Burgess
2	Creditors	480.00		Adjust from customer account	Jordan Burgess (supplier)

Figure 8.35 – Adjusting a balance between a customer and a supplier using a journal

Once the journal has been saved, the values can be allocated to the bill or invoice by creating a payment that totals zero, allocating the amounts as appropriate.

Summary

In this chapter, we've shown that although at first glance QuickBooks may appear up to date and even have the bank reconciled, it's important that all areas should be checked fully before we start preparing accounts of any kind.

You should now have a good understanding of the following:

- Basic accounting principles and concepts
- How often QuickBooks should be checked
- Basic reports to check and how these can be adapted
- Common errors that occur and how to fix them

When it comes to preparing our end-of-year accounts, we've made a start by checking for inconsistencies and have been able to make some corrections.

In our next chapter, we'll be looking more at how we can improve the consistency in our financial reporting; this will focus mainly on our profit and loss. As we progress further, *Chapter 10, Reconciling the Balance Sheet,* will look more closely at the balance sheet to ensure all areas have been fully agreed upon and reconciled.

9
Enhancing the Consistency of Your Financial Statements

In *Chapter 8*, *Best Practices when Reviewing Financial Records*, we started by looking at some best practices for reviewing financial records, uncovering some common errors, and making corrections and adjustments where necessary.

Continuing with our theme of reviewing our accounting entries, we may need to make some enhancements. At this stage, we've just covered the basics, and that means making sure that the bank accounts have been fully reconciled and that the customer and supplier balances have been checked and are up to date.

In this chapter, we will cover the following topics:

- Common errors associated with chart of accounts
- Common errors associated with products and services
- Using journals to adjust for accruals and prepayments
- Using other options – Classes, Locations, and Tags

Now that we have some understanding of accounting principles and concepts, we can check our reports to ensure that these principles and concepts are being followed. *Consistency* is probably one of the most important principles to get right.

If this was our first year using QuickBooks Online, it might not be possible to compare historical values using QuickBooks reporting, unless data was converted or historical information was imported.

If that were the case, we would need to manually compare values to either those reported in previous systems or to financial reports prepared by an accountant.

In *Chapter 2*, *Useful Tips and Tricks Every QuickBooks User Should Know*, we covered the use of chart of account codes in detail. If our chart of accounts has not been set up correctly, reporting can not only look a little messy, but the difference between reporting either a profit or a loss can be quite substantial.

Let's start by looking at some of the most common errors that are made with chart of accounts, repair them, and check what difference it makes.

Common Errors Associated with Chart of Accounts

Whenever possible, it's a good idea to keep our chart of accounts simple and the number of account categories in use down to a bare minimum. However, there is likely to be a time when there doesn't seem to be a category that *fits* the transaction you are trying to record.

If entries were being recorded from the bank feed and the option to **Add new** category is selected, the default **Account Type** will be **Cash at bank and in hand**:

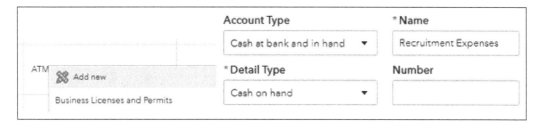

Figure 9.1 – Category set up using the incorrect account type

An inexperienced user, or somebody adding accounts in haste, could easily create a new chart of account category with an incorrect type.

The new account example shown in the preceding screenshot was required because a payment of £3,458.30 needed to be recorded for Recruitment Expenses. With this incorrect **Account Type** in use, the entry would have no impact on **Profit and Loss** and will appear on our **Balance Sheet** as a bank:

Figure 9.2 – Recruitment expenses created as a bank

It is important to fully review every value against every category regarding **Profit and Loss** and **Balance Sheet** – not only to ensure the figures displayed are correct but also to ensure that they are being displayed on the correct report and within the correct area of the report.

The following screenshot shows the correct settings for Recruitment Expenses:

Figure 9.3 – Selecting the correct account type

With regards to **Detail Type**, what is selected here will determine how figures are grouped if you are using QuickBooks Online to produce tax returns (this option will vary in different regions). If a third-party app is being used to create financial statements and tax returns, it also helps if **Detail Type** is set up correctly.

> Tip
>
> Using **Detail Type** will not affect the position of a category on reports. **Account Type** determines exactly which report will hold the value and where it will be grouped.

Where an account has been set up incorrectly, the account can be edited to the correct type (there are some limitations when it is not always possible). If a type is changed, you will receive the following warning:

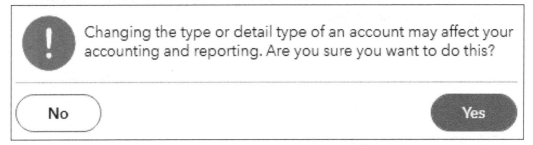

Figure 9.4 – Warning when changing the account's type

To make sure that QuickBooks produces reports correctly, with `Recruitment Expenses` appearing in **Profit and Loss** instead of **Balance Sheet**, the warning would be accepted.

If, after reviewing **Profit and Loss** and **Balance Sheet**, we are happy that all the categories in use have the correct **Account Type**, we can check if we have more categories in use than we need.

Unnecessary use of Chart of Account Categories

Occasionally, chart of account categories that were perhaps used in the past that are still active may get used in error. To prevent this from happening, we can make them inactive, as explained in *Chapter 2, Useful Tips and Tricks Every QuickBooks User Should Know*.

If two very similar categories are in use but only one is required, we can use the **Merge** option. In the following example, there are two chart of account categories in use for `Insurance Expense` and `Insurance Expense-General Liability`:

| Insurance Expense | | 750.00 | | |
| Insurance Expense-General Li... | 750.00 | | 750.00 | 750.00 |

Figure 9.5 – Two categories in use for insurance

Using the example shown in the preceding screenshot, it has been agreed that only `Insurance Expense` is required. It's not necessary to edit any transactions because using the **Merge** option will ensure that all the transactions from both categories will appear under this one heading.

The option to **Merge** is not visible within any menus. It will become available after you choose to **Edit** the **Name** of the account that you no longer wish to use so that it's the same as the one you wish to keep.

So, here, we would edit the chart of account category for `Insurance Expense-General Liability` and replace **Name** with `Insurance Expense`. Upon saving, we will be given the option to **Merge**:

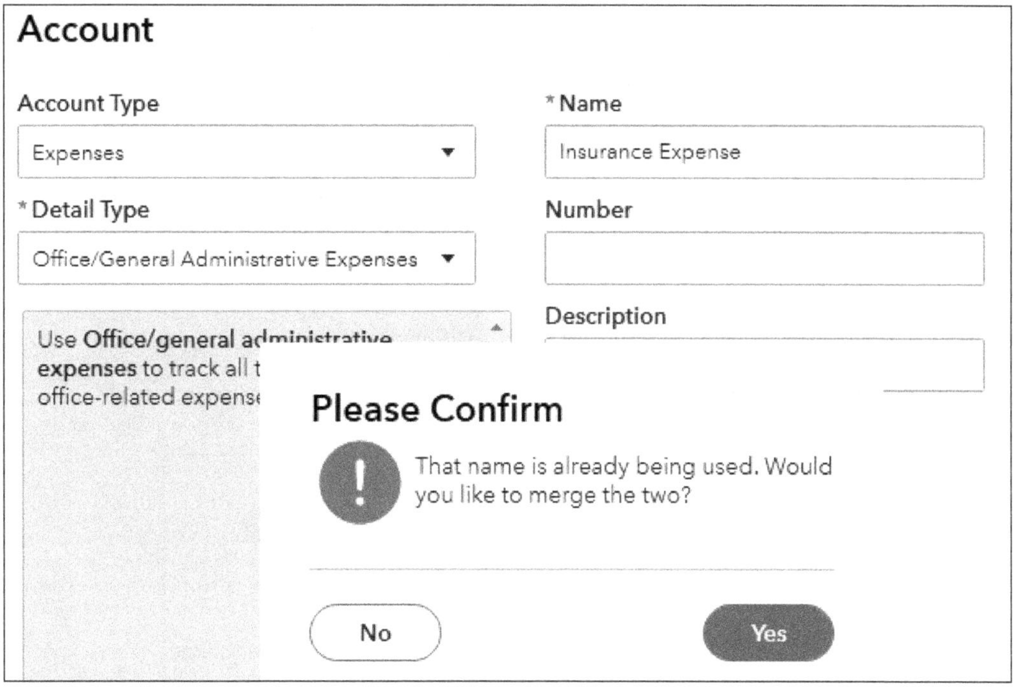

Figure 9.6 – Using the Merge feature

Accepting the merge for this account would now result in a consistent cost being charged against a single category every month.

> **Tip**
>
> The Merge function works in the same way for products and services, as well as customers and suppliers. So, if other areas of QuickBooks have become a little messy, the Merge feature can help tidy them up.

So far, we've learned that if chart of account categories have been set up with incorrect **Account Types**, there can be an impact on how profit figures are reported. In addition, if we have too many similar categories, they can be easily merged.

As part of our review, some invoices and sales receipts may appear within the wrong areas of our profit and loss report. Let's see what we can do to correct those entries.

Common Errors associated with Products and Services

All Products and Service items are linked to at least one chart of account category. The most common use of a Product or Service item is when creating an invoice because it is not possible to code an invoice directly to a chart of account code.

The benefit of using a Product or Service item is that you can have lots of different service offerings, but they could all have the sales figures credited to the same chart of account category, such as `Fees` or `Sale of products`.

For QuickBooks reporting, it may be the business owner's preference to use many different chart of account categories to reflect different income types. This isn't necessary when you can run reports such as **Sales by Product/Service Summary**.

The following profit and loss report shows the use of five different chart of account categories for **Income**:

▼ Income	
Billable Expenses Income	50,581.00
Fees	17,244.91
Markup	10,550.05
Sales of Product Income	9,747.45
Services	1,200.00
Total Income	**£89,323.41**

Figure 9.7 – Income categories in use

It's been found that some **Product/Service** items are being directed to the wrong chart of account category. Clicking on the value of 50,581 for Billable Expenses Income, we can see that charges for catering and venue rental are crediting this account when they should be directed to Services:

Promotional items - engraved pa…	Billable Expenses Income	Debtors - USD	1,250.00	33,893.50
Venue Rental	Billable Expenses Income	Debtors - USD	2,500.00	36,393.50
promotional items -- misc engra…	Billable Expenses Income	Debtors - USD	937.50	37,331.00
Catering -- food & beverage	Billable Expenses Income	Debtors - USD	12,500.00	49,831.00
Entertainment for the event	Billable Expenses Income	Debtors - USD	750.00	50,581.00
				£50,581.00

Figure 9.8 – Service items appearing within the incorrect category

To correct these entries, we can edit the **Product/Service** item, amend **Income account** to Services, and ensure that the **Also update this account in historical transactions** box is ticked:

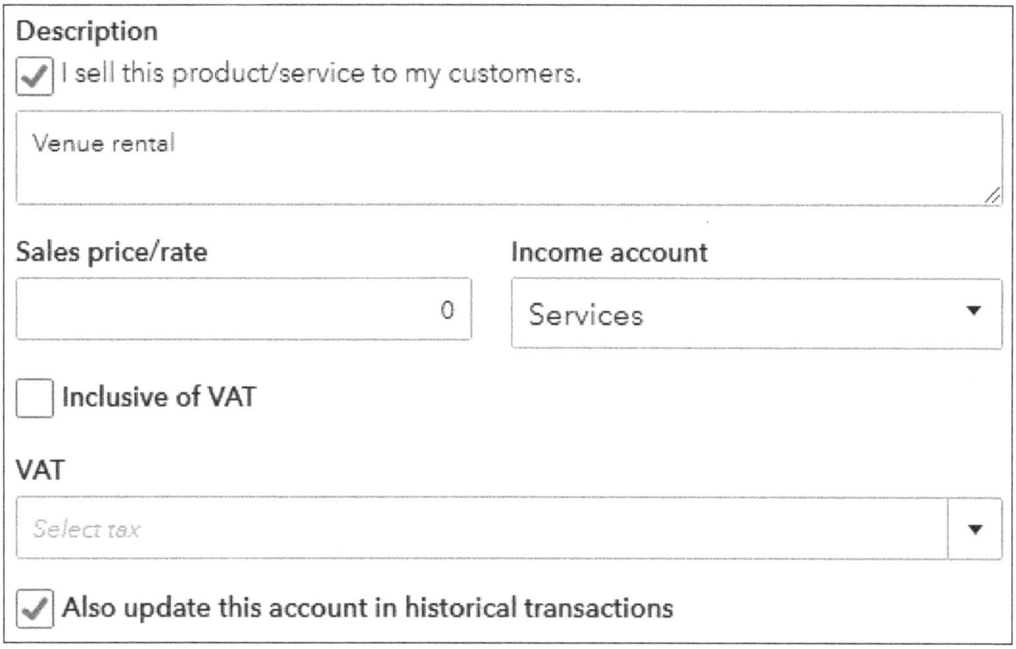

Description

[✓] I sell this product/service to my customers.

Venue rental

Sales price/rate	Income account
0	Services ▼

[ ] Inclusive of VAT

VAT

| Select tax | ▼ |

[✓] Also update this account in historical transactions

Figure 9.9 – Editing the income account and updating historical transactions

After editing the **Product/Service** items for `Catering` and `Venue Rental` so that they use **Income account**, which is set to `Services`, and choosing to **Also update this account in historical transactions**, the **Profit and Loss** report displays the same total value for **Income**, but the allocations to the account categories are different:

▼ Income	
Billable Expenses Income	7,343.50
Fees	17,244.91
Markup	10,550.05
Sales of Product Income	9,747.45
Services	44,437.50
Total Income	**£89,323.41**

Figure 9.10 – Revised profit and loss once the Product/Service items have been updated

> **Note**
>
> Due to the complexities of stock/inventory, editing a Product/Service item of this type will not provide an option for you to update historical transactions.

Now that we've made some adjustments to the way our Products/Services have been set up and reviewed transactions within our **Profit and Loss** report, it may be necessary to make some manual adjustments to the way our income or expenditure is currently being reported. To do this, we'll need to create some *accruals* or *prepayments*.

Prepayments, Accruals, and Deferred Income

In *Chapter 8, Best Practices When Reviewing Financial Records*, we introduced some standard accounting principles and concepts, including *the matching concept, the accruals concept*, and *income recognition*.

These concepts are similar in the sense that the values that are reported on a profit and loss report might not reflect the dates invoices were raised or the supplier bills were received. Instead, values are adjusted to reflect dates when work was carried out, or to a period that it relates to, regardless of when the fees were charged.

Let's look at an example of a large consultancy company. They are working for an international corporate client. They have been advised to raise an invoice in advance for the next quarter for £60,000.

After raising the invoice, the income within the **Profit and Loss** report will immediately show a value of £60,000 against 1 month:

	AUG 2021	SEP 2021	OCT 2021	TOTAL
▼ Income				
Services	60,000.00			£60,000.00
Total Income	£60,000.00	£0.00	£0.00	£60,000.00

Figure 9.11 – Profit and loss showing all the fees in a single month

Although this invoice was raised in August and paid in the same month, it would be incorrect to report all this income in 1 month if you're producing monthly reports. If the business didn't have a lot of other work planned, it could report that August was a good month and that September and October were poor in comparison.

This really wouldn't be the case here because the business is being paid in advance for work that they have not done yet, so some of this income will need to be *deferred*. This will improve *consistency* within our accounting and will *match* costs such as payroll expenses, which will be paid in later months.

To be able to defer the income, an appropriate balance sheet account will be required for **Deferred income**. Go ahead and make one:

Figure 9.12 – Account settings for deferred income

If the income for each month is to be set at £20,000, at the end of August, it will be necessary to defer a value of £40,000. We will need to create a **Journal entry**, as follows:

	#	ACCOUNT	DEBITS (GBP)	CREDITS (GBP)	DESCRIPTION
Journal date					
31/08/2021					
⠿	1	Deferred income		40,000.00	Defer two months income
⠿	2	Services	40,000.00		Defer two months income

Figure 9.13 – Journal to defer income for 2 months

This entry will reduce the value of the income on our **Profit and Loss** report by £40,000. With our **Journal entry** saved and left on the screen, the option to **Reverse** will be available at the bottom of the screen. Selecting this option will create another journal dated the first day of the following month but reversing the debits and credits.

We can reverse the entire amount, but since we want to adjust over 2 months, the values can be edited after selecting the **Reverse** option:

	#	ACCOUNT	DEBITS (GBP)	CREDITS (GBP)	DESCRIPTION
Journal date					
01/09/2021					
⠿	1	Deferred income	20,000.00		Adjust income - one month
⠿	2	Services		20,000.00	Adjust income - one month

Figure 9.14 – Reverse deferred income for 1 month

With the reversed journal saved and shown on the screen, by selecting **More** and then **Copy** from the bottom of the journal screen, a duplicate of the journal shown in the preceding screenshot will be created for October 1, 2021.

If we look at the detailed movements of the account for Deferred income, it will appear as follows:

DATE	TRANSACTION TYPE	MEMO/DESCRIPTION	AMOUNT	BALANCE
▾ Deferred income				
31/08/2021	Journal Entry	Defer two months income	40,000.00	40,000.00
01/09/2021	Journal Entry	Adjust income - one month	-20,000.00	20,000.00
01/10/2021	Journal Entry	Adjust income - one month	-20,000.00	0.00
Total for Deferred income			£0.00	
TOTAL			£0.00	

Figure 9.15 – Movements within Deferred income

These entries show the first journal that was created to remove the income value from the **Profit and Loss** report, followed by two further journals that release the income. This results in consistent income values being reported every month:

	AUG 2021	SEP 2021	OCT 2021	TOTAL
▾ Income				
Services	20,000.00	20,000.00	20,000.00	£60,000.00
Total Income	£20,000.00	£20,000.00	£20,000.00	£60,000.00
GROSS PROFIT	£20,000.00	£20,000.00	£20,000.00	£60,000.00

Figure 9.16 – Revised profit and loss after journal adjustments

The same principles need to be applied if expenses are prepaid. It is common for subscriptions and insurance payments to be paid 12 months in advance. Let's take a quick look at some of the setup required.

Adjusting prepayments

Sometimes, suppliers will bill for goods or services in advance of a period that they relate to. One example can be an organization receiving a bill for a 2-year professional membership subscription.

This single bill, when entered into QuickBooks, will create a cost that will immediately appear within 1 month. This cost should be apportioned so that the charge is evenly spread across all the relevant months.

If the total charge was £2,400 to begin with, the total cost would appear against the subscriptions in 1 month. This would need adjusting so that each month reflects a cost of £100 instead:

	JAN 2021	FEB 2021	MAR 2021	APR 2021
Subscriptions	2,400.00			
Subscriptions	100.00	100.00	100.00	100.00

Figure 9.17 – Subscription charges before and after prepayments have been adjusted

Before we can adjust for prepayments (also known as prepaid expenses), we will need the relevant chart of account category to be in place:

Figure 9.18 – Chart of account for Prepayments

If we had incurred an insurance cost that was £1,200 for 12 months, the first thing we could do is create a journal to prepay all or 11 months of the total annual cost. If the cost was incurred part way through a month, you may want to apportion by a specified number of days. For simplicity, we will prepay the entire year. This would require a **Journal entry** to *debit* Prepayments and *credit* Insurance for the entire amount.

For a prepayment that needs to run over 12 months, it will make things much easier to create a recurring transaction. If you're creating one from scratch, access the *gear icon* and select **Recurring transactions** from the **LISTS** menu.

Within the **Recurring transactions** area, select the **New** option, which can be found at the top right of the screen. For this example, we need to select **Journal Entry**:

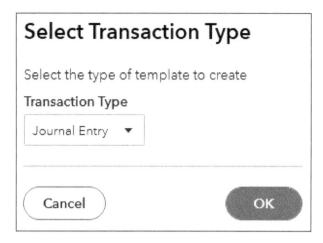

Figure 9.19 – Creating a recurring journal entry

In the top section of a recurring template screen, you can add a **Template name**, select its **Type**, and its various **Interval** options.

In the lower section of a recurring entry screen, you can choose how the entry should be created each month. With this example, it would be *debit* Insurance and *credit* Prepayments – £100 on each line:

Figure 9.20 – Recurring options

> **Tip**
> Although recurring entries can be created from the **Recurring transactions** list area, the option to use **Make recurring** can be found at the bottom of most manual data entry screens.

We have an initial journal entry of £1,200 that *debits* Prepayments and *credits* Insurance, followed by 12 journals of £100 each that *credits* Prepayments and *debits* Insurance. Our **Balance Sheet** will be in line, and there will be a *consistent* monthly charge for insurance on our **Profit and Loss** report.

The following table lists some of the different balance sheet categories that we can create to adjust income and expenditure, improving consistency in our profit and loss reporting:

Account Name	Type	Detailed Type	Notes
Accrued income	Current assets	Other current assets	The initial journal will debit this account and credit income.
Prepayments	Current assets	Other current assets	The initial journal will debit this account and credit expenses.
Accrued expenses	Current liabilities	Current liabilities	The initial journal will credit this account and debit expenses.
Deferred income	Current liabilities	Current liabilities	The initial journal will credit this account and debit income.

To recap a little, here are some examples of when we may need to create **journal entries** for the different accounts listed in the preceding table:

- **Accrued Income**:

  Services or products have been provided to a customer in one period, but the invoice was raised in a later period. There could be many reasons why this timing issue occurs. It could be that somebody simply forgot to raise an invoice, or that it has taken time to work out how much to charge a customer. This might involve looking at the costs that were incurred in a particular period first.

- **Prepayments**:

  Costs have been incurred in one period that relates to future periods. Subscriptions, insurance, license fees, and rent are good examples of costs that are billed in advance.

- **Accrued Expenses**:

  We can account for costs that relate to a specific period that may not have been fully calculated or perhaps billed later, and adjustments can be made to bring these in line. Common adjustments include accruals for accountancy fees, commissions payable, and possibly interest charges if statements are only received annually. Also, like accrued income, it could be that a supplier has sent a bill late. We may need to accrue for those costs so that they match the month in which income was generated.

- **Deferred income**:

  This is the opposite of prepayments. Invoices could be raised to customers in advance of the time when goods or services are provided. Adjustments are required to ensure that the income that's reported is in line with the relevant period. It should also match any costs that have been incurred.

After reviewing our profit and loss to check the associated costs match the income, and that there is consistency with how entries are being recorded, we are getting close to ensuring that the balance sheet is fully reconciled.

Before we do that, let's look at some other options that can enhance the reporting of our business.

Using Classes, Locations, and Tags

So far, we've concentrated on looking at a standard profit and loss report, but it could be that an organization needs to break the information down on the profit and loss report even further.

Although an organization may operate as one entity for tax and statutory reporting, it may have offices in different locations or consist of different departments. They may even have a mixture of both.

Charities may need to record the use of different *funds*. These are known as *restricted* and *unrestricted funds*. In addition to using a chart of account category, they may need to indicate when income or expenditure needs to be allocated to a specific fund type.

When we have an organization that requires an extra level of reporting, we may need to look at using some of the other features available. **Classes**, **locations**, and **tags** provide us with additional data fields to complete when creating a transaction, as well as enhanced levels of reporting.

Let's start by looking at classes and locations.

Classes and locations

If we take an example of a car dealership, they could operate as one business but may have showrooms and workshops at different branches. We could associate the different branches to locations in QuickBooks.

In addition, the business has different *departments*; that is, sales, marketing, parts, workshop, human resources, and finance. Classes could be used to help monitor the spending against the different departments.

The major benefit of using classes or locations (or both) is that it is not necessary to create lots of different chart of account categories for all the different areas we wish to report against. We can keep those short and prevent our reports from running over multiple pages.

First, we need to enable the **Track classes** and **Track locations** options, which can be found on the **Advanced** tab of **Account and Settings**:

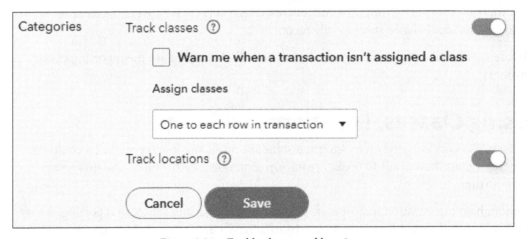

Figure 9.21 – Enable classes and locations

> **Note**
> A *Plus* level subscription is required to use this feature.

With **Classes** and **Locations** enabled, they will appear as options within **All lists,** which can be accessed from the **LISTS** option via the *gear icon*. From this area, you can easily create new classes and locations as you need them. You can also create new classes and locations from within a transaction using the **Add new** option if the name you require does not exist yet:

> **Tip**
>
> If you add a new location from within the **LISTS** area, more options will become available to use with that **Location**. This includes using different contact information, which could be useful if you're sending invoices out from different branches.

Location Information

* Name

Cambridge

☐ Is sub-location

☐ This location has a different title for sales forms.

☐ This location has a different company name when communicating with customers.

☐ This location has a different address where customers contact me or send payments.

☐ This location has a different email address for communicating with customers.

☐ This location has a different phone number where customers phone me.

Figure 9.22 – Location options when creating from an all lists area

When creating a transaction such as an invoice or a bill, different fields are available to record a single location and a mixture of classes. This is because this option can be used on each row:

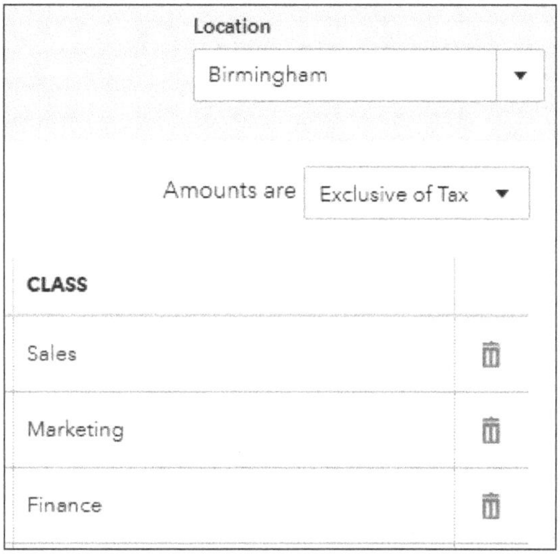

Location

Birmingham ▼

Amounts are   Exclusive of Tax ▼

CLASS

Sales   🗑

Marketing   🗑

Finance   🗑

Figure 9.23 – Using a location and classes on an invoice

> **Note**
> Like **Location**, you can choose to limit the use of one **Class** per transaction.
> This option can be selected by going to **Account** and then **Settings**.

If you are creating transactions from within the bank feed and need to allocate costs to multiple classes, you will need to use the **Split** option. **Location** will appear at the top of the screen, and **Class** can be selected on each line:

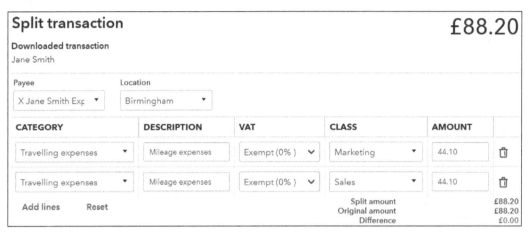

Figure 9.24 – Using Class and Location on a Split bank feed transaction

When creating a **Journal entry**, it is possible to enter multiple locations. The option to select a **Class** and **Location** is available on the far right of every line in a journal entry. This is useful when you're creating a journal entry for wages and salaries:

LOCATION	CLASS	
Birmingham	Sales	🗑
London	Sales	🗑
Cambridge	Finance	🗑

Figure 9.25 – Class and Locations used on a journal entry

Now that the settings for classes and locations have been enabled and we are using the additional fields when creating transactions, we would benefit from being able to report against the different classes and locations in use.

Reporting against Classes and Locations

From the **Reports** center, which can be accessed from the *left navigation* panel in QuickBooks, you have the option to search for reports. Simply type the word `class` or `location` into this box and you will get a list of reports that are already available by default:

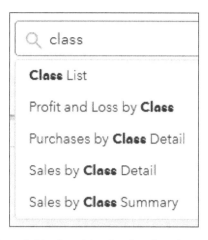

Figure 9.26 – Searching for class-based reports

As well as searching for reports, the option to **Display columns by** (as shown in *Figure 8.3* in *Chapter 8, Best Practices When Reviewing Financial Records*) can be used to change the columns to be displayed by **Class** or **Location**.

When detailed reports are being viewed, using the **Customize** option, it is possible to **filter** against specific **Classes** and **Locations** so that you can tailor your report to provide the information exactly as you need it.

If we view the **Profit and Loss** report by **Class,** the different classes will appear at the top of the report, and the account categories will be listed down the left:

Profit and Loss All Dates					
	FINANCE	MARKETING	SALES	NOT SPECIFIED	TOTAL
▼ Income					
Fees	4,850.00	7,425.00	11,561.56	200.00	£24,036.56
Sales				112.50	£112.50
Takings				3,489.94	£3,489.94
Uncategorised Income				12,500.01	£12,500.01
Total Income	£4,850.00	£7,425.00	£11,561.56	£16,302.45	£40,139.01

Figure 9.27 – Profit and Loss by Class

Any transactions that have not been assigned to a class make up the values that appear in the **NOT SPECIFIED** column. To prevent transactions from being coded without a class, you can select the warning shown when enabling the class feature.

> **Note**
> If a lot of transactions have been added without a class but they should have been assigned to one, users with an *Accountant Login* will have additional tools that can **Reclassify** transactions in a batch.

So far, we've looked at running the **Profit and Loss** report by **Class**, but is it possible to do the same with a **Balance Sheet**? Let's find out next.

Viewing the Balance Sheet by Class or Location

You may find that you could run into a problem trying to view the **Balance Sheet** by **Class**. The reason is that QuickBooks has what's known as *Sources* and *Targets*. Account categories such as **Banks**, **Credit Cards**, **Accounts Receivable**, and **Accounts Payable** would be referred to as *Sources*.

QuickBooks Online is a full double-entry bookkeeping system, but it is only possible to assign a class or location to the account category that is being *targeted*. This means that the bank side of a double entry would not have a class coded for it.

Let's say you are preparing accounts for a charity and you are using classes to record spending against different fund types. The bank balances reconcile perfectly, but the values are not shown under the correct fund headings.

If we look at the **Total Cash at bank and in hand** and **Total Debtors** sections of the balance sheet, all the values appear as **NOT SPECIFIED**:

Balance Sheet As of July 31, 2021				
	GENERAL UNRESTRICTED FUNDS	RESTRICTED FUNDS	NOT SPECIFIED	TOTAL
Fixed Asset				
Total Fixed Asset				**£0.00**
▾ Cash at bank and in hand				
Business Bank Account			22,815.85	£22,815.85
Contra Account			0.00	£0.00
Petty cash			100.00	£100.00
Shopify control Account			5,200.00	£5,200.00
US Dollar Bank Account			107.89	£107.89
Total Cash at bank and in hand	**£0.00**	**£0.00**	**£28,223.74**	**£28,223.74**
▾ Debtors				
Debtors			13,177.10	£13,177.10
Debtors - EUR			0.00	£0.00
Debtors - USD			0.00	£0.00
Total Debtors	**£0.00**	**£0.00**	**£13,177.10**	**£13,177.10**

Figure 9.28 – Balance Sheet by Class

If we have different bank accounts for different funds, we'll know where the values should appear on this report. For debtors, this might not be as easy, but sub-customers, as explained in *Chapter 6, The Secret to Success with Projects in QuickBooks Online*, could be used as a way of group different customer types:

A/R Ageing Summary As of August 28, 2021						
	CURRENT	1 - 30	31 - 60	61 - 90	91 AND OVER	TOTAL
▾ 001 - Unrestricted Donations						£0.00
Joe Wells	1,206.00					£1,206.00
Kari Steblay	810.00			656.40		£1,466.40
Leonardo Rodriguez	1,218.00		3,500.00			£4,718.00
Total 001 - Unrestricted Donations	**3,234.00**		**3,500.00**	**656.40**		**£7,390.40**

Figure 9.29 – Using sub-customers to group Accounts Receivable

If we want to ensure that our balance sheet reports exactly as required, we can create a simple journal entry. For each account category that is reporting incorrect figures, we need to debit and credit the same values to it. However, one line entry will include the class and the other will be left blank:

#	ACCOUNT	DEBITS (GBP)	CREDITS (GBP)	DESCRIPTION	NAME	VAT	CLASS
1	Business Bank Account	22,815.85		correct class report			General Unrestricted Funds
2	Business Bank Account		22,815.85	correct class report			
3	Debtors	7,390.40		correct class report	001 - Unrestricted Donations		General Unrestricted Funds
4	Debtors		7,390.40	correct class report	001 - Unrestricted Donations		
5	Debtors	5,786.70		correct class report	Restricted Donations		Restricted Funds
6	Debtors		5,786.70	correct class report	Restricted Donations		

Figure 9.30 – Journal to adjust the Balance Sheet report by Class

After saving the journal entry shown in the preceding screenshot, our balance sheet will now display values beneath the correct fund types for Business Bank Account and Debtors:

Balance Sheet As of July 31, 2021				
	GENERAL UNRESTRICTED FUNDS	RESTRICTED FUNDS	NOT SPECIFIED	TOTAL
Fixed Asset				
Total Fixed Asset				£0.00
▼ Cash at bank and in hand				
Business Bank Account	22,815.85		0.00	£22,815.85
Contra Account			0.00	£0.00
Petty cash			100.00	£100.00
Shopify control Account			5,200.00	£5,200.00
US Dollar Bank Account			107.89	£107.89
Total Cash at bank and in hand	£22,815.85	£0.00	£5,407.89	£28,223.74
▼ Debtors				
Debtors	7,390.40	5,786.70	0.00	£13,177.10
Debtors - EUR			0.00	£0.00
Debtors - USD			0.00	£0.00
Total Debtors	£7,390.40	£5,786.70	£0.00	£13,177.10

Figure 9.31 – Revised Balance Sheet report by Class

So far, we've looked at editing some reports so that values can be displayed by class or location, depending on the option selected. But what if you would like to try and combine both income and expenditure by class and location on one report? Well, this is possible, but we will need to run a **Custom Summary Report**.

The Custom Summary Report

Without making any changes to it, **Custom Summary Report** looks very much like a **Profit and Loss** report, but there are some additional options. Just below the **Report period** selection is the option to choose to **Display rows by** and **Display columns by**:

Figure 9.32 – Custom Summary Report options

With these options selected, we will be presented with a profit summary that combines the use of both a class and a location:

	FINANCE	MARKETING	SALES	NOT SPECIFIED	TOTAL
Birmingham	4,850.00	-44.10	-6,809.10		£ -2,003.20
Cambridge		11,561.56			£11,561.56
London		-4,496.40	7,425.00		£2,928.60
Not Specified				-5,493.76	£ -5,493.76
TOTAL	£4,850.00	£7,021.06	£615.90	£ -5,493.76	£6,993.20

Custom Summary Report
All Dates

Figure 9.33 – Custom Summary Report

Clicking on any of the summary values presented will produce a detailed report listing all income and expenditure transactions that produce the profit/loss for the combined class and location.

Earlier in this section, we mentioned that a *Plus* level subscription is required to use classes and locations. There is another feature that may be useful and is available with any of the subscription types. This is the ability to use **Tags**.

Tags

Tags are a relatively new addition to QuickBooks Online and can be used for many different purposes. The possibilities are endless. All transactions can be tagged except for journal entries.

Regardless of why we use a tag, it's about increasing the discoverability of an entry within QuickBooks Online, which helps us improve and make it easier to find the different accounting entries that we are looking for.

Here are a few suggestions for using tags:

- Monitoring income and expenditure against a project (if you're not using the **Project** feature)

- Monitoring expenditure against events, such as staff parties

- Flagging transactions that require further clarification (such as *Accountant please check*)

- Flagging transactions that require proof of purchase (missing receipts)

The option to use **Tags** is normally enabled by default. If you don't see the option to use tags when creating a transaction, it can be enabled within **Account and Settings** by going to **Sales form content**, which can be found in the **Sales** tab, and **Bills and expenses**, which can be found in the **Expenses** tab.

The useful thing about tags is that you can attach multiple tags to a transaction. In the following example, which has been taken from an expense, the entry has been flagged with three tags—`Missing receipt`, `More info required`, and `Staff parties: Xmas parties`:

9.34 – Using Tags on an expense

When you're creating a transaction and you need to apply a tag but the name you require is not in place yet, simply **Start typing to add a tag**.

Now that tags have been applied to some accounting entries, we want to be able to report against them in some way. Let's look at how that is done in the following section.

Reporting against Tags

You can find summary information for the tags that have been used from within the **Banking** area. The top left of the **Tags** center displays a summary of **MONEY IN**, while the right-hand side where a tag has been applied shows **MONEY OUT**. At the time of writing, all the values on this screen are displayed inclusive of tax:

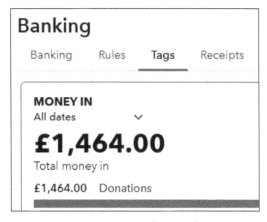

Figure 9.35 – Top-left view of Tags

In the lower section of the **Tags** center, you will find various options to search for tags and create new tags. You can create up to 300 tags and 40 tag groups. Using a group is useful if you need to be able to quickly run a report for multiple tags of a similar type.

Below the summary information of **MONEY IN** and **MONEY OUT** where **Tags** have been applied, you will see a list of all the **TAGS AND TAG GROUPS** properties that have been set up. It's also possible to see the number of transactions that have had a specific tag applied:

See all untagged transactions	
TAGS AND TAG GROUPS	**TRANSACTIONS**
⌃ ● Staff parties (3)	1 transaction
▌ Staff parties : Birthday Pa...	
▌ Staff parties : Summer Pa...	
▌ Staff parties: Xmas parties	1 transaction
Donations	1 transaction
Missing receipt	1 transaction
More info required	1 transaction
6 of 300 tags created. 1 of 40 tag groups created. Learn more about tag limits	

Figure 9.36 –Tags and Tag Groups

The preceding screenshot shows that a **Tag Group** has been created for `Staff parties` that includes `Summer parties`, `Xmas parties`, and `Birthday parties` as tags.

One of the *ungrouped tags* is `Missing receipt`. If the organization has a policy where a receipt should be attached to every transaction, the tag will remain in place until a receipt has been found and attached. Then, the transaction can be edited and the tag can be removed.

As well as being able to view the summary of gross income and expenditure from the **Tags** center, **Display columns by** on the **Profit and Loss** report can be used to choose a report against a **Tag Group** or any **Ungrouped tags**:

Figure 9.37 – Reporting against Ungrouped Tags

In *Figure 9.34*, we created an expense and applied three tags. Two of those were **Ungrouped tags** for `MISSING RECEIPT` and `MORE INFO REQUIRED`. The cost of the expense was £750 plus VAT. As both tags were applied to a single transaction, the cost will appear in both columns:

	MISSING RECEIPT	MORE INFO REQUIRED
Income		
Total Income		
GROSS PROFIT	£0.00	£0.00
▼ Expenses		
Staff welfare	750.00	750.00
Total Expenses	£750.00	£750.00

Figure 9.38 – Profit and Loss displayed by Ungrouped Tags

Hopefully, this section has given a small insight into how tags can be used. Like classes and locations, tags broaden how we can report in QuickBooks without creating a lot of unnecessary chart of account categories.

Now, let's summarize what we've covered in this chapter.

Summary

As part of reviewing our profit and loss and Balance Sheet, we have learned that any chart of account categories that have been set up with an incorrect **Account Type** could significantly impact how profit/loss figures are reported.

If too many unnecessary chart of account categories have been created, we can merge accounts, and where Product/Service items have been set up incorrectly, a quick edit can update all historical transactions.

Once we are satisfied that everything has been set up correctly, some inconsistencies in our reports may occur, either due to **Invoices** being raised in advance or **Bills** being received in advance. To ensure our bookkeeping records follow some standard accounting concepts and principles, we may need to create journal entries to adjust how income and expenditure are being reflected within a particular financial period.

Finally, we learned that an organization may require income and expenditure to be broken down into further detail for internal purposes. To avoid creating dozens and dozens of unnecessary chart of account codes, we can use features such as classes, locations, and tags, which will take our reporting options to the next level.

Before accounts can be fully signed off, every figure that's reported on the Balance Sheet should be checked carefully and reconciled. The next chapter follows that process and includes some useful tips that help close the period much easier.

10
Reconciling the Balance Sheet

When we talk about *reconciling the balance sheet*, we mean we must be able to explain every figure that is reported. The balance sheet is a summary of assets and liabilities, but it is important to agree on all of the details that make up the totals held against each balance sheet category before accounts can be finalized at a period end.

During this chapter, you will learn the following:

- Different balance sheet categories used in **QuickBooks**
- Basic concepts used when agreeing values on the balance sheet
- Basic reports used when checking values held on the balance sheet
- Advanced techniques used when reconciling balance sheet categories
- Advanced reporting options used to report against balance sheet categories

It's important to check whether the values held on the balance sheet are correct – we can never accept values as they appear without reviewing them in detail. The final figures in our balance sheet may impact profit and the amount of tax payable.

A good example being that loan payments are being made every month, but no interest has been accounted for on the loan. This would result in the loan balance being incorrect and the profit being overstated until an adjustment is made for the interest.

Before we start checking the balance sheet in detail, first of all, we should be familiar with the different balance sheet categories and what we normally expect to find within them. Listing every possible type could take up an entire chapter, so we'll just look at some of those that are used the most.

Different Balance Sheet Categories

When creating any chart-of-account category in QuickBooks, it is mandatory to choose an **Account Type** and a **Detailed Type,** and then you must give the account a **Name.** Choosing the **Account Type** is really the most important. This will determine within which section of a report the account category will appear. The **Detailed Type** is really to give you a guide of what sort of accounts usually fall within this group.

The following table lists the Account Type categories in QuickBooks against the different balance sheet categories that can be created:

QUICKBOOKS ACCOUNT TYPE (UK / US)	EXAMPLES OF DIFFERENT BALANCE SHEET ACCOUNT CATEGORIES
Debtors / Accounts receivable	Trade debtors – customer balances.
Current Assets / Other Current Assets	Undeposited Funds, Stock/Inventory, Work-in-Progress, Prepayments, Accrued Income, Retentions, Staff Loans, Director's loans (overdrawn), Inter-Company Loans.
Cash at bank and in hand / Bank	Current Bank Accounts, Savings, Petty Cash.
Tangible Assets / Fixed Assets	Capital Expenditure and Provision for Depreciation.
Non-current Assets / Other Assets	Goodwill, Intangible Assets, Investments, Loans Provided Payable after 12 months.
Creditors / Accounts Payable	Trade creditors – supplier balances.
Credit card	Credit cards.
Current Liabilities / Other Current Liabilities	Accruals, Deferred Income, Hire Purchase Loans, Bank Loans, Director's Loans, Inter-company loans, Payroll Liabilities, Tax Liabilities.
Non-current Liabilities / Long-Term Liabilities	Loans Payable after 12 months, Mortgages.
Equity	Retained Earnings, Revaluation Reserves, Capital / Current Accounts used for Sole Traders and Partnerships, Opening Balance Equity (used for Opening Balance adjustments).

> **Note**
>
> The terminology for Account Types may vary slightly in different regions. For example, the UK has an Account Type called `Tangible Assets`, where most other regions have `Fixed Assets`.

You'll no doubt be able to come up with a few more examples of balance sheet account categories. If you have done, think about which Account Type they would fall under.

Now that we are familiar with some of the different categories that can be found on the balance sheet, let's start looking at some of the basics of balance sheet reconciliation.

Agreeing Values on the Balance Sheet (Basics)

As we know, the balance sheet is a summary of the various assets held and liabilities owed by an organization. Reconciling all the different values that, when combined, agree to the totals on the balance sheet can be easier to do in some areas than it is in others.

When checking the balance sheet or profit and loss values, it can sometimes be easier to use the **Trial Balance report**. The trial balance is a list of all categories in use, with the balances recognized at a specified period. The balance sheet values appear in the top section of the report, with **Retained Earnings** always being the last balance sheet category, followed by the profit and loss categories.

Let's start by checking the balances that will require the least amount of work.

Reconciling Debtors/Accounts Receivable (Current Assets – Trade Debtors)

This should be nice and simple. All that is required is to view the **Accounts Receivable Ageing Summary Report** at the date of the financial period end. If the figures don't immediately match, check the following:

- The ageing method is set to **Report date**.
- The tick-box for **Show unrealized gain or loss** has not been selected.

- If the **Accounts Receivable Ageing Summary Report** contains foreign customers, it will be necessary to combine the values of all `Debtors/Accounts Receivable` values as they appear on the **Trial Balance**.

A/R Ageing Summary As of September 30, 2021						
	CURRENT	**1 - 30**	**31 - 60**	**61 - 90**	**91 AND OVER**	**TOTAL**
AJ Music (France)		2,035.15				£2,035.15
Christina Nystrom					1,506.00	£1,506.00
Christopher Mocko					1,038.00	£1,038.00
Colin Minnis					366.00	£366.00
Kumud Kokal					852.00	£852.00
NX Supplies (U.S.)		721.01				£721.01
TOTAL	**£0.00**	**£2,756.16**	**£0.00**	**£0.00**	**£3,762.00**	**£6,518.16**
Debtors						3,762.00
Debtors - CAD						0.00
Debtors - EUR						2,035.15
Debtors - USD						721.01

Figure 10.1 – Accounts Receivable report with debtor values taken from trial balance

Figure 10.1 shows that the three debtor values reported on the **Trial Balance** equal the total value reported on the **Accounts Receivable Summary Report**.

Creditors/Accounts Payable (Current Liabilities – Trade Creditors)

For our supplier balances, we will be checking the exact same things that we have for our customers, but instead run the **Accounts Payable Ageing Summary Report**, and, where necessary, combine different `Creditor/Accounts Payable balances` when the **Multicurrency** feature is in use.

> **Tip**
>
> When running either an **Accounts Payable Ageing Summary Report** or **Accounts Receivable Ageing Summary Report**, you can set the **Ageing Method** to be **Current** or **Report Date**.
>
> This means that if a report was run today for the date of March 31, 2021, **Report date** will display the balances on March 31, 2021. The **Current** ageing method will display if those balances are still unpaid.
>
> Viewing the current position of balances from a previous period can help to decide if any adjustments or provisions for bad debts are required.

Reconciling Bank Accounts and Credit Cards

It is highly recommended that bank accounts and credit cards are reconciled monthly as a bare minimum. For larger organizations with greater volumes of transactions, this action could be required weekly or even daily.

Basically, we must agree that the bank or credit card balance being reported in QuickBooks agrees to the balance shown on a bank or credit card statement. When QuickBooks has been linked to a bank account, this process can be much quicker. Regardless of whether bank feeds are in use, the principle is the same.

The option to **Reconcile** can be accessed from a few different places:

- From the left-hand navigation panel within **Accounting**
- From within the Gear icon, below the **TOOLS** menu
- From within **Banking**, selecting **Go to bank register** and then **Reconcile**

Whichever route you choose, you'll need to select the **Account** you wish to reconcile, the **Ending balance*** (taken from a bank/card statement), and an **Ending date*** (date of the bank/card statement).

In the following example, the balance per the `Business Bank Account` statement was £369.40 on `May 31, 2021`.

Reconcile an account

Open your statement and let's get started.

Which account do you want to reconcile?

Account

| Business Bank Account | ▼ | GBP |

Add the following information

Beginning balance	**Ending balance ***	**Ending date ***
0.00	369.40	31/05/2021

Start reconciling

Figure 10.2 – Entering initial reconciliation information

In the example shown in *Figure 10.2*, the **Beginning balance** is 0.00. This indicates the account has never been reconciled before, and an **Opening balance** was not added within the chart-of-account settings.

Tip

If an account contains a beginning balance but you are not sure what it relates to, there is a high possibility it was automatically created when linking the account. One of the easiest ways to check is to make a note of the balance and then view all transactions entered into `Opening Balance Equity` (or the `Retained Profit Balance Forward Account`). This account will contain one side of the **Journal entry** made that creates the balance. If necessary, you can **Delete** the **Journal entry**.

With the bank statement information in place, we need to select **Start reconciling**. If our bank account is linked to QuickBooks and transactions have been created using the bank feed information, we should find the account *instantly reconciles*.

£369.40 STATEMENT ENDING BALANCE	–	£369.40 CLEARED BALANCE		£0.00 DIFFERENCE

£0.00 BEGINNING BALANCE	–	£2,159.40 4 PAYMENTS	+	£2,528.80 4 DEPOSITS

DATE ▲	CLEARED DATE	TYPE	PAYEE	MEMO		PAYMENT (GBP)	DEPOSIT (GBP)	
06/05/2021	06/05/2021	Transfer		Transfer $2,500 US Dollars		1,910.00		●
06/05/2021	06/05/2021	Receive Payment	Joe Wells				363.60	●
08/05/2021	08/05/2021	Receive Payment	Jay Walker				180.00	●
09/05/2021	09/05/2021	Deposit		Credit Card Receipts			150.00	●
10/05/2021	10/05/2021	Deposit		Bank Deposit 000123			1,835.20	●
15/05/2021	15/05/2021	Expense		McDonalds		6.00		●
15/05/2021	15/05/2021	Expense	Staples	Staples		182.40		●
15/05/2021	15/05/2021	Expense		Petrol		61.00		●

Figure 10.3 – Reconciled bank account

Where a transaction has been created or matched to an entry found on a bank statement feed, the small green folder icon will appear on the line of that entry. When that happens, the entry will automatically be ticked as *Reconciled* on the far right of the screen. *Figure 10.3* shows that all values are ticked and there is a **DIFFERENCE** of 0.00. This means the account is fully reconciled and we can select **Finish now**.

That example was straightforward, and when banks are maintained properly the process should really only take a minute. However, it's not always plain sailing, so let's look at when reconciling the bank may take a bit longer than normal.

When does the bank reconciliation have a difference?

There are a few reasons why things don't always agree as they should when reconciling a bank account. Some of these differences can be easy to sort, and others take a little longer to solve. The following steps and tips should help if the bank doesn't instantly reconcile:

- If bank feeds are not in use, you must reconcile the bank the old-fashioned way by printing the bank statements off and then manually ticking each entry in QuickBooks once agreed to the entries checked on the bank statement.

- Ensure the **Ending Date** and **Ending Balance** is correct. If the bank has an overdrawn balance, make sure a negative value has been used. The **Edit info** option within the reconciliation screen can be used to edit the bank statement date and balance being used.

- Ensure the **Beginning Balance** is correct. If this is a new bank account that has not been in use for long, you would expect the beginning balance to be 0.00. If it's the first time the account has been reconciled since converting to QuickBooks, perhaps the opening balance is missing, which could cause a difference. If the account has been reconciled before, the **Beginning Balance** should be the same as the **Ending Balance** of the last reconciliation. If it had changed, you would receive a warning to alert you to this fact.

- With a difference still showing, try clicking on the title of the **PAYMENT** or **DEPOSIT** columns, which will sort the columns by value. This can help spot any possible duplicate entries. If two entries do appear to be the same, compare them to those on the bank statement. Duplicate entries can be **Deleted**.

	PAYMENT (GBP) ▲	DEPOSIT (GBP)	
	6.00		
	61.00		
	182.40		

Figure 10.4 – Sorting the payment column within reconciliation

- It may be necessary to **Clear filter / View all**. If a bank reconciliation was dated May 31, 2021, the reconciliation screen will initially only display transactions to this date. It could be possible that a transaction entered manually with a date of June 5, 2021, has been matched to a transaction that was dated in May. Removing the filter will display all unreconciled transactions.

▽▼   ✕ Statement ending date   Clear filter / View all
DATE   CLEARED DATE   TYPE   REF NO.

Figure 10.5 – Clearing the filter to view all unreconciled transactions

- With the filter removed, sort the transactions by **Cleared Date** (the date a transaction clears the bank) and compare to the **Date** used in QuickBooks. A transaction should never be *future-dated*. This means it should not be given a date later than when it appeared on the bank statement.

Figure 10.6 – Compare the QuickBooks date to the cleared date

- If after thoroughly checking through the above points, the problem remains, then it's possible that information is missing. If bank feeds are in place and you are trying to reconcile a whole year's worth of transactions in one go, break it down into smaller chunks. This will involve using the **Edit info** option, changing the **Ending Date** and **Ending Balance** and ensuring the relevant Statement ending date filter is in place. It may be necessary to go back six months or more before you find a date and balance that agrees. Once this has been done, start by reconciling the bank one month or even one week at a time until a reconciliation difference occurs. When you do have a difference, it will then be necessary to manually reconcile the bank for a particular period until you can discover where the errors lie. This will mean all the transactions must first of all be unticked before checking items on the bank statement, and ticking entries one-by-one in QuickBooks as you agree them.

- If you find some transactions missing, you will need to manually create them to reconcile the bank account. If you discover a large period of data missing, it may be necessary to obtain bank statements in CSV or a similar format and import them via the **Banking** area before you can continue to reconcile the bank account.

To summarize, if you have problems reconciling the bank, you must ensure the following:

- Check previous reconciliations to ensure they are all in line.

- Check the beginning and ending dates/balances entered are correct.

- Check that there is no duplication of data.

- Check there are no future dated transactions.

- Check there are no missing transactions.

If it is not possible to solve a bank difference quickly, it may be necessary to untick all transactions on the bank reconciliation. Then, work through the process manually, checking entries as they appear on the bank statement and applying the reconciliation tick in QuickBooks.

Now that the bank has been reconciled, we may need to produce a report if the bank statement balance doesn't agree exactly with QuickBooks.

How can the bank be reconciled, but the Balance Sheet does not agree?

This is the overall purpose of the *bank reconciliation*. It is very common for the bank statement to show a different balance to the value reported on the balance sheet. The main reason is all down to timing.

If a check for £200 was written on May 31, 2021, the entry will be recorded in QuickBooks with this date. However, it is unlikely to clear the bank until June 2021. On May 31, this would be an unreconciled item, meaning the balance sheet would report a £200 difference.

Using this as an example when reconciling the bank, we would see that all the entries that agree with the bank statement will be ticked, and the one entry that has not yet cleared the bank will be left unticked.

Figure 10.7 – Bank with one unreconciled item

As the image in *Figure 10.7* shows, the bank is fully reconciled with a **DIFFERENCE** of 0.00. One of the lines on this reconciliation has not been ticked because it has not yet cleared through the bank.

After selecting the option to **Finish now** to complete the reconciliation, you will be taken back to the main **Reconcile an account** screen. In the top-right of this screen is an option to view **History by account**.

This will produce a summary list of all bank reconciliations saved against this account. The screen will show the following information:

- **STATEMENT ENDING DATE**: Bank statement date of reconciliation.
- **RECONCILED ON**: Date the reconciliation was performed.

- **ENDING BALANCE**: The ending bank balance of the reconciliation.

- **CHANGES**: Indicates if any transactions have been changed since the reconciliation was performed.

- **AUTO ADJUSTMENT**: Indicates that the bank was not reconciled properly, and the **Adjust now** option was selected as a *quick fix*.

- **ACTION**: Various actions can be performed, such as **View report**.

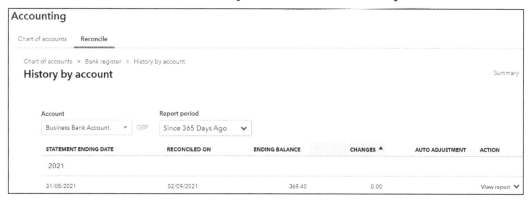

Figure 10.8 – Reconciliation history by account

Choosing to **View report** will produce a detailed **Reconciliation Report** for the account selected. This will show in detail any differences between the balance per the bank statement and the balance per the balance sheet (the **Register balance**).

The same logic can be applied to loans, let's see how this works.

Loans and Mortgages

When a business has been provided with a loan of any kind (*as per Figures 8.30, and 8.31 in Chapter 8, Best Practices When Reviewing Financial Records*), entries will be required to repay the loan, and adjust it for any interest that is to be charged. Some loans are provided with a fixed interest calculation, and others could have a variable rate applied.

Regardless of how interest is calculated, it is a good idea for consistency within the profit and loss to create an entry each month that will reflect a pro-rata monthly interest charge. A simple **Journal** to *debit* interest charges on the **Profit and Loss** and *credit* the loan on the **Balance Sheet** could be created that you can choose **Make recurring**.

Creating the journal adjustments for interest will mean there is no necessity to split the payment made from the bank account between capital and interest. It is advisable to create loan payments as a **Transfer** from bank to loan. You could also create a **Bank Rule** to reflect the expected future payments.

At the end of a financial year, the loan account should reflect all payments and interest charges. Upon receipt of a loan statement, it may be necessary to create an additional journal, or edit the last journal entry to agree the loan balance before reconciling the loan in the exact same way as the bank account.

> **Tip**
>
> Some financial institutions will allow QuickBooks Online to link to a loan account in the same way that bank feeds are obtained. This can be useful to help ensure the current loan balance is accurate.

We can use the **Reconcile** tool to check the balances of all bank accounts, credit cards, loans, and much more. We're keeping things simple for now, so let's move on to stock/inventory.

Reconciling Stock (Inventory)

Where inventory is being used within **QuickBooks Online**, there should be very little to do in this area. In *Chapter 4, Recording Income for Retail Businesses*, within the section *Considerations for inventory*, we covered how we can adjust quantities and revalue stock where stock tracking within QuickBooks Online is in use.

Where users are taking advantage of the stock control features in QuickBooks, producing the **Stock/Inventory Valuation Summary Report** at a specified date should agree back to the stock value reported on the balance sheet on the same date.

Some businesses will not use any of the stock control features available within QuickBooks, and may prefer to use a third-party app, or may not track inventory at all in any detail. Periodically, stock will be checked, counted, and valued, and the balance sheet will be updated using a **Journal Entry**.

The **Journal Entry** is often a very simple entry consisting of two lines. One line will affect the balance sheet category for stock/inventory, and the other will adjust a profit and loss category being Cost of Sales or similar. A *debit* to the balance sheet category will increase the value of stock, a *credit* to the balance sheet will reduce the value.

> **Tip**
>
> If a **Journal entry** is being used to adjust stock, the valuation is likely to have been calculated within Excel or similar. Don't forget that **Excel** documents, **Word** documents, **PDFs**, and other images can be attached to a **Journal entry** for future reference.

Essentially, whether QuickBooks inventory is in use or not, any report used that shows the stock value at a specified date should agree back to the figure on the balance sheet as of the same date. If not, use a **Journal entry** to align both reports.

At this point, everything reconciled should be relatively straightforward. Bank accounts, customers, suppliers, and inventory. If bank accounts are checked on a regular basis, what we've covered so far should only take a few minutes if we are ensuring all is in line for our year-end accounts.

The next report is still another simple one and reflects the drawings of the business owner. Depending on the structure of the business, this may be known as the *drawings* or *director's loan*. Let's take a look at that next.

Director's loans or drawings

During a financial year, a business owner will usually need to withdraw money from the business to fund their lifestyle. It is not always the case, especially for start-ups, as investment is often required to get a business off the ground and cash may be introduced by a director or partner of the business.

A *limited company* will usually have `Director's loans` set up within **Current Liabilities**. *Sole proprietors and partnerships* will have a mixture of `Current Accounts`, `Capital Accounts`, and `Drawings` that fall within **Equity** on the balance sheet.

In the following example, we will use director's loans, but the same methods can be used for other scenarios.

Within **Current Liabilities** on the QuickBooks balance sheet, the `Director's loan` account reports a balance of £25,750.

Current Liabilities	
Director's loan account	25,750.00
VAT Control	3,185.38
Total Current Liabilities	**£28,935.38**

Figure 10.9 – Director's loan on the balance sheet

As with any account category reported on the **Balance Sheet** or **Profit and Loss**, clicking on the value displayed will provide a full breakdown of all transactions created within a specified period. This detailed information is displayed on what is known as a **Transaction Report** in QuickBooks.

For this example, the year-end is July 31, 2021, so we are interested in the movements between August 1, 2020, and July 31, 2021. If there was a balance on this account on July 31, 2020, it will be represented as the **Beginning Balance**.

Clicking on the balance alone is likely to display far more columns on the **Transaction Report** than you are likely to need. If the report is being produced for the business owner to review, it needs to be made as easy to review as possible.

Too many columns can be confusing to view and can lead to unnecessary questions and delays when trying to get accounts completed. For this report, it is recommended to **Customize** and use the **Rows/Columns** options to remove any columns that are not required.

> **Tip**
>
> The default on a **Transaction Report** is to display all movements within an **Amount** column. Sometimes it can help to remove this column and replace it with separate **Debit** and **Credit** columns.

The following **Transaction Report** has been **Customized**, leaving only the most important information visible:

DATE	MEMO/DESCRIPTION	DEBIT	CREDIT	BALANCE
Director's Loan				
August 2020 - July 2021				
▼ Director's loan account				
Beginning Balance				25,000.00
31/08/2020	Monthly payment on account	£1,500.00		23,500.00
30/09/2020	Monthly payment on account	£1,500.00		22,000.00
31/10/2020	Monthly payment on account	£1,500.00		20,500.00
30/11/2020	Monthly payment on account	£1,500.00		19,000.00
31/12/2020	Monthly payment on account	£1,500.00		17,500.00
31/01/2021	Monthly payment on account	£1,500.00		16,000.00
28/02/2021	Monthly payment on account	£1,500.00		14,500.00
31/03/2021	Monthly payment on account	£1,500.00		13,000.00
30/04/2021	stationery costs paid for by director		£250.00	13,250.00
30/04/2021	Monthly payment on account	£1,500.00		11,750.00
22/05/2021	purchase of TV (personal)	£500.00		11,250.00
31/05/2021	Monthly payment on account	£1,500.00		9,750.00
30/06/2021	Extra holilday cash	£1,000.00		8,750.00
30/06/2021	Monthly payment on account	£1,500.00		7,250.00
31/07/2021	Monthly payment on account	£1,500.00		5,750.00
31/07/2021	Dividends allocated to director		£20,000.00	25,750.00
Total for Director's loan account		**£19,500.00**	**£20,250.00**	
TOTAL		**£19,500.00**	**£20,250.00**	

Figure 10.10 – Customized Director's Loan report

In *Chapter 5*, *Handling Client Money*, the section for *Reporting against client funds* covers how a **Transaction Report** can be customized in more detail if you need to refer to it. *Figure 5.30* shows how **Rows/Columns** are edited.

As with all reports, if this is a report to be used in the future, don't forget to click **Save customization** so that the report can be accessed from **Custom reports**, found within the *Report Center* at any time (as shown in *Figure 5.32*).

Expert Tip

It's a good idea to review drawings/director's loans on a regular basis. Perhaps set up a memorized report to be automatically emailed to the relevant people on a regular basis to check.

If you choose the option to **Edit** a report listed in the **Custom reports** area, you can enable an **email schedule** and choose the report frequency using **SET RECURRENCE**. You can send to multiple email addresses (separate each using a comma) and the report can be sent either as a PDF or attached in Excel:

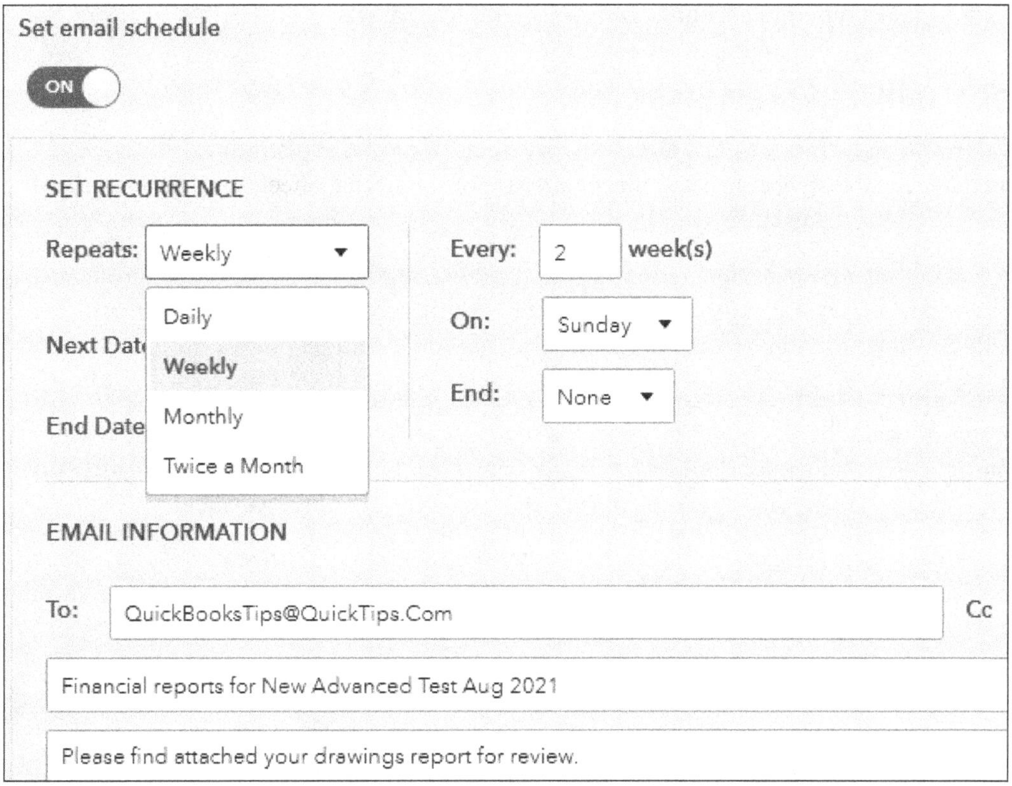

Figure 10.11 – Enabling a recurring report

> **Tip**
> Recurring reports are useful when a business owner has little or no need to log in to QuickBooks. Automatically sending emails to those that require financial information on a regular basis can save a lot of time. Remember though, bookkeeping must *always* be kept up to date when automated reporting is in place.

Up until this point, we've looked at balance sheet categories where the information should be readily available in QuickBooks. In some instances, understanding exactly what makes up a particular balance is not so straightforward. Let's look at some examples of this in the next section.

Advanced Balance Sheet Reconciliations

There are some balance sheet accounts that will take much more time to reconcile than others. The degree of difficulty in working out what makes up certain balances is likely to depend on the size of the business, which may affect the volume of transactions that are adjusted against different accounts. Let's start with fixed assets.

Reconciling Fixed Assets

Fixed Assets, also known as *tangible assets*, are items of capital expenditure. This can sometimes involve investing a significant amount of spend that affects cash flow or might require a loan of some kind.

The cost of such assets, such as a delivery van, will not immediately impact the profit and loss. The cost of, say, £20,000, could be spread evenly across the profit and loss over the length of what is called its *estimated useful life*. This could be four years.

Depreciation is used to adjust the profit and loss over the required timeframe. In this example, it would be £5,000 per year, or £416.67 per month. This asset would require a Journal entry that would *debit* Depreciation (**Other expense**) within the **Profit and Loss**, and *credit* Accumulated Depreciation within the **Balance Sheet**.

▾ Fixed Asset	
▾ Tangible assets	
▾ Motor vehicles	20,000.00
Depreciation - vehicles	-416.67
Total Motor vehicles	**19,583.33**
Total Tangible assets	**£19,583.33**

Figure 10.12 – Fixed assets on the balance sheet

If a business only had one asset, then using a few chart-of-account codes for the cost, depreciation, and disposal entries may suffice. However, many businesses can have hundreds or even thousands of assets, so using a single chart-of-account category for each is not manageable.

All fixed asset purchases should be recorded on a *fixed asset register*. This records when assets are purchased, disposed, and how much depreciation has been provided, reporting a total net book value for all assets held. The values of assets reported on the asset register should always agree to the totals reported on the balance sheet.

QuickBooks Online does not contain its own fixed asset register. The information is usually recorded using one or several spreadsheets, and the balances are checked with the totals shown in the fixed asset area in QuickBooks.

The third-party app *nettTracker* can automatically handle all the accounting requirements when it comes to reporting fixed assets and reconciling values on the balance sheet. Full details can be found by visiting www.nett-tracker.com.

Now that our fixed assets totals on the balance sheet agree to the fixed asset register, we'll move on to look at other areas that require reconciliation.

Reconciling Accruals, Prepayments, and Deferred Income

The three balance sheet accounts named in this section heading are all used to adjust our profit and loss in some way. As we learned in *Chapter 9*, *Enhancing the Consistency of Your Financial Statements*, various journal entries may be required to correct the consistency of monthly or annual reporting.

Over time, these different balance sheet accounts will contain both debit and credit entries, and it can be difficult to work out exactly what the remaining balance relates to.

Let's take the account for Prepayments (*Prepaid Expenses*). The financial year is running from August to July. We are about to prepare the accounts for July 31, 2021.

On July 31, 2020, the following values made up the balance within Prepayments:

Purpose	Value	Months remaining
Software subscription	£3,600	36 months
Membership subscription	£750	3 months
Insurance	£400	2 months
31 July 2020 total	£4,750	

The following image reflects all entries shown within a **Transaction Report** for Prepayments as of July 31, 2021. The **Beginning Balance** agrees with our summary of prepayments from the prior year. Since then, some prepayments have been released back to the profit and loss, and new prepayments have been created.

DATE	TRANSACTION TYPE	MEMO/DESCRIPTION	SPLIT	AMOUNT	BALANCE
▾ Prepayments					
Beginning Balance					4,750.00
31/08/2020	Journal Entry	Monthly software costs	-Split-	(100.00)	4,650.00
31/08/2020	Journal Entry	Insurance adjust	-Split-	(200.00)	4,450.00
30/09/2020	Journal Entry	Insurance adjust	-Split-	(200.00)	4,250.00
30/09/2020	Journal Entry	monthly membership	-Split-	(250.00)	4,000.00
30/09/2020	Journal Entry	Monthly software costs	-Split-	(100.00)	3,900.00
31/10/2020	Journal Entry	Monthly software costs	-Split-	(100.00)	3,800.00
31/10/2020	Journal Entry	monthly membership	-Split-	(250.00)	3,550.00
30/11/2020	Journal Entry	Monthly software costs	-Split-	(100.00)	3,450.00
31/12/2020	Journal Entry	Monthly software costs	-Split-	(100.00)	3,350.00
31/01/2021	Journal Entry	Monthly software costs	-Split-	(100.00)	3,250.00
28/02/2021	Journal Entry	Monthly software costs	-Split-	(100.00)	3,150.00
31/03/2021	Journal Entry	Monthly software costs	-Split-	(100.00)	3,050.00
30/04/2021	Journal Entry	Monthly software costs	-Split-	(100.00)	2,950.00
31/05/2021	Journal Entry	Monthly software costs	-Split-	(100.00)	2,850.00
30/06/2021	Journal Entry	Monthly software costs	-Split-	(100.00)	2,750.00
30/06/2021	Journal Entry	Insurance prepaid	-Split-	600.00	3,350.00
31/07/2021	Journal Entry	Monthly software costs	-Split-	(100.00)	3,250.00
31/07/2021	Journal Entry	monthly membership	-Split-	(250.00)	3,000.00
31/07/2021	Journal Entry	10 months magazine subscription	-Split-	500.00	3,500.00
Total for Prepayments				£ (1,250.00)	
TOTAL				£ (1,250.00)	

Figure 10.13 – Transaction report for Prepayments

The ending balance is £3,500, but it is not very clear what this relates to exactly. To improve how we can report against the account for Prepayments, we are going to **Reconcile** it. Yes, this means it will be reconciled using the same tools used to reconcile banks and credit cards.

Before we go ahead and reconcile the account for `Prepayments`, we are going to make one simple adjustment to it. As of July 31, 2020, there was one value for prepayments that exceeded the period of 12 months. This means that after one year, there will still be 24 months where a software subscription has been paid in advance.

We are going to summarize this value by creating a *contra* **Journal entry** that will *debit* and *credit* the same account – `Prepayments`.

Journal date						Journal no.
31/07/2021						adjust

	#	ACCOUNT	DEBITS (GBP)	CREDITS (GBP)	DESCRIPTION
⠿	1	Prepayments	2,400.00		24 months software subscription left
⠿	2	Prepayments		2,400.00	adjust prepayments

Figure 10.14 – Journal adjustment

When reconciling accounts used for adjustments, we will always reconcile using an ending balance of `0.00`. This is to ensure that all related *debits* and *credits* are matched correctly.

The journal used in *Figure 10.14* will help us with our reconciliation. The account for `Prepayments` contained an original *debit* entry of £3,600. £1,200 has been *credited* during the year, so the *credit* above will be matched in our reconciliation, leaving only the £2,400 outstanding at the end of the financial year. This relates to the software subscription costs that will be adjusted to the profit and loss over the next 24 months.

As already mentioned, to reconcile the account for `Prepayments`, we use the same tools as those used for reconciling our banks and credit cards. However, the **Ending balance** is always `0.00`.

Reconcile an account

Open your statement and let's get started.

Which account do you want to reconcile?

Account

Prepayments ▼	GBP

Add the following information

Beginning balance	Ending balance *	Ending date *
0.00	0.00	31/07/2021

Figure 10.15 – Reconciling Prepayments

Once in the main reconciliation screen, the corresponding journal debit and credit entries are ticked until the **DIFFERENCE** agrees to 0.00. For example, the original prepayment of £3,600 (*debit*): twelve journals of £100 (*credit*) and the £2,400 credit per *Figure 10.14*. Unmatched items will relate to prepayments to be adjusted in the future, with one of them being the journal debit of £2,400.

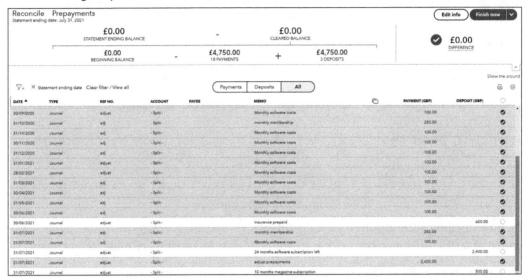

Figure 10.16 – Debits and credits agreed within Prepayments reconciliation

With a **DIFFERENCE** of 0.00, the **Finish now** option is selected, and we can improve the report we viewed in *Figure 10.13*.

With our **Transaction Report** open for Prepayments, we need to click **Customize** and choose to **Filter** by **Cleared**, selecting **Uncleared** from the dropdown.

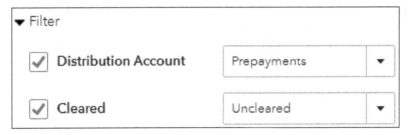

Figure 10.17 – Filter against Uncleared items

Doing this will remove any entries that have been reconciled, leaving only those entries that have a combined total that will agree back to the value displayed on the balance sheet.

Prepayments August 2020 - July 2021					
DATE	TRANSACTION TYPE	MEMO/DESCRIPTION	SPLIT	AMOUNT	BALANCE
▾ Prepayments					
30/06/2021	Journal Entry	Insurance prepaid	-Split-	600.00	600.00
31/07/2021	Journal Entry	24 months software subscription I...	-Split-	2,400.00	3,000.00
31/07/2021	Journal Entry	10 months magazine subscription	-Split-	500.00	3,500.00
Total for Prepayments				£3,500.00	
TOTAL				£3,500.00	

Figure 10.18 – Revised Prepayments report with Uncleared filter in place

Both reports shown in *Figure 10.13* and *Figure 10.18* have the same ending balance of £3,500, but *Figure 10.18* only displays the transactions we are interested in reviewing.

> **Tip**
>
> It's advisable to reconcile as many of your balance sheet accounts as you can in the same way – payroll liabilities, deferred income, accrued income, accruals, and retentions. All these accounts should be reconciled to a balance of 0.00, matching the appropriate debits and credits. You will then be able to produce the filtered reports for uncleared items that makes it so much easier to understand all values held on the balance sheet.

Another account in regular use could be Undeposited Funds. Let's look at that next.

Reconciling undeposited funds

In *Chapter 4*, *Recording Income for Retail Businesses*, we used Undeposited Funds for some transactions. Payments can be recorded as being received into Undeposited Funds before the payment is later deposited to the bank.

Undeposited Funds is a self-reconciling account, and you cannot use the reconciliation tool on this account. You will also find (at the time of writing) that when viewing the **Transaction Report** for this account, it is not possible to filter the uncleared transactions. However, there is something else that you can do to agree with the totals.

The first thing to do is to go to the **Chart of Accounts** and find Undeposited Funds within the list. On the far right of the screen will be the option to view the **Account History**. Selecting this option will take you to the **Bank Register** for this account.

DECREASE (GBP)	INCREASE (GBP)	✓ ▲	VAT	BALANCE (GBP)
	£266.20		-Split-	£1,713.20
	£829.00		-Split-	£1,447.00
£114.20		R		£618.00

Figure 10.19 – Part view of Register for Undeposited Funds screen

Within this screen, there is a column that contains the **Reconciliation** status of each transaction. There can be three levels of **Reconciliation** status, and these are as follows:

- **Reconciled**: **R** – when a transaction is fully marked as reconciled.
- **Cleared**: **C** – a transaction may have cleared the bank but not fully reconciled.
- **Uncleared**: (blank) – not reconciled.

On the far left of the **Asset Account History** screen is an option to create a filter (shown in the following screenshot). This will allow you to filter this screen to display only transactions that have a **Reconcile Status** of Not Reconciled.

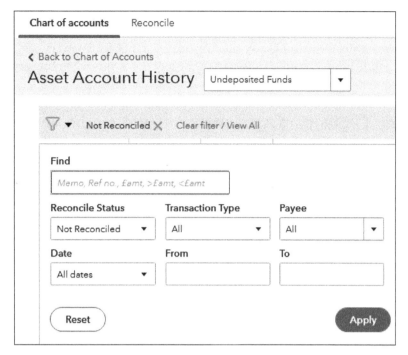

Figure 10.20 – Filtering Asset Account History

This filtered list can be exported into Excel. The total value of the transactions in this list will agree with the balance sheet total as of today's date.

> **Note**
> It's not easy to report against undeposited funds retrospectively, so it's advisable to check these values on, or very soon after, the financial year-end date.

Our last area to reconcile in this chapter is for **VAT**. For **GST**/sales tax, similar principles should apply. The chart-of-account names will just be a little different.

Reconciling VAT

Before we look at some different scenarios, here's a reminder of how VAT works in QuickBooks. If this feature has been enabled within Taxes, VAT will be applied to income and expenditure when given the appropriate VAT coding.

Transactions given VAT codes affect the VAT Control account and will appear on a VAT return that will summarize all the data. When a VAT return is filed or submitted to the appropriate government agency, a journal is created that will adjust the balance of the liability to the VAT Suspense account.

When a VAT return is marked as paid, it is the VAT Suspense account that is affected.

Like many areas within QuickBooks, reconciling this account could be very easy or might require a little more thought. Let's start off by looking at this when things are straightforward.

VAT Scenario 1 – Standard Accounting with VAT periods in line with year-end

With standard accounting in place, the VAT amounts will appear on the VAT return regardless of whether they have been paid or not. This means if the VAT return has not yet been filed, the balance on the VAT return should agree exactly to the VAT Control on the balance sheet.

Here is an extract from a balance sheet on October 31, 2021:

▾ Debtors	
Debtors	36,667.10
Debtors - EUR	0.00
Debtors - USD	0.00
Total Debtors	**£36,667.10**
▾ Current Assets	
Prepayments	3,500.00
Stock Asset	5,568.00
Undeposited Funds	1,713.20
Total Current Assets	**£10,781.20**
NET CURRENT ASSETS	**£72,160.04**
▾ Creditors: amounts falling due within one year	
▾ Trade Creditors	
Creditors	10,654.54
Creditors - EUR	0.00
Creditors - USD	1,421.35
Total Trade Creditors	**£12,075.89**
▾ Current Liabilities	
Director's loan account	25,750.00
VAT Control	4,767.88
VAT Suspense	1,705.07

Figure 10.21 – Extract of balance sheet

The **VAT Control** account reports a liability of £4,767.88. If we were to look at the VAT liability within **Taxes** at this date, let's see what amount is showing as due to be filed:

Figure 10.22 – VAT liability on a standard basis

This first scenario shows that the VAT return for a given period should agree with the VAT Control balance on the same date. If viewing the balance sheet six months or a year after the return was submitted, there could be a difference because of timings.

Supplier bills entered against a VAT period that has been closed will create an *exception* and will be captured in future VAT returns.

If VAT is filed on a *cash basis*, a little more work is required to reconcile the figures.

VAT Scenario 2 – Cash Accounting for VAT with periods in line with year-end

When VAT is accounted for on a cash basis, values are submitted on a VAT return that reflect the date the amounts have been paid. If a customer invoice has been raised during a VAT period but not paid, the values will not be included within the VAT return.

It is usually the accounting standard to prepare financial reports on an accrual basis, except in some circumstances where very small businesses are concerned. This will mean at any given point in time, the amount of VAT shown as payable on a *cash-based* VAT return will not agree to the total shown on the **VAT Control** being reported on an accrual basis.

There are two things that you can do to check the accuracy of values being reported on both the VAT return and the balance sheet when on a cash basis:

- View the balance sheet on a cash basis.

- Run reports against unpaid debtors and creditors to account for unpaid VAT.

The first option is very easy, and just involves changing the **Accounting method** on the **Balance Sheet** report.

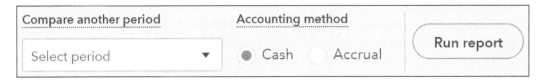

Figure 10.23 – Change Accounting method

After changing the **Accounting method** and selecting **Run report**, all balance sheet values will report on a cash basis. The VAT Control balance should agree back to the VAT return in the same way it should when comparing a VAT return filed on a standard basis to the VAT Control reported on an accrual basis.

More than anything, this is a sense check that things are working as they should. However, when preparing accounts on an accrual basis, a more detailed reconciliation is required.

Reconciling VAT using values from Unpaid Debtors and Creditors

Reconciling the VAT Control account fully takes a little bit more work. It's very similar to reconciling a bank account, but you'll need to do this manually outside of QuickBooks.

In summary:

VAT Return Value + VAT on unpaid debtors – VAT on unpaid creditors = **VAT Control**

With VAT settings switched to *cash*, our return produces a different value:

Figure 10.24 – VAT liability value on a cash basis

To obtain the unpaid VAT values for debtors and creditors, we will have to choose to **Customize** a report, starting with the **Accounts Receivable Ageing Detail Report**. Within our **Rows/Columns** options, we can add an extra column for **Outstanding VAT**:

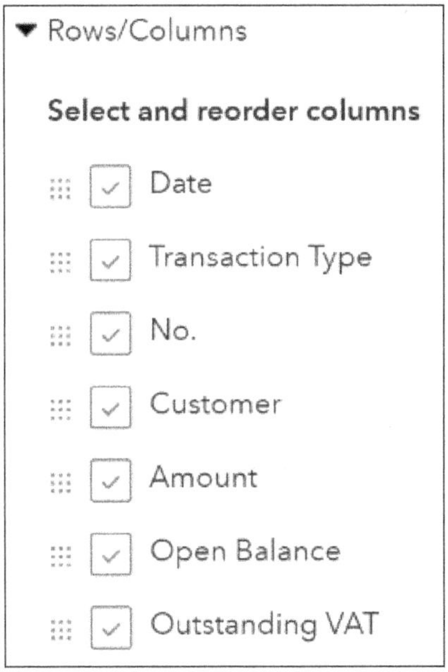

Figure 10.25 – Customize Rows/Columns menu with the Outstanding VAT option

With the additional column selected, the **Accounts Receivable Ageing Detail Report** will display the unpaid VAT values against each invoice and provide a total:

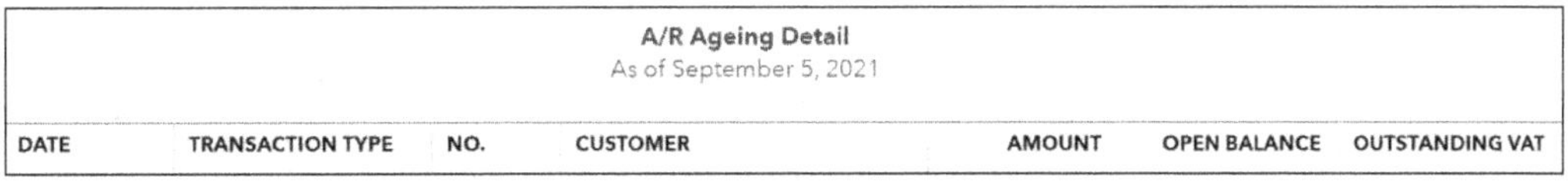

			A/R Ageing Detail			
			As of September 5, 2021			
DATE	TRANSACTION TYPE	NO.	CUSTOMER	AMOUNT	OPEN BALANCE	OUTSTANDING VAT

Figure 10.26 – Customized A/R Ageing Detail Report

Customizing the report to provide the information we need is only necessary if the organization uses different rates of VAT, or perhaps some of the balances within **Accounts Receivable** contain unallocated credits.

Where every unpaid invoice is created using the same VAT rate, a simple calculation could be used.

For an **Accounts Receivable** balance of £36,667.10, with a standard rate of VAT of 20%, we divide £36,667.10 by 1.2. This yields a net value of £30,555.92 (the .2 being the *20%*. If the rate was *15%*, we would divide by *1.15*).

Then, multiply £30,555.92 by 20% to produce a VAT value of £6,111.18.

The values we are interested in from *Figure 10.21* are **Debtors/Accounts Receivable**, £36,667.10, **Creditors/Accounts Payable**, £12,075.89, and the **VAT Control** amount of £4,767.88.

The **VAT Suspense** value in this example relates to previous VAT returns filed, but not paid.

We have worked out roughly what we expect the VAT value on **Debtors** to be (£6,111.18). If we know all **Creditors – USD** are zero rated, we can try to apply the same calculations used to work out the VAT on the **Creditors** amount of £10,654.54 to be £1,775.76.

Using the figures manually calculated, we can try and create our VAT reconciliation on a cash basis:

Details	Value
VAT return on a cash basis	-£530.10
Add VAT calculated on unpaid debtors	£6,111.18
Deduct VAT calculated on unpaid creditors (exc. USD)	-£1,775.76
Total VAT liability manually calculated	£3,805.32
VAT control account on QuickBooks	£4,767.88
Difference	-£962.56

From the preceding calculation, it immediately appears that we have a huge discrepancy when trying to reconcile VAT on a cash basis. This is because we've not looked at the information in full detail.

We may know for a fact that all customer invoices will have the standard rate of VAT applied, but for suppliers that is often not the case. If we were to customize reports to obtain unpaid VAT values, our reconciliation should look a little better. The following image displays the value of unpaid **Creditors** with the VAT amount:

£10,654.54	£813.20
£10,654.54	£813.20

Figure 10.27 – Creditors and VAT value

After obtaining the correct value with regards to the unpaid VAT values for **Creditors/ Accounts Payable**, we can try reconciling the VAT again:

Details	Value
VAT return on a cash basis	-£530.10
Add VAT calculated on unpaid debtors	£6,111.18
Deduct VAT calculated on unpaid creditors (exc. USD)	-£813.20
Total VAT liability manually calculated	£4,767.88
VAT control account on QuickBooks	£4,767.88
Difference	£0.00

It may be that even after obtaining all detailed reports, there is still a difference when performing this reconciliation retrospectively. This could be the result of exceptions caused by timing differences. If the difference is not material, you may choose to ignore it, as long as the VAT agrees moving forward.

If you are unsure about checking and reconciling VAT, it is advisable to seek assistance from an accounting professional.

Scenario 3 – VAT quarter-end not in line with Year-End

When looking at the previous VAT scenarios, we've taken the VAT quarter-end to be October 31, 2021. Other VAT quarters would end in January, April, and July. What do we do if the financial year-end doesn't fall on one of these months?

Using the same VAT quarter-ends, we'll take the year-end to be June 30, 2021. The year-end falls in the middle of the VAT return filed for May-July, which created a liability of £1,705.07. This return was filed on a cash basis:

Paid returns ▼			
01/05/2021	31/07/2021	05/09/2021	£1,705.07

Figure 10.28 – VAT liability for July 2021

Our financial year-end being June 30, 2021, we will need to review the VAT Control figure reported on the balance sheet at that date. As the VAT return within this VAT quarter was prepared on a cash basis, the balance sheet report is using the same method here:

Figure 10.29 – VAT Control value, June 30, 2021

As is the case here, the VAT reconciliation is being performed retrospectively, so we can't simply run the VAT return for a desired period. However, there is another report that we can check. This is known as the **VAT/Tax Liability Report**:

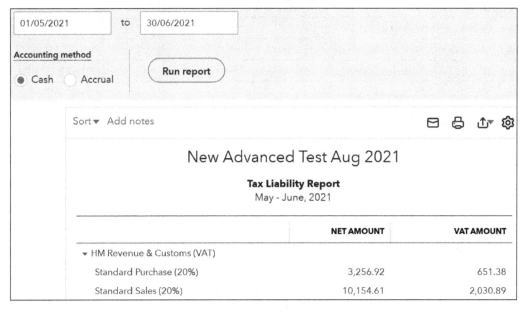

Figure 10.30 – VAT Liability Report

You can see from the image in *Figure 10.30* that the report has been run for the specified period of two months (May-June) using the cash **Accounting method**. Some manual calculation is required here, as we need to deduct the **Standard Purchase** VAT of £651.38 away from the **Standard Sales** VAT of £2,030.89, which gives a total of £1,379.51.

To fully reconcile between the cash VAT and accrual accounting method, we would then do exactly as we did in the *VAT scenario 2* within this section.

With our final balance sheet reconciliation complete, let's summarize what we've covered in this chapter.

Summary

In this chapter, we've learned that every single account category that appears on the balance sheet should be reconciled fully. This simply means it is fully understood what any figure reported represents.

Simply printing a lengthy report is not good enough when it may comprise lots of debits and credits that eventually contra (cancel each other out), so it's important we are left with just the current values visible.

Some balance sheet reports should be simple to reconcile, and these are as follows:

- Bank accounts and credit cards
- Trade debtors and creditors
- Undeposited funds
- Stock
- Payroll liabilities
- VAT (when standard and in-line with year-end dates)

Other balance sheet accounts that may require more work:

- Fixed assets
- Accruals, prepayments, deferred income, accrued income
- VAT on a cash basis

As with everything, reconciling the balance sheet is made much easier if the bookkeeping has been done well and everything is up to date, and even better when the balance sheet is checked every quarter or month instead of just on an annual basis.

There is another balance sheet account that we should check before preparing year-end accounts, and that is **Retained Earnings**. You shall learn all about this account, closing the year, and the audit trail in *Chapter 11, Closing the Year-End, the Audit Log, and More*.

11
Closing the Year-End, the Audit Log, and More

Throughout this book, you have learned how opening balances are created when setting up a QuickBooks file, how different features can be applied to specific business types, and the types of things to look out for when reviewing financial data.

We'll now focus on what we do as we close down a financial period, with a few extra tips thrown in for good measure.

Within this chapter, we will cover the following topics:

- Bookkeeping checklists
- Closing a financial year/period
- Retained Earnings
- The Audit log feature
- Using Management Reports at year-end

If you are an accountant or bookkeeper and have a QuickBooks Online Accountant subscription, you will have access to additional tools that are not available to other users, as illustrated in the following screenshot:

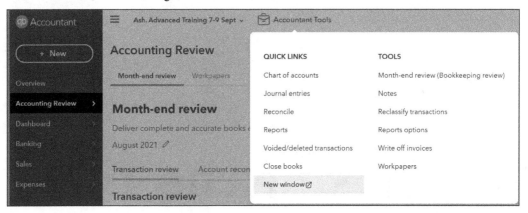

Figure 11.1 – Accountant Tools section

The **Accountant Tools** section is useful when it comes to reviewing data at the end of a financial period. **Reclassify transactions** will allow you to amend a lot of transactions in bulk (this feature is available to everybody using *QuickBooks Advanced*), so this can be a huge time saver when making corrections to improve consistency.

> **Tip**
> Supplier/vendor transactions listed in the **Expenses** tab within QuickBooks or transactions listed in the **Transaction List** against a supplier/vendor can also be re-categorized in bulk by selecting transactions and using **Batch Actions**. This feature is available to all.

Month-end review and **Workpapers** are editable checklists of things that can be used when checking all the information within a QuickBooks company file.

If you don't have an Accountant subscription, you will not have access to these features, but that doesn't need to stop you from creating your own *bookkeeping checklist*. Let's look at the sorts of lists we can compile.

Bookkeeping Checklists

When it comes to preparing accounts for a company, there can be lots to do, and very often many other things are going on at the same time. It's generally a good idea to compile a list of what you need to review and reconcile.

This saves the heartache of thinking that everything is completed and ready to go and then realizing something has been missed.

The tables shown next contain some examples of what should be reviewed at the end of a financial period. As you complete your review and reconciliation, you could add appropriate notes if necessary.

If these checklists are saved, when it comes to the next period to review, they can help remind you of why certain adjustments were made previously.

The following table shows a sample balance sheet review checklist:

Tick	BALANCE SHEET	Notes
	Main Bank Account Reconciled	
	Other Bank Accounts Reconciled	
	Credit Cards Reconciled	
	Undeposited Funds Reviewed	
	Customer Balances Checked	
	Supplier Balances Checked	
	Value-Added Tax (VAT)/Goods and Services Tax (GST) Sales Tax Reconciled	
	Employee Liabilities Reconciled	
	Accruals Reconciled	
	Prepayments Reconciled	
	Accrued Income Reconciled	
	Deferred Income Reconciled	
	Director's Loans Reviewed	
	Inter-company Loans Reconciled	
	Loans/Hire Purchase (HP) Agreements Reconciled	
	Stock/Inventory Checked and Reconciled	
	Work-In-Progress (WIP) Updated and Reconciled	
	Fixed Assets Reviewed, Updated, and Reconciled	
	Goodwill Adjusted	
	Other Taxes Adjusted and Reconciled	
	Compare Balance Sheet to Prior Year	

The following table shows a sample **profit and loss (P&L)** review checklist:

Tick	P&L	Notes
	Review Sales Reports	
	Review Cost of Sales Reports	
	Review P&L by Month	
	Check for Consistency	
	Check for Relevance	
	Check for Personal Transactions	
	Check for Fixed Assets Coded to P&L	
	Check Chart of Account Categories Used	
	Costs Accrued Where Required	
	Costs Prepaid Where Required	
	Income Accrued Where Required	
	Income Deferred Where Required	
	Gross Profit Compared to Previous Year	
	Net Profit Compared to Previous Year	

The checklist is split between the balance sheet and the P&L. This is not to say that the balance sheet must be checked fully first. In some areas, there would need to be some back and forth between the two.

For example, the P&L would need to be checked first to discover whether any income needed to be deferred. This entry would then adjust our balance sheet.

Now that the P&L and balance sheet have been fully reviewed and appropriate adjustments made, we are able to **Close the books**.

Closing The Financial Year/period

QuickBooks Online doesn't contain a full mandatory year-end process of any kind. When a QuickBooks company file has been set up within **Account and Settings**, by selecting the **Advanced** tab, the **First month of financial year** option is selected.

If January is selected in the **First month of financial year** option, then December will automatically become our last month. When running any financial report, the financial-year date defaults will be based on these settings, which you can view in the following screenshot:

Account and Settings

Company

Billing & Subscription

Sales

Expenses

Advanced

Accounting

First month of financial year ⑦   January ▼

First month of tax year   Same as financial year ▼

Accounting method ⑦   Accrual ▼

Close the books ⑦

Default tax rate selection ⑦   Exclusive of Tax ▼

Cancel   Save

Figure 11.2 – Financial-year settings

Within this area, you will find the **Close the books** option. You can select this option at any time and turn it on or off as needed. No journal entries will be created as a result of closing the books. Selecting this option will prevent any accounting entries from being created with a date on or before that specified in the **Closing date** setting. You can see this option in the following screenshot:

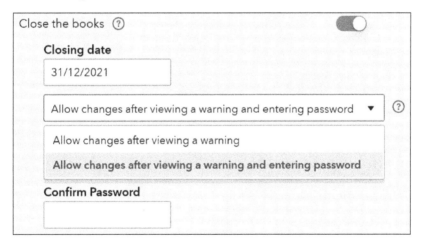

Figure 11.3 – Setting a closing date

There are two options to choose from when closing the books. The first means that any attempt to create an entry dated on or before the closing date can be easily overridden after viewing a warning.

The second option requires that a password be entered to override the warning.

> **Tip**
> It's advisable to close the books with a password if other users are accessing the same QuickBooks company file. Don't worry if you forget the password—if you were able to set one, it means you are an *Admin* user and can change the password at any time.

If we have reached the end of our financial year and closing the books just prevents further entries from being made to that period, you may wonder how the P&L account resets for the new year. This is all down to the **Retained Earnings** account, so let's look at reconciling this final balance sheet account.

Retained Earnings

The **Retained Earnings** account in QuickBooks Online will automatically calculate what the **Retained Profit** value should be. This will be a cumulative balance of profits from previous financial years.

Let's take an example of a company that has a current financial year ending September 30, 2021. The following screenshot has been extracted from the bottom of the **Profit and Loss** report:

NET OPERATING INCOME	£52,403.12
▾ Other Expenses	
Unrealised Gain or Loss	0.00
Depreciation Expenses	5,000.04
Dividends	31,000.00
Exchange Gain or Loss	9.92
UK Corporation Tax	9,956.57
Total Other Expenses	**£45,966.53**
NET OTHER INCOME	£ -45,966.53
NET INCOME	£6,436.59

Figure 11.4 – Extract from the Profit and Loss report

The **Profit and Loss** report is reporting a final **NET INCOME** figure of £6,436.59. This is after interest, depreciation, dividends, and tax are calculated.

> **Tip**
>
> It helps to create categories that are not part of day-to-day operations using the **Other Expenses** account type to ensure that they appear in the lower section of the **Profit and Loss** report. Bank interest received or government grants should be set up using the **Other Income** account type to ensure there is no confusion with turnover.

If we switch over to the **Balance Sheet** report for the same company at the same date, we can see 6,436.59 is displayed against the **Profit for the year** field, as illustrated in the following screenshot:

TOTAL NET ASSETS (LIABILITIES)	£15,904.59
▾ Capital and Reserves	
Ordinary share capital	1,000.00
Retained Earnings	8,468.00
Retained profit balance forward account	0.00
Profit for the year	6,436.59
Total Capital and Reserves	**£15,904.59**

Figure 11.5 – Balance sheet extract: September 30, 2021

With this example having a year-end date of September 30, 2021, the amount of 8,468.00 reported against **Retained Earnings** would be the value of profits after the deduction of tax and dividends brought forward from September 30, 2020.

Important: Before finalizing the accounts for a year, you must always check that the value of **Retained Earnings** has not changed since the accounts were last submitted. If it has, we may need to review the **Audit log** option—we'll cover that in the next section.

> **Note**
>
> The **Retained profit balance forward account** category is also known as **Opening Balance Equity**. This category should only be used to create opening balances and should always balance to 0.00 after all necessary adjustments have been made.

The following screenshot shows the **Balance Sheet** report for the same company with a date of October 1, 2021. Before any entries have been made in the new financial year, we can see that the prior year profit figure has automatically rolled into the value reported for **Retained Earnings**:

TOTAL NET ASSETS (LIABILITIES)	£15,904.59
▾ Capital and Reserves	
Ordinary share capital	1,000.00
Retained Earnings	14,904.59
Retained profit balance forward account	0.00
Profit for the year	
Total Capital and Reserves	**£15,904.59**

Figure 11.6 – Balance sheet extract: October 1, 2021

The **Retained Earnings** account is fine for limited companies and corporations, but for some business types, further considerations are required. Let's see how we handle those.

What if the business is a sole proprietor or partnership?

Sole proprietors and partnerships don't retain profits. At the end of each financial year, any profits or losses made are adjusted to the current account of the business owner when operating as a sole proprietor. It's the same for partnerships, and adjustments are split appropriately between the partners.

The **Advanced** section of **Account and Settings** includes a **Company type** option. Depending on the region, this can affect the type of tax form that can be produced in QuickBooks but will not affect the way that the **Retained Earnings** account works.

This means that some manual adjustments will be required. Let's take an example of a sole proprietor. The following screenshot displays the lower section of a balance sheet at the end of the financial year, this being September 30, 2021:

TOTAL NET ASSETS (LIABILITIES)	£10,094.49
▾ Capital and Reserves	
Capital Account - Ash	10,468.00
▾ Current Account - Ash	-1,000.00
Drawings	-22,500.00
Total Current Account - Ash	**-23,500.00**
Retained Earnings	0.00
Retained profit balance forward account	0.00
Profit for the year	23,126.49
Total Capital and Reserves	**£10,094.49**

Figure 11.7 – Balance sheet of a sole proprietor

The **Retained Earnings** account reports a balance of 0.00, due to this being adjusted for the previous year. Taking all the accounts to be agreed and accepted, we need to make adjustments to the **Drawings** figure of 22,500.00 and the **Profit for the year** figure of 23,126.49. To do this, we are going to use a journal entry, as illustrated in the following screenshot:

Journal date				Journal no.	
01/10/2021				adjust	

	#	ACCOUNT	DEBITS (GBP)	CREDITS (GBP)	DESCRIPTION
⋮⋮⋮	1	Current Account - Ash:Drawings		22,500.00	adjust drawings for year
⋮⋮⋮	2	Current Account - Ash	22,500.00		adjust drawings for year
⋮⋮⋮	3	Retained Earnings	23,126.49		adjust profits to owner
⋮⋮⋮	4	Current Account - Ash		23,126.49	adjust profits to owner

Figure 11.8 – Journal entry to adjust drawings and profits

It's important to note that the date of the journal entry is the **first day of the new financial year**. This ensures that the balance sheet and the trial balance will still reflect current year movements. Using this date will ensure that the balances for **Drawings** and **Retained Earnings** are correctly reset to 0.00 for the new financial year, as illustrated in the following screenshot:

TOTAL NET ASSETS (LIABILITIES)	£10,094.49
▼ Capital and Reserves	
Capital Account - Ash	10,468.00
▼ Current Account - Ash	-373.51
Drawings	0.00
Total Current Account - Ash	**-373.51**
Retained Earnings	0.00
Retained profit balance forward account	0.00
Profit for the year	
Total Capital and Reserves	**£10,094.49**

Figure 11.9 – Balance sheet capital and reserves for a sole trader at the start of the new year

Figure 11.9 shows that the total shown in **Total Capital and Reserves** is the same as in *Figure 11.7*. This is after adding the journal entry from *Figure 11.8* that has adjusted **Retained Earnings** and **Drawings** to 0.00.

Whether a business operates as a sole proprietor, partnership, or limited company, occasionally it can be decided to change the financial year-end date. Let's look at how that will affect reporting when using QuickBooks Online.

What happens if the financial year-end is changed?

If a company decides to change the month in which the financial year will end, it will be necessary in QuickBooks to change the **First month of financial year** field, as shown in *Figure 11.2*. However, please bear in mind that a **Trial Balance** report will only contain values for income and expenditure within a 12-month window.

For example, if a financial year-end was changed from September 2021 to December 2021, then we would need to report for a 15-month period of October 1, 2020 to December 31, 2021, this being if the accounts were last filed and submitted on September 30, 2020.

Although QuickBooks will allow us to enter this date range into the **Trial Balance** report, P&L categories will only report totals for a 12-month period (January-December 2021). Values from October to December 2020 will be included within **Retained Earnings**.

In this scenario, it will be necessary to combine information from the **Profit and Loss** report using custom dates from October 1, 2020 to December 31, 2021, with the balance sheet having an end date of December 31, 2021.

The **Profit in Year** value on the balance sheet is ignored, as the total from the **Profit and Loss** report would be used. The **Retained Earnings** value needs to reflect the value on October 1, 2020 instead of January 1, 2021, this being the date that QuickBooks will calculate the figures from.

Let's quickly run an example starting with a P&L run for a 15-month period, as follows:

Figure 11.10 – P&L for 15 months

Now that we have a report that has provided total profits after tax and other expenses, we can run the **Balance Sheet** report on December 31, 2021, as illustrated in the following screenshot:

Balance Sheet Report

‹ Back to report list
Report period

| Custom ▼ | 31/12/2021 | to | 31/12/2021 |

TOTAL NET ASSETS (LIABILITIES)	**£40,649.58**
▾ Capital and Reserves	
Ordinary share capital	1,000.00
Retained Earnings	7,918.00
Retained profit balance forward account	0.00
Profit for the year	31,731.58
Total Capital and Reserves	**£40,649.58**

Figure 11.11 – Balance Sheet report at revised year-end

The **Balance Sheet** report is producing incorrect figures for **Retained Earnings** and **Profit for the year**, so we will need to make some corrections, as shown in the following table:

Total net assets reported December 31, 2021 in Figure 11.11	40,649.58
Share capital	1,000.00
Retained earnings from Figure 11.5 (October 1, 2020)	8,468.00
Profits for 15 months reported in Figure 11.10	31,181.58
Total capital and reserves as reported in Figure 11.8	40,649.58

> **Tip**
> If you're trying the preceding calculations and finding that the values do not add up, it's likely that journals have been entered directly against **Retained Earnings** instead of using the appropriate income or expense category.
> Running the **Transaction Detail by Account** report, selecting **Customize**, and choosing to filter against **Distribution Account** for **Retained Earnings** will help identify any entries made.

The balance sheet should always report the correct **Total Capital and Reserves** amount. However, the split between **Retained Earnings** and **Profit for the year** is unlikely to be correct when changing the **First month of financial year** option, or when reporting against periods that are not in line with an expected 12-month pattern.

Now that we understand what closing the books does and how **Retained Earnings** works, let's look at what we can do if the value of **Retained Earnings** from the prior year doesn't appear as it should. This is where the **Audit log** feature is our friend.

The Audit Log feature

The **Audit log** feature within QuickBooks holds a lot of information. It is not simply a list of transactions but also shows dates and times when users log in or out, when customers and suppliers are added, when reports are customized, and a whole lot more.

The **Audit log** feature records every single action that is carried out in QuickBooks. You can search for the **Audit log** feature within reports, and it can also be accessed from the *Gear icon*, below the **TOOLS** menu.

Ideally, when a financial period has been fully brought up to date and figures have been reported, we should **close the books** to prevent further changes being made to previous periods.

When it's time to finalize the accounts for a financial year, the **Retained Earnings** balance should correspond to the total retained profits carried forward from the previous year.

Occasionally, entries may get edited, deleted, or added, and this will affect the **Retained Earnings** value if dated in a previous financial year. This can still happen if the books are closed and any warnings are overridden. However, by using the **Audit log** feature and customizing some reports, it's possible to discover what has been changed.

Let's take the example balance sheet from *Figure 11.6*. On October 1, 2021, the **Retained Earnings** figure is reported as being 14,904.59. The following table contains actions that will affect this balance:

Original Retained Earnings balance on October 1, 2021	14,904.59
Deleted Expense dated August 1, 2021	997.60
Deleted Invoice dated September 4, 2021	-10,000.00
Added Journal for Dividends dated September 30, 2020	-1,500.00
Edited Supplier Bill from June 2021 from £111.00 to £211.00	-100.00
Adjusted Retained Earnings balance October 1, 2021	4,302.19

You can see how the actions listed in the previous table have affected the **Retained Earnings** account, as shown in the following extract from the **Balance Sheet** report:

▼ Capital and Reserves	
Ordinary share capital	1,000.00
Retained Earnings	4,302.19
Retained profit balance forward account	0.00
Profit for the year	
Total Capital and Reserves	**£5,302.19**

Figure 11.12 – Adjusted Retained Earnings figure on the Balance Sheet report

By listing the changes, we can see how the adjusted **Retained Earnings** figure has been calculated, but if you had only just run the **Balance Sheet** report, working out what has caused the difference would require some investigation. We can start by looking at the **Audit log** feature.

Let's say that we know that the accounts were prepared on September 8, 2021. This means that any changes to the data in QuickBooks are likely to have happened from September 9, 2021. Sometimes, looking for voided/deleted transactions is a good place to start.

With the **Audit log** feature open, we can use the **Filter** option to limit the amount of activity being reported. In the following example, we are looking for **Transactions** and have selected to search for only those that are **Voided** or **Deleted**:

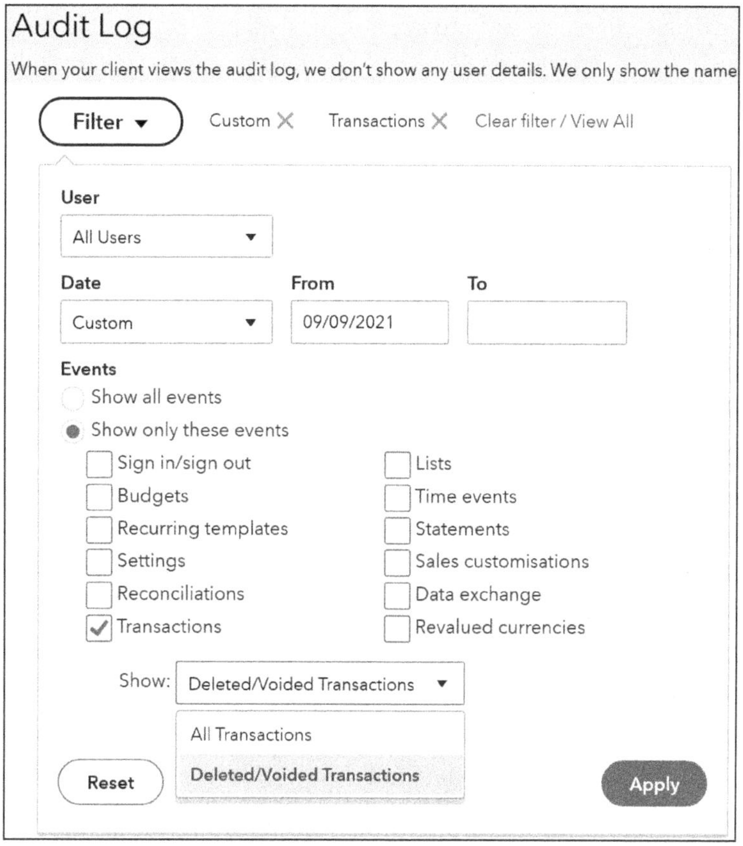

Figure 11.13 – Filtering the Audit log feature

> **Note**
>
> The **Date** value in the **Audit log** feature is not the *transaction date*—it is the system date when an event took place. In a detailed report, this would be the **Last Modified Date** value. Also, users with the **Accountant Tools** functionality have a shortcut to **Deleted/Voided Transactions**.

The filter used in *Figure 11.13* has produced the following information:

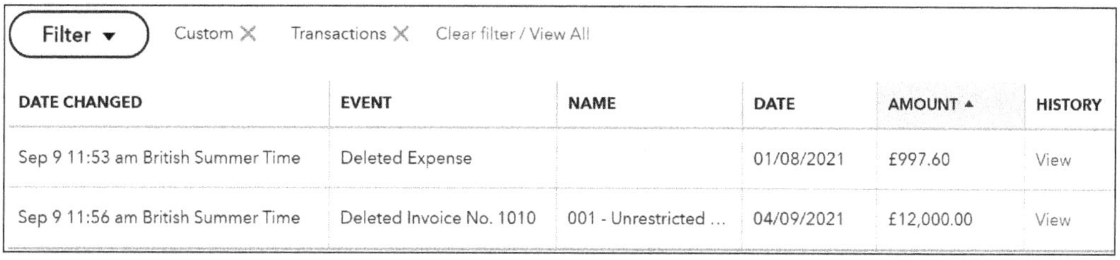

DATE CHANGED	EVENT	NAME	DATE	AMOUNT ▲	HISTORY
Sep 9 11:53 am British Summer Time	Deleted Expense		01/08/2021	£997.60	View
Sep 9 11:56 am British Summer Time	Deleted Invoice No. 1010	001 - Unrestricted ...	04/09/2021	£12,000.00	View

Figure 11.14 – Results from the filtered audit log

This contains the deleted expense and invoice previously listed in the table. Note that the amount in the audit log is reported as £12,000.00 as this was the invoice total including VAT. Only the net value will affect our **Retained Earnings** balance.

Using the **View** option within the **HISTORY** column of the **Audit log** feature, it is possible to see any changes made to a transaction since it was originally created. All the events are listed with the most recent at the top of the screen, as illustrated in the following screenshot:

> **History of this transaction:** Invoice No. 1010 ID: 208
>
> ▶ **Sep 9 11:56 am British Summer Time:** Deleted by qbt002@qbtrguk.com null
>
> ▶ **Sep 4 12:47 pm British Summer Time:** Added by qbt002@qbtrguk.com null

Figure 11.15 – Audit history of a transaction

Clicking on the black arrow to the left of a particular date will provide full details of the original entry. Entries can be edited and saved multiple times. Each change will be listed, and any changes made to a transaction will be highlighted.

Using a similar filter, but this time selecting the **All Transactions** option, the following information is produced:

DATE CHANGED	EVENT	NAME	DATE	AMOUNT ▲	HISTORY
Sep 9 12:02 pm British Summer Time	Edited Bill No. bill no 24	Vodafone	30/06/2021	£253.20	View
Sep 9 11:53 am British Summer Time	Deleted Expense		01/08/2021	£997.60	View
Sep 9 11:56 am British Summer Time	Deleted Invoice No. 1010	001 - Unrestricted ...	04/09/2021	£12,000.00	View
Sep 9 9:41 am British Summer Time	Edited Journal Entry No. adjust		31/10/2021		View
Sep 9 9:13 am British Summer Time	Added Journal Entry No. 5		31/12/2021		View
Sep 9 11:58 am British Summer Time	Added Journal Entry No. adjust		30/09/2020		View

Figure 11.16 – All transactions in the audit log

With the **Audit log** feature on screen, clicking on any column header will sort the data by that column. **DATE CHANGED** is the system date being filtered against, and **DATE** in this view is the transaction date.

You may notice that journal entries do not show a value, which can mean more time is required when checking entries. Sometimes, we can work out what has changed by customizing a report. Let's do that next.

Customizing reports to investigate changes to previous periods

The **Transaction Detail by Account** report can be very useful. You can search for this report from within the **Reports Center**, as illustrated in the following screenshot:

Figure 11.17 – Searching for the Transaction Detail by Account report

Once this report has been opened, not only can we set a transaction date range that can cover multiple years, but we can also add a filter to look for when a transaction was last modified, as illustrated in the following screenshot:

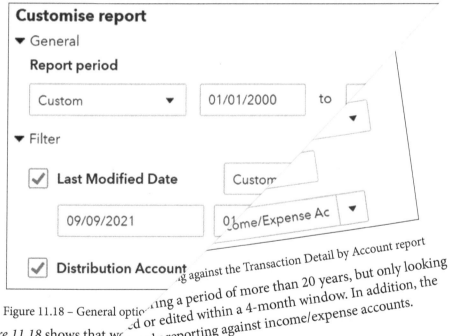

Figure 11.18 – General optio... ...ing a period of more than 20 years, but only looking

Figure 11.18 shows that w... ...d or edited within a 4-month window. In addition, the
at which transactions v... ...on is only reporting against income/expense accounts.
Distribution Acco...

If we also change the **Rows/Columns** in use, the report now only displays the data we need to see, as illustrated in the following screenshot:

	Transaction Detail by Account			
	Created/Edited: 9 September, 2021 - 1 January, 2022			
DATE	**TRANSACTION TYPE**	**SPLIT**	**AMOUNT**	**LAST MODIFIED**
▾ Telephone				
30/06/2021	Bill	Creditors	211.00	09/09/2021 12:02:01 PM
Total for Telephone			**£211.00**	
▾ Dividends				
30/09/2020	Journal Entry	-Split-	1,500.00	09/09/2021 11:58:07 AM
Total for Dividends			**£1,500.00**	

Figure 11.19 – Transaction Detail by Account report with filters in place

This report will show transactions that have been added, edited, and voided. The report shown in *Figure 11.19* contains a bill that was changed from being £111.00 plus VAT to £211.00 plus VAT. To work out what had changed, we would have to open this transaction.

the bottom of all transaction data-entry screens, you will see a **More** menu where
dit History option can be found. This will list all events associated with this
n, as shown in *Figure 11.15*.

ompare the original entry to the current values in place, as illustrated in the
ot. All changes made to a transaction will be highlighted:

...INT	OPEN BALANCE		ACCOUNT	AMOUNT	OPEN BALANCE
Telephone			Creditors	133.20	133.20
	253.20		Telephone	111.00	0.00
VAT Control	-42.20		VAT Control	-22.20	0.00

Figure 11.20 – Comparing curre...original entry in Audit History

As mentioned earlier, *voided transactions wi...* ...ithin the **Transaction Detail by**
Account report, but *deleted transactions will not b...* ...ain the main difference.

Voided and deleted transactions – what is the ...nce?

An option to void or delete a transaction is found within the **More** ...the bottom of
most transaction data-input screens. Here are the key differences.

When you choose to void a transaction, all the data is left in place except for the values, which are adjusted to 0.00. The transaction will remain visible on all reports and, if associated with a customer or supplier, will also remain visible within the customer and supplier areas.

When you delete a transaction, it is removed from QuickBooks fully, apart from being flagged as a deleted transaction within the **Audit log** feature.

It is usually advisable to void errors made with customers, especially invoices, as this can make things easier if you need to investigate any differences in the future. Deletion is best used if perhaps a straightforward duplication has been made and one entry needs to be removed—for example, a supplier bill or expense entered twice in error. Simply deleting the duplicate entry often makes the most sense.

The last three chapters have all been concerned with reporting, reviewing, and reconciliations. At the beginning of this chapter, it was shown that users with an **Accountant** login have additional tools. This book concentrates on features that are available to all users.

Management Reports is a feature available to all and is a great way to produce a document that contains all your year-end reports.

Using Management Reports at Year-End

Throughout this book, we've run and customized various reports, and any report that is likely to be used in the future can be saved using the **Save customization** option. When you do save a report, the **Add this report to a group** option is available, as illustrated in the following screenshot:

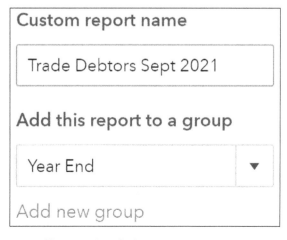

Figure 11.21 – Saving a report to a group

Saving reports to a group is useful if they have been prepared for a specific purpose. Not only will they be grouped neatly within the **Custom reports** area, but it also makes it much easier when searching for a report, as the following screenshot illustrates:

Q year end

Year End:Balance Sheet - Sept 2021 : Customised

Year End:Trade Debtors Sept 2021 : Customised

Year End:Trial Balance - Sept 2021 : Customised

Figure 11.22 – Searching for year-end reports

While checking and reconciling different account categories, we can save all the necessary reports that provide our supporting documentation: details that correspond with figures being summarized on the balance sheet.

Saved reports in a group will appear within **Custom reports**, listed in alphabetical order. This is illustrated in the following screenshot:

Standard	Custom reports	Management reports	
NAME		**CREATED**	**DATE RANGE**
⟩ **Year End**			
Balance Sheet - Sept 2021		Ashley Beetson	01/10/2020-30/09/2021
Profit and Loss Sept 2021		Ashley Beetson	01/10/2020-30/09/2021
Reconciled Prepayments Sept 2021		Ashley Beetson	01/01/2000-30/09/2021
Trade Creditors Sept 2021		Ashley Beetson	30/09/2021
Trade Debtors Sept 2021		Ashley Beetson	30/09/2021
Trial Balance - Sept 2021		Ashley Beetson	30/09/2021-30/09/2021

Figure 11.23 – Custom reports saved to a group

Without using the **Management Reports** section at all, it is possible to export an entire group of reports into **Portable Document Format (PDF)** files using the **Export As PDF** option from within the **ACTION** menu, as illustrated in the following screenshot:

Figure 11.24 – Exporting a group of reports

Using **Management Reports** to produce a single document containing all our reports provides us with a few more options. We're not going to detail every feature of **Management reports**; instead, we will just point out some of the most useful ones.

You should be presented with some default management reports. There is no **Add new** option for this feature. Instead, you need to choose between **Edit** or **Copy** options for an existing report, as illustrated in the following screenshot. **Basic Company Financials** is usually the best place to start:

Figure 11.25 – Copying an existing management report

Once a management report has been copied, it will be added to a list of management reports and will have a suffix of -1. You can see from the following screenshot that our copied report is named `Basic Company Financials-1`:

NAME	CREATED BY	LAST MODIFIED
Basic Company Financials-1	Ash Beetson	Sep 10, 2021 09:48 AM
Basic Company Financials	QuickBooks	

Figure 11.26 – Copied management report added to list

Now that the management report has been copied, we can choose **Edit** from the **Action** menu. Once opened, the name of the report can be edited in the top left of the screen. In this example, we are changing the name to **Year End Report Pack - September 2021**:

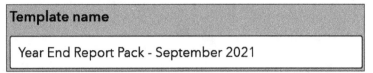

Figure 11.27 – Management report template name edited

> Tip
> Even if the financial year has not actually passed, you can start editing these reports. This can make things easier and save time later if part of a report is prepared in advance.

In the top right-hand corner of the **Management Reports** feature is a **Report period** option. This date would be used when adding a **Standard** QuickBooks-generated report. Any **Custom** reports that you choose to include will be based on the date customizations the report was saved with.

When creating a management report, five sections can be accessed, and these are represented by different tiles that we need to click on where changes are required. These are listed here:

- **Cover page**
- **Table of contents**
- **Preliminary pages**
- **Reports**
- **End notes**

Here is a summary of each section—we will only go into detail where the **Reports** section is concerned:

- The **Cover page** section will allow us to change the style of the front cover, include a company logo, and edit various titles.
- The **Table of contents** section simply lists what is being included within the document.
- Within **Preliminary pages**, we can add notes. This would help anybody else reading the document understand any values reported that require a detailed explanation.

- **Reports** will contain all the reports we wish to include within the document.

- **End notes** is used to add any further notes and explanations at the end of the document if desired.

The area we are most interested in is the **Reports** section, so let's look at that in more detail.

Including reports in a management report

First, if you have edited or copied an existing report, it is likely there will be some reports already in place. The default **Basic Company Financials** report contains **Profit and Loss**, **Balance Sheet**, and **Statement of Cash Flows** sections.

If you have created your own custom reports to use, you will probably want to delete some, if not all, of the reports already in place. This is very easy to do. All you need to do is click on the report listed in the section, and on the far right, there will be a small trash-can icon you can use to delete the report, as illustrated in the following screenshot:

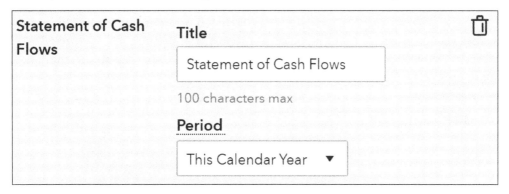

Figure 11.28 – Choosing to edit or delete a report

Any report that you wish to include within the management report is added by clicking on the blue text that is worded **Add new report**, as illustrated in the following screenshot:

Figure 11.29 – Using the Add new report option

When adding a new report, you can choose to type in the name, and QuickBooks will search for it. Any saved custom reports will appear at the top of the list. If they are part of a group, the group name will prefix the report name, as illustrated in the following screenshot:

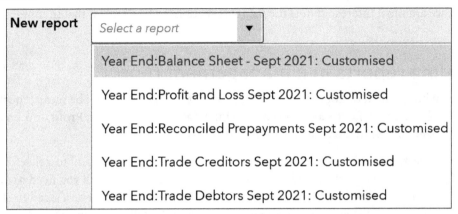

Figure 11.30 – Selecting a report to be added

Once you have selected a report that needs to be included, you can amend the **Title** field to how you want it to appear in the management report. You should check the period being used and, depending on the report type selected, you can choose between the **Compare previous year** and **Compare previous period** options, as illustrated in the following screenshot:

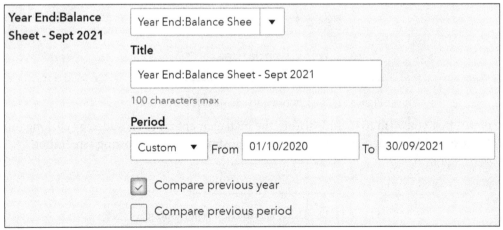

Figure 11.31 – Checking reporting options

Add further reports as required. Ensure that you click **Save** while making edits. If you are getting a management report ready in advance, you can always add further reports later.

Finishing touches to the Management Report

If detailed explanations are needed, add them to your **Preliminary pages** or **End notes** options.

While editing a management report, an **Advanced** option is available at the bottom of the screen. Selecting this option will allow you to edit how specific text appears on the report. It is also possible to change the order in which pages appear by clicking and dragging the small grid box to the left of each page description, as illustrated in the following screenshot:

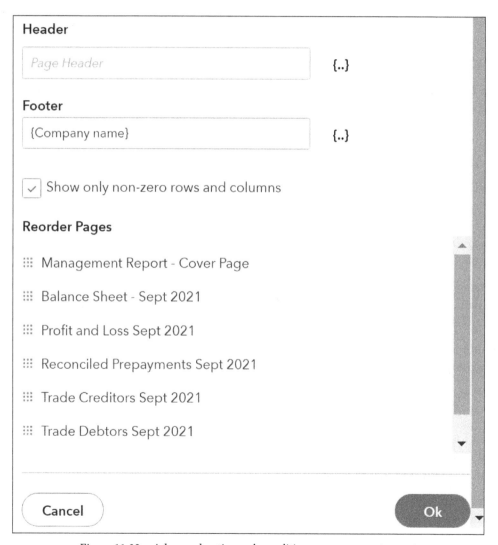

Figure 11.32 – Advanced options when editing a management report

With your management report saved, as shown in *Figure 11.25*, you can click **Send** to send the report to somebody directly by email from within QuickBooks, and a PDF document will be attached. Alternatively, you can select **Export as PDF** or **Export as DOCX** (Word document) if further edits are required.

Producing reports of any kind has absolutely no effect on data. Editing various reports is a great way to learn more about how different types of data are stored in QuickBooks.

Whether it's creating detailed filters in transaction reports or producing a set of management reports for the directors of a business, it's a good idea to experiment to see what you can produce. The more you practice, the easier it gets.

Summary

In this chapter, we have looked at some of the things we can do when we are closing a financial period. We've used the following tools and features within QuickBooks:

- Closing the books
- The **Retained Earnings** account
- The **Audit Log** feature
- Management Reports

Utilizing different features can generally make life easier. Closing the books to prevent data from being entered or changed in previous financial periods is an absolute must.

Understanding how the value in Retained Earnings is calculated can avoid confusion when running reports that extend beyond 12 months, or when an accounting year-end needs to be changed.

The audit log can help us identify when changes are made to accounting entries, or whether any have been voided and deleted.

Finally, we can produce management reports to pull all the relevant information together in one document.

The last four chapters of this book have looked at best practices when reviewing financial records, enhancing the consistency of financial statements, reconciling the balance sheet, and ending with closing the books.

With everything in place at the end of a financial year, you should have confidence that values reported in future financial years are accurate and appear in QuickBooks as expected.

Other Books You May Enjoy

If you enjoyed this book, you may be interested in these other books by Packt:

Mastering QuickBooks 2021

Crystalynn Shelton

ISBN: 978-1-80020-404-1

- Discover the new features of QBO and find out what the QBO line-up offers.
- Get to grips with bookkeeping concepts and the typical bookkeeping and financial accounting cycle.
- Set up QuickBooks for both product-based and service-based businesses.
- Track everything from billable and non-billable time and expenses to profit.
- Generate key financial reports for accounts, customers, jobs, and invoice items.

Hands-On Microsoft Teams

João Ferreira

ISBN: 978-1-80107-527-5

- Perform scheduling and manage meetings, live events, and webinars.

- Create and manage Microsoft Teams templates to streamline company processes.

- Deal with permissions and security issues in managing private and public teams and channels.

- Extend Microsoft Teams using custom apps, Microsoft 365, and PowerShell automation.

- Build your own Teams app with App Studio without writing any code.

Packt is searching for authors like you

If you're interested in becoming an author for Packt, please visit authors. packtpub.com and apply today. We have worked with thousands of developers and tech professionals, just like you, to help them share their insight with the global tech community. You can make a general application, apply for a specific hot topic that we are recruiting an author for, or submit your own idea.

Hi!

I am Ash Beetson author of *Professional Tips and Workarounds for QuickBooks Online*. I really hope you enjoyed reading this book, found the content useful, and helps you get the most out of using QuickBooks Online.

It would really help me (and other potential readers!) if you could leave a review on Amazon sharing your thoughts on *Professional Tips and Workarounds for QuickBooks Online*.

Your review will help me to understand what's worked well in this book, and what could be improved upon for future editions, so it really is appreciated.

Best Wishes,

Ashley Beetson

Index

VAT (sales tax) 117
voided transactions 302

Z

zero-total Bill
  using, to adjust project 162

CPSIA information can be obtained
at www.ICGtesting.com
Printed in the USA
LVHW062253190322
713875LV00010B/677

9 781801 810371